SUCCESSFUL
USE OF
TEACHING
PORTFOLIOS

SUCCESSFUL USE OF TEACHING PORTFOLIOS

Peter Seldin
and Associates

Anker Publishing Company, Inc.
Bolton, MA

SUCCESSFUL USE OF TEACHING PORTFOLIOS

ISBN 0-9627042-5-3

Composition by Deerfoot Studios.
Cover design by Marianna Montuori.
Printing and binding by Goodway Graphics.

Anker Publishing Company, Inc.
176 Ballville Road
P.O. Box 249
Bolton, MA 01740-0249

ABOUT THE AUTHOR

Peter Seldin is Distinguished Professor of Management at Pace University, Pleasantville, New York. A specialist in the evaluation and development of faculty performance, he has designed and conducted seminars for faculty and administrators in colleges and universities throughout the United States and in twenty countries around the world.

Seldin has made more than two hundred presentations at national and international conferences and often serves as a faculty member in programs offered by the American Council on Education and the American Assembly of Collegiate Schools of Business.

His well-received books include *The Teaching Portfolio* (1991), *How Administrators Can Improve Teaching* (1990, with associates), *Evaluating and Developing Administrative Performance* (1988), *Coping With Faculty Stress* (1987, with associates), *Changing Practices in Faculty Evaluation* (1984), *Successful Faculty Evaluation Programs* (1980), *Teaching Professors to Teach* (1977), and *How Colleges Evaluate Professors* (1975). He has contributed numerous articles on the teaching profession, evaluating and developing performance, and academic culture to such publications as the *New York Times* and *Change* magazine.

CONTENTS

About the Author   *v*

Contributors   *ix*

Preface   *xi*

1. The Teaching Portfolio Concept   1

2. Preparing the Teaching Portfolio: A Firsthand Report   15

3. The Key Role of the Mentor   19

4. How Portfolios are Used in Nine Institutions   27

5. Evaluating Teaching Portfolios for Personnel Decisions   71

6. Answers to Common Questions About the Teaching Portfolio   87

7. A Roundtable Discussion of the Portfolio and its Results   95

8. Sample Portfolios From Across Disciplines   101

   Index   211

CONTRIBUTORS

PATRICIA A. ALEXANDER, Professor of Educational Psychology and Educational Curriculum and Instruction, Texas A & M University

LINDA F. ANNIS, Professor of Educational Psychology, Ball State University

VALERIE M. BALESTER, Assistant Professor of English, Texas A & M University

JOHN BARBER, Professor of History, Ball State University

NINA CARIS, Director of Introductory Programs, Department of Biology, Texas A & M University

ELAINE K. FERRARO, Associate Professor of Sociology and Director of Social Work Program, Columbia College

THERESA W. FOSSUM, Assistant Professor, Department of Small Animal Medicine and Surgery, Texas A & M University

VIVIA LAWTON FOWLER, Instructor of Religion, Columbia College

LAURIE HOPKINS, Associate Professor of Mathematics, Columbia College

MARDEE JENRETTE, Director, Teaching/Learning Project, Miami-Dade Community College

RICHARD C. KREJCI, Assistant Professor of Physical Education, Columbia College

BARBARA J. MILLIS, Assistant Dean, Faculty Development, University of Maryland University College

ROBERT D. NARVESON, Professor of English, University of Nebraska-Lincoln

CHARLOTTE NELSON, Associate Professor of Music (Voice), Shenandoah Conservatory of Shenandoah University

M. CAROL O'NEIL, Research Associate, Office of Instructional Development and Technology, Dalhousie University

DONALD W. ORR, Assistant Professor of Mathematics, Miami-Dade Community College

WILLIAM L. PERRY, Associate Provost and Dean of Faculties, Professor of Mathematics, Texas A & M University

MARIAN M. POSEY, Director, Faculty Resource Center, Murray State University

JONATHAN S. RAYMOND, Dean of Faculty, Gordon College

JEROLD J. SAVORY, Dean of Faculty, Columbia College

CLEMENT A. SELDIN, Associate Professor of Elementary Education, University of Massachusetts at Amherst

DONNIE J. SELF, Professor and Head, Department of Humanities in Medicine, Texas A & M University

RAY SHACKELFORD, Professor of Industry and Technology and Director, Teaching the Technology of Teaching Program, Ball State University

CHRISTINE D. TOWNSEND, Associate Professor of Agricultural Education, Texas A & M University

RONALD C. WARNER, Professor of Modern Languages and Classics and Coordinator of German, Ball State University

JAMES WILKINSON, Director, Derek Bok Center for Teaching, Harvard University

W. ALAN WRIGHT, Executive Director, Office of Instructional Development and Technology, Dalhousie University

KENNETH J. ZAHORSKI, Professor of English and Director of Faculty Development, St. Norbert College

JOHN ZUBIZARRETA, Associate Professor of English, Columbia College

PREFACE

An historic change is taking place in higher education: Teaching is being taken more seriously. Countless colleges and universities are reexamining their commitment to teaching and exploring ways to improve and reward it. As for faculty, they are being held accountable, as never before, to provide indisputable evidence of the quality of their classroom instruction.

In the past, factual information on teaching has been skimpy at best. The typical professor has been unable to present solid evidence of what they do in the classroom, much less why it is done. The result: the general and routine approach to evaluate classroom teaching has relied almost exclusively on student ratings, perhaps supplemented by a testimonial letter or two. But experience now tells us there is much more to teaching than what is critiqued on student rating forms buttressed by one or two pat-on-the-back testimonials.

The best way this writer knows to get at both the complexity and individuality of teaching is the teaching portfolio. What is the teaching portfolio? It is a gathering of documents and other materials highlighting the professor's classroom teaching and suggesting its scope and quality. It can be used to present the evidence, the hard evidence, on teaching effectiveness. It is flexible enough to be used for personnel decisions and/or to provide the stimulus and structure for self-reflection about teaching areas in need of improvement.

Today, the portfolio approach is experiencing explosive growth. An estimated 400 colleges and universities in the United States are now using or experimenting with it. That is a stunning jump from the estimated 75 institutions using it just two years ago. Significantly, among the users or experimenters with portfolios today are institutions of every size, shape, and mission.

Previous books exploring the teaching portfolio have taken a broad how-to approach and have been geared primarily to describing the kinds of material that could go into a portfolio. This book has a different thrust.

- ◆ It details in depth the experience with portfolios of nine institutions.
- ◆ It provides time-tested strategies and proven advice for getting started with portfolios.
- ◆ It offers practical suggestions on using portfolios for improved teaching performance or personnel decisions.
- ◆ It not only spells out the important points to consider in evaluating portfolios but also provides field-tested forms for doing so.
- ◆ It offers seventeen model teaching portfolios from across disciplines.

In short, *Successful Use of Teaching Portfolios* offers college and university administrators and faculty the kind of ready-to-use, hands-on information required to foster the most effective use of portfolios.

It is written for presidents, provosts, academic vice-presidents, deans, department chairs, and faculty. They are the essential partners in developing successful teaching portfolio programs. Graduate students, especially those planning careers as faculty members, should also find this book stimulating and useful.

OVERVIEW OF THE CONTENTS

Chapter One discusses the teaching portfolio concept, how it differs from all other approaches to evaluate and improve teaching, what is included and what is not included in a portfolio, why the content depends on the purpose for which the portfolio is to be used, and how and why the portfolio movement is blossoming across the country.

Chapter Two is a personal report by an associate provost on his portfolio preparation, the process, what he learned about himself as a teacher of mathematics, and why he is a strong advocate of the portfolio.

Chapter Three examines the key role of the mentor and describes the collaborative three-meetings approach to developing a polished portfolio. It also provides practical advice on the selection of a mentor and how institutions can "grow" their own on-campus mentors.

Chapter Four describes in important detail how nine institutions, large, small, public and private, have implemented portfolios. It takes a hard, real-world look at purposes, strategies, tough decisions, what worked and what didn't, today's practices and tomorrow's plans.

Chapter Five spells out how to plan and implement a viable system to evaluate teaching portfolios for personnel decisions, what should be evaluated, and how it should be done. Also explored are vital criteria and crucial differences between strong and weak portfolios. Field-tested forms to evaluate teaching from portfolios are in the appendix to this chapter.

Chapter Six offers pragmatic answers to many questions commonly raised about developing and using portfolios. Here are guidelines for getting started and a discussion on how the portfolio differs from the usual faculty report to administrators. Also, how much time it takes to produce a portfolio, how to produce what administrators are really looking for, why portfolios are different from each other, and why an elegant portfolio cannot disguise poor teaching.

Chapter Seven presents a roundtable discussion by four faculty members whose personal experience in preparing portfolios has given them insights into their teaching.

Chapter Eight contains the actual teaching portfolios of seventeen professors from different disciplines and institutions.

ACKNOWLEDGMENTS

I am grateful to Pace University for its unflagging support of this book. Special thanks go to Irving McPhail, Arthur Centonze, Frieda Reitman, and Don Streever for their continuing encouragement and assistance.

I applaud the writers who contributed to this book for their professionalism and good-humored acceptance of deadlines and rewrites. Working with them has truly been my pleasure.

Peter Seldin
Croton-on-Hudson, New York
January, 1993

THE TEACHING PORTFOLIO CONCEPT

Peter Seldin

INTRODUCTION

An important and welcome change is taking place on college and university campuses: Teaching is being taken more seriously. Countless institutions are reexamining their commitment to teaching and exploring ways to improve and reward it. As for faculty, they are being held accountable, as never before, to provide solid evidence of the quality of their classroom instruction.

The familiar professorial paradox is crumbling on many campuses. Traditionally, college professors were hired to teach, but were rewarded for research. While this is still true in many institutions, especially those with strong graduate schools, it has been largely swept away on campuses stressing undergraduate education. Today, teaching may still be in second place in the race with research but the gap is slowly closing.

There is an explosive growth to the movement to take teaching seriously. Interest is evident from the overcrowded conferences and second and third printings of books on improving and evaluating teaching. It can be seen in the recently issued reports by such institutions as Berkeley, Dartmouth, Michigan, Penn State, and Stanford, all chorusing the pressing need for closer attention to the quality of teaching. Moreover, institutions are finding the funds to support the teaching renaissance. Stanford University, for example, set aside $7 million for programs aimed at rewarding and improving teaching (Mooney, 1991); the University of Pennsylvania's Wharton School offered a $15,000 cash award ("No Such Problems...,") and the University of Missouri-Columbia $10,000 ("10 Top Teachers Get Recognition...,") to recognize and reward outstanding faculty teaching.

What is behind the new emphasis on teaching? Faculty and administrators who chafed at the inequity of teaching and research played a part. The growing number of students and parents facing the swiftly escalating annual costs of higher education led to demanding questions about the quality of teaching. And the insistent viewpoint that teaching is actually an expression of scholarship, that scholarship does not confine itself to the cutting edge of research but also lives in intimate knowledge and teaching of the research in the classroom (see *Scholarship Revisited*, Boyer, 1990), added to the pressure on campuses.

But perhaps the most compelling force for the new seriousness about teaching is the strident demands for teaching accountability from newly aroused legislatures and institutional governing boards. Facing an unrelenting budgetary squeeze, they are taking fresh, almost inquisitorial interest, in knowing how faculty members spend their time and about their effectiveness as teachers.

In short, the movement to improve and reward teaching and to take it seriously has become a groundswell across the nation. It has enlisted state legislatures, boards of trustees, financial donors, academic administrators, faculty members, parents and students to press colleges and universities to scrutinize more carefully the classroom performance of each professor.

Unfortunately, factual information on teaching performance is at best often skimpy. The typical professor has little solid evidence about what they do in the classroom and how well they do it. True, they probably have student ratings but that's about all and student ratings alone fall far short of a complete picture of one's classroom performance. They may have a curriculum vitae but typically that lists publications, honors, research grants and other scholarly accomplishments and says very little about teaching.

Yet in the absence of factual information about teaching, how can it be evaluated? How can it be rewarded? How can it be improved? And how can institutions give the teaching function its proper role and value in the educational process?

Is there a way for colleges and universities to respond simultaneously to the movement to take teaching seriously and to the pressures to improve systems of teaching accountability? The answer is yes. A solution can be found by turning to the teaching portfolio. It is an approach increasingly recognized and respected.

WHAT IS A TEACHING PORTFOLIO?

It is a factual description of a professor's teaching strengths and accomplishments. It includes documents and materials which collectively suggest the scope and quality of a professor's teaching performance.

The portfolio is to teaching what lists of publications, grants and honors are to research and scholarship. As such, it allows faculty members to display their teaching accomplishments for examination by others. And, in the process, it contributes both to sounder personnel decisions and to the professional development of individual faculty members (Seldin, 1991). As a result, it provides a strong signal that teaching is an institutional priority.

Why would a faculty member want to prepare a teaching portfolio? They might do so in order to spell out for the record, the hard evidence and specific data about their teaching effectiveness. That is a clear advantage when an evaluation committee examines academic credentials for tenure and promotion decisions. Or they might do so in order to provide the needed structure for self-reflection about areas of their teaching needing improvement.

An important point: the teaching portfolio is *not* an exhaustive compilation of *all* the documents and materials that bear on teaching performance. Instead, it culls from the record *selected* information on teaching activities and solid evidence of their effectiveness (Seldin, 1991). And, importantly, just as in a curriculum vitae, all claims in the portfolio should be supported by firm empirical evidence.

To the skeptical professor who hesitates to spend valuable time preparing a teaching portfolio, Lemm (1992) offers this answer: As faculty, he says, we are trained to document our research and publication activities. We update our curriculum vitae as we strive for tenure and promotion. But we don't document our teaching, nor are we expected to do so. Doesn't it make sense to document teaching activities with the same care and vigor we document research and scholarship? The portfolio enables a professor to present evidence of teaching achievements in an orderly, efficient, and persuasive way.

The logic behind portfolios is straightforward. Earlier assessment methods, such as student ratings or peer observations, were like flashlights. That is, they illuminated only the teaching skills and abilities that fell within their beams. As such, they shed light on only a small part of a professor's classroom performance. But with portfolios, the flashlight is replaced by a searchlight. Its beam discloses the broad range of teaching skills, abilities, attitudes and philosophies.

Edgerton, Hutchings, and Quinlan (1991) make the case for teaching portfolios in this way:

1. Portfolios provide documented evidence of teaching that is connected to the specifics and contexts of what is being taught.
2. They go beyond exclusive reliance on student ratings because they include a range of evidence from a variety of sources such as syllabi, samples of student work, self-reflections, reports on classroom research, and faculty development programs.
3. In the process of selecting and organizing their portfolio material, faculty think hard about their teaching, a practice which is likely to lead to improvement in classroom performance.
4. In deciding what should go into a portfolio and how it should be evaluated, institutions necessarily must address the question of what is

effective teaching and what standards should drive campus teaching practice.

5. Portfolios are a step toward a more public, professional view of teaching. They reflect teaching as a scholarly activity.

The teaching portfolio is increasingly recognized and respected. Among the many presidents of academic institutions and associations supporting the portfolio approach are Derek Bok, former Harvard University president; Donald Kennedy, President of Stanford University; Ernest Boyer, President of the Carnegie Foundation for the Advancement of Teaching (see *Scholarship Revisited*, 1990); and Lynne Cheney, Chairman of the National Endowment for the Humanities (see *Tyrannical Machines*, 1990).

The teaching portfolio concept has gone well beyond the point of theoretical possibility. It has been used in Canada (where it is called a teaching dossier) for nearly fifteen years. Today it is being adopted or pilot-tested in various forms by an increasing number of American institutions.

Although reliable numbers are hard to come by, it is estimated that as many as 400 colleges and universities in the United States are now using or experimenting with portfolios. That is a stunning jump from the approximately 75 institutions thought to be using portfolios just two years ago. Among the current users or experimenters with portfolios are: Texas A&M University, Columbia College (South Carolina), University of Maryland, Miami-Dade Community College (Florida), St. Norbert College (Wisconsin), New Community College of Baltimore (Maryland), the University of Nebraska, and Murray State University (Kentucky).

THE IMPORTANCE OF COLLABORATION

Should portfolios be developed by the professor working alone or should they be collaborative efforts? From mounting experience, we know now that they are best prepared in consultation with others. The reason, says Seldin (1991) and Bird (1989) is because portfolios prepared by the professor working alone do not include the collegial or supervisory support needed in a program of teaching improvement. And, importantly, there is none of the control or corroboration of evidence that is essential to sustain personnel decisions. That is why portfolio development *should* involve interaction and mentoring in the same way that a doctoral dissertation reflects both the efforts of the candidate and the advice of the mentor.

Who might serve as a mentor? A department chair, a colleague or a faculty development specialist could fill the role. They discuss with the professor such key questions as: Which areas of the teaching-learning process are to be examined? What kinds of information do they expect to collect? How is the information to be analyzed and presented? Why are they preparing the portfolio?

One caution: Whoever serves as portfolio consultant/mentor must have wide knowledge of procedures and current instruments to document effective teaching. In this way the consultant can assist the faculty member by providing suggestions and resources, and maintaining support during the preparation of the portfolio (Seldin, 1991). This point is discussed in detail, this volume, in the chapter by Annis.

A second caution: Because faculty members and institutional contexts differ widely, there is no one "best" way to structure the collaboration. Edgerton, Hutchings and Quinlan (1991) offer these approaches:

1. A buddy system in which two faculty pair up for a semester to visit each other's classes, talk to their students, confer on syllabi, exercises, and exams and then assist each other in documenting their teaching in their respective portfolios.
2. A mentoring system where the older, more experienced professor works directly with a younger colleague in assisting them as they develop their portfolio.
3. A departmentally-based portfolio project in which discussions about teaching can be more sharply focused and richer because they are focused on the discipline.

Since "teaching tends to be a private, solitary activity," Edgerton, Hutchings and Quinlan (p.51) conclude that "collaboratively-designed portfolios are an antidote to this isolation and a way to promote collegial exchange focused on the substance—the scholarship—of teaching."

Although some professors will prepare their portfolios in collaboration with their department chair, experience tells us that most will end up working with someone else. Therefore it is of special importance that a periodic, written exchange of views between the chair and the professor take place about: 1) teaching responsibilities; 2) other duties related to teaching; 3) the general content and structure of the portfolio; and 4) how teaching performance is to be reported. "Otherwise," cautions Seldin (1991, p.6) "there is a danger that the department chair may erroneously conclude that the data submitted overlook areas of prime concern and may even cover up areas of suspected weaknesses."

SIX STEPS TO CREATE A TEACHING PORTFOLIO

Experience suggests that most faculty members rely on the following step-by-step approach in creating their portfolios. It is based on the work of Shore and others (1986), Seldin (1991), and O'Neil and Wright (1992).

Step 1. Clarify Teaching Responsibilities. Typically, this covers such topics as courses currently taught and those taught in the recent past, teaching-related activities such as serving as faculty advisor to student organizations, or advising individual graduate or undergraduate students. It is based on the exchange of memos between the department chair and the faculty member.

Step 2. Select Items for the Portfolio. Based on the teaching responsibilities described in Step 1, the professor selects items for inclusion in the portfolio which are directly applicable to their teaching responsibilities.

Step 3. Prepare Statements on Each Item. Statements are prepared by the professor on activities, initiatives, and accomplishments on each item. Back-up documentation and appendices are referenced, as appropriate.

Step 4. Arrange the Items in Order. The sequence of the statements about accomplishments in each area is determined by their intended use. For example, if the professor intends to demonstrate teaching improvement, such activities as attending faculty development workshops and seminars should be stressed.

Step 5. Compile the Support Data. Evidence supporting all items mentioned in the portfolio should be retained by the professor and made available for review upon request. These would include, for example, letters from colleagues and students, original student evaluations of teaching, samples of student work, invitations to contribute articles on teaching in one's discipline. Such evidence is *not* part of the portfolio but is back-up material placed in the appendix or made available upon request.

Step 6. Incorporate the Portfolio into the Curriculum Vitae. Lastly, the portfolio is then inserted into the professor's curriculum vitae under the heading of "Teaching" or "Instruction." Departmental guidelines will determine its precise location in the c.v. in relation to the sections on "Research" and "Service."

CHOOSING ITEMS FOR THE PORTFOLIO

There are many possibilities from which items can be selected that are especially relevant to the professor's particular teaching situation. The items chosen also depend, to some degree, on whether the portfolio is prepared for purposes of improvement or personnel decision, and on any format or content requirements of a professor's department or institution.

Based on empirical evidence, it is clear that certain items turn up in portfolios with much more frequency than others. From personal review of more than 400 portfolios prepared by professors in both public and private institutions, the writer can assert that certain items appear again and again.

Material from Oneself
   ✦ Statement of teaching responsibilities, including course titles, numbers, enrollments, and a brief description of the way each course was taught.
   ✦ Representative course syllabi detailing course content and objectives, teaching methods, readings, homework assignments.
   ✦ Description of steps taken to improve teaching, including changes resulting from self-evaluation, reading journals on teaching improvement, participation in programs on sharpening instructional skill.
   ✦ Instructional innovations and evaluation of their effectiveness.
   ✦ A personal statement by the professor describing teaching goals for the next five years.

Material from Others
+ Student course or teaching evaluation data which produce an overall rating of effectiveness or suggest improvements.
+ Statements from colleagues who have observed the professor in the classroom.
+ Documentation of teaching development activity through the campus center for teaching and learning.
+ Statements from colleagues who have reviewed the professor's teaching materials, such as course syllabi, assignments, testing and grading practices.
+ Honors or other recognition such as a distinguished teaching award.

The Products of Good Teaching
+ A record of students who succeed in advanced study in the field.
+ Student publications or conference presentations on course-related work.
+ Testimonials from employers or students about the professor's influence on career choice.
+ Student scores on pre- and post-course examinations.

These are the most commonly selected items but by no means are they the only ones to appear in portfolios. Some professors, for reasons of discipline or institution or personal predilection, choose a different content mix.

Some Items that Sometimes Appear in Portfolios
+ Description of curricular revisions, including new course projects, materials, and class assignments.
+ Self-evaluation of teaching-related activities.
+ Contributing to, or editing, a professional journal on teaching the professor's discipline.
+ A statement by the department chair assessing the professor's teaching contribution to the department.
+ Invitations to present a paper on teaching one's discipline.
+ A videotape of the professor teaching a typical class.
+ Participation in off-campus activities related to teaching in the professor's discipline.
+ Evidence of help given to colleagues leading to improvement of their teaching.
+ Description of how computers, films, and other non-print materials are used in teaching.
+ Statements by alumni on the quality of instruction.
+ Examples of graded student essays along with the professor's comments on why they were so graded.

How much information and evidence is needed to fairly represent a professor's teaching performance? There is no simple answer. Each professor must set the balance scale between "too much" and "not enough" information. However, for most professors, six to eight pages plus supporting appendix material is sufficient.

The appendix material needs careful attention to be sure all the statements on teaching accomplishments are adequately supported. In deciding what to include, it is best not to engage in overkill. O'Neil and Wright (1992) suggest that the professor maintain a file of all relevant records on teaching. The best examples should be chosen for the portfolio and evaluators informed that additional evidence is available upon request.

Keep in mind that the portfolio is a living document that changes over time. New items are added. Others are removed. Updating a portfolio becomes a simple matter of dropping items pertaining to teaching into a file drawer just as is now done for research and service. Little time or effort is involved. When the research and service sections of the curriculum vitae are being updated, simply do the same for the teaching section.

USING THE PORTFOLIO FOR PERSONNEL DECISIONS

Because each portfolio is unique, like a fingerprint, no two are exactly alike. The content and organization differ from one professor to another. This approach works well if the portfolio is used for improvement purposes. But it works less well if the portfolio is used for personnel decisions.

One way, says Seldin (1989), to lay the problem to rest is to require those portfolios used for tenure and promotion decisions, or for teaching excellence awards, to include certain mandated items along with the elective ones. Among the institutions adopting this approach are Murray State University (Kentucky), Pace University Business School (New York), Marquette University (Wisconsin) and the University of Colorado at Boulder.

At Murray State University, for example, all faculty are expected to include in their portfolios: 1) a reflective statement; 2) course syllabi, 3) examinations; 4) graded assignments; and 5) student rating reports.

At the Pace University Business School, faculty are urged to include: 1) a statement of teaching philosophy, 2) student evaluations and comments, 3) teaching awards, 4) innovative course materials and technologies, 5) course syllabi and exams, and 6) evidence of the integration of contemporary business theory and practice into classroom instruction.

Since teaching is now being taken more seriously, professors looking for recognition as superior teachers stand to benefit by providing tenure and promotion committees with their teaching portfolios. It provides evaluators with hard-to-ignore information on *what* they do in the classroom and *why* they do it. And by so doing, it avoids looking at teaching performance as a derivative of student ratings.

Does the teaching portfolio approach really make any difference? See the chapter by Shackelford in this volume and consider the typical comments from professors whose portfolios were used for purposes of personnel decisions:

> *A history professor in New Jersey:* "Teaching is more important here now. My promotion to full professor was largely due to my portfolio. It gave the P & T committee an analysis, prioritizing, and valuing of what I do in the classroom."

> *A sociology professor in California:* "I knew I was a good teacher but no one else did until they read my portfolio. I got tenure!"

> *A foreign language professor in Nebraska:* "In the last two years I've won three teaching awards at the state and international level. Without the portfolio, none of this would have happened."

How do members of promotion and tenure committees feel about teaching portfolios? Consider the following comments from members of committees:

> *A committee member in Georgia:* "It took time to learn how to evaluate portfolios. But once we did, the richness of the data on teaching made our job a hell of a lot easier."

> *A committee member in Texas:* "No doubt about it, we just make better tenure and promotion decisions with portfolios."

It is important to keep in mind that use of the portfolio for personnel decisions is only occasional. Its primary purpose is to improve teaching performance.

USING THE PORTFOLIO TO IMPROVE TEACHING

It is in the very process of creating the collection of documents and materials that comprise the portfolio that the professor is stimulated to: 1) reconsider personal teaching activities; 2) rethink teaching strategies; 3) rearrange priorities; and 4) plan for the future (Seldin and Annis, 1990). Agreement comes from Edgerton, Hutchings, and Quinlan (1991), who say that portfolios possess a special power to involve faculty in reflecting on their own classroom practices and how to improve it.

There are three important reasons why the portfolio is such a valuable aid in professional development: 1) It is grounded in discipline-based pedagogy, that is, the focus is on teaching a particular subject to a particular group of students at a particular time; 2) The level of personal investment in time, energy, and commitment is high (since faculty develop their own portfolios) and that is a necessary condition for change; and 3) It stirs many professors to reflect on their teaching in an insightful, refocused way. (See the section on Gordon College by Raymond, this volume, for further discussion on portfolios as an aid in faculty development.)

When used for improvement purposes, the portfolio contains *no* mandated items. Instead, it contains only items chosen by the professor working in collaboration with a consultant/mentor. The professor may decide, for example, to improve one particular course and include such items as: 1) A summary of instructional methods used; 2) Specific course objectives and the degree of student achievement of those objectives; 3) A full-period videotape of a typical class; 4) student ratings containing both diagnostic and summative questions. (See the Barber and Perry portfolios, this volume, for examples of portfolios prepared for teaching improvement.)

The bottom-line question, of course, remains. Do portfolios actually improve teaching? The most candid answer is frequently yes but not always. Experience on campus after campus suggests that if the professor is motivated to improve, knows how to improve, or where to go for help, improvement is quite likely. Consider these comments:

> *A marketing professor in Oregon:* "I hadn't really thought about my teaching before. But preparing a portfolio made me think about why I do what I do in the classroom. Now I'm breaking out of the old, tired examples and cases. I'm trying new things."

> *A biology professor in South Carolina:* "I confess I was very skeptical at first. But the portfolio led me to rethink my entire approach to teaching. For the better, I must add."

> *A mathematics professor in Illinois:* "I only wish I had learned about the portfolio concept twenty years ago. It sure would have improved my teaching."

> *An educational psychology professor in Florida:* "I believe that every new and experienced faculty member can improve their teaching by preparing a portfolio. It's not a quick-fix approach. But it sure is helpful."

USING PORTFOLIOS FOR OTHER PURPOSES

Some professors prepare portfolios in order to take them on the road as they seek a different teaching position. Generally, the portfolio is submitted in advance of an interview as an aid to presenting a more complete teacher to the institution. And some institutions are now requiring portfolios from professors applying for teaching positions.

Portfolios are now widely used to help determine winners of awards for outstanding teaching or for merit pay consideration. And excerpts from portfolios are increasingly used in successful faculty grant applications.

GAINING ACCEPTANCE OF THE PORTFOLIO APPROACH

To say that the teaching portfolio approach is useful is one thing, but to get the approach off the ground is quite another. To begin with, there are social and attitudinal problems. Some professors automatically resist by evoking various academic traditions. They say that faculty members are not comfortable as self-promoters, don't need to raise "defensive" documentation, and have neither the time nor the desire to keep a record of their classroom achievements. O'Neil and Wright (1992) dispose of these arguments by pointing out that the world of college and university teaching is undergoing change. In an age of accountability, the portfolio is an instrument focused on effective teaching, and that professors: 1) Must produce better evidence of contributions; 2) Need "positive" documentation to support accomplishments; and 3) Need to convey those accomplishments clearly and persuasively to third-party inspection outside their immediate fields.

Caution: Not only do some professors decline to embrace the portfolio concept, but some administrators also enlist as nay-sayers. Administrators at some institutions are immediately negative at the sight of strangers bearing new ideas, and the portfolio concept is no exception. People being people, some operate comfortably in well-worn grooves and resist almost any change. Others resist out of an unspoken fear that somehow they are threatened.

If the portfolio approach is ultimately to be embraced, an institutional climate of acceptance must first be created. How can that be done? The following guidelines are based on years of practical experience and the work of Edgerton, Hutchings, and Quinlan (1991), Millis (1991), Seldin (1991), and O'Neil and Wright (1992). They should be helpful in creating such a climate of acceptance.

1. The portfolio concept must be presented in a candid, complete, and clear way to every faculty member and academic administrator.
2. Professors must have a significant hand in both the development and the operation of the portfolio program. They must feel, with justification, that they "own" the program.
3. The primary purpose of the portfolio program should be to improve the quality of teaching.
4. The institution's most respected faculty should be involved from the outset. That means the best *teachers* because their participation attracts other faculty to the program. It also means admired teachers who are also prominent *researchers* because their participation will signal both the value of portfolios and their willingness to go public with the scholarship of their teaching.
5. The portfolio should be field-tested on a handful of prestigious professors. The fact that faculty leaders are willing to try the concept will not be lost on others.
6. Top-level academic administrators must give their active support to the portfolio concept. They must be publicly committed to the program and provide whatever resources are necessary so it operates effectively.
7. Sufficient time—a year or even two years—must be allowed for acceptance and implementation. Use the time to modify procedures, standards, and techniques. But keep moving forward. Don't allow the portfolio concept to stall in a futile search for perfection.
8. The portfolio approach must *not* be forced on anyone. It is much better to use faculty volunteers.
9. If portfolios are used for personnel decisions, or for determining teaching

award winners, all professors must know the criteria and standards by which portfolios will be evaluated. And those who evaluate portfolios must be clear on those criteria and standards and abide by them.

10. It is wise to allow room for individual differences in developing portfolios. Disciplines differ. So do styles of teaching.

11. Encourage collaboration. A mentor from the same discipline can provide special insights and understandings as well as departmental practices in dealing with portfolios. On the other hand, a mentor from a different discipline can often help clarify the institution's viewpoint, the "big picture." That can be significant since portfolios submitted for personnel decisions will be read by faculty from other disciplines.

SOME FINAL THOUGHTS

For the past several years, the writer has crisscrossed the country explaining the teaching portfolio. I've visited scores of colleges and universities of differing sizes, shapes, and missions and discussed with promotion and tenure committees, department chairs, deans, and faculty, the place of portfolios in the evaluation of teaching *and* as a powerful tool for teaching improvement.

And I've had the pleasure of working as mentor to more than 200 professors across disciplines as they prepared their personal portfolios. This extensive involvement, not just as a theorist but also as a practitioner, has led me to conclude that while we are still short many answers to the portfolio puzzle, we have discovered some of the answers and are on the edge of discovering more. Let me share some of what we've learned.

We know that the portfolio concept has gone well beyond the point of theoretical possibility. More and more institutions—public and private, large and small—are today emphasizing, nurturing, and rewarding teaching through portfolios. Some colleges and universities use them to improve teaching. Others use them in tenure and promotion decisions. Still others use portfolios both for improving teaching and for personnel decisions. It's clear that portfolios are being used—and used successfully—in a variety of different ways. (See Chapter 4, this volume, on the varying ways colleges and universities are using portfolios.)

We know that a teaching portfolio *cannot* gloss over terrible teaching. Why? Because the preparer cannot document effective teaching performance. The evidence is just not there. A fancy cover and attractive printer fonts cannot overcome weak performance in the classroom for a professor any more than it can for a student. On the other hand, for an excellent teacher, the portfolio offers an unmatched opportunity to document classroom practices that have previously gone unrecognized and unrewarded.

We know that portfolio models and mentors must be available to professors as they prepare their own portfolios. The models enable them to see how others—in a variety of disciplines—have put together documents and materials into a cohesive whole. At the same time, since most faculty come to the teaching portfolio concept with no previous experience with the concept, the resources of a mentor, someone with wide knowledge of ways to document teaching, should be made available to faculty.

We know that the portfolio should include selected information. It is not an exhaustive compilation of all the documents and materials that bear on teaching performance. Instead, it presents *selected* information on teaching activities and accomplishments.

We know that the primary purpose of the portfolio is to improve classroom teaching and only occasionally for personnel decisions. Does it actually help improve teaching? On campus after campus, the answer is gratifyingly and frequently, yes. The reason is that the very process of collecting and sifting documents and materials that reflect a professor's teaching, gets them thinking about what has worked and what hasn't in the classroom. And why they do what they do in the classroom. It forces them to review their activities, strategies, and plans for the future.

We know that the time and energy it takes to prepare a portfolio are well worth the benefits. That is the conclusion from the experience of hundreds of faculty in many colleges and universities in preparing portfolios. The fact is, it usually takes no more than a few days to put together. And, on the plus side, the benefits are considerable.

What are those benefits? The teaching portfolio offers professors the chance to describe their teaching strengths and accomplishments for the record. That is a clear advantage when evaluation committees examine the record for personnel decisions.

But the portfolio concept does more than that. Many professors find that the process of portfolio development, itself, acts as a stimulant to self-improvement. And, importantly, many colleges and universities find that portfolios are a useful means to underscore *teaching* as an institutional priority (Seldin, 1992).

Especially in light of the national movement to take teaching seriously, I think readers will agree that these are important benefits.

BIBLIOGRAPHY

Bird, T. "The Schoolteacher's Portfolio," In L. Darling-Hammond and J. Millman (Eds.) *Handbook on the Evaluation of Elementary and Secondary Schoolteachers.* Newbury Park, CA: Sage, 1989.

Boyer, E.L. *Scholarship Revisited.* Princeton, NJ: Carnegie Foundation for the Advancement of Teaching, 1990.

Cheney, L.V. *Tyrannical Machines.* Washington, DC: National Endowment for the Humanities, 1990.

Edgerton, R., Hutchings, P. and Quinlan, K. *The Teaching Portfolio: Capturing the Scholarship in Teaching.* Washington, DC: American Association for Higher Education, 1991.

Lemm, R. "The I Ain't Got No Teaching Dossier Blues." *The Point.* 1 (2), Charlottetown, PEI: University of Prince Edward Island, February, 1992.

Millis, B. "Putting the Teaching Portfolio in Context," In K. Zahorski (Ed.), *To Improve the Academy.* Stillwater, OK: POD/New Forums Press, 1991.

Mooney, C. "Stanford Unveils Plan Designed to Elevate Status of Teaching." *Chronicle of Higher Education,* March 31, 1991, p. A15.

"No Such Problems Plague the University of Pennsylvania's Wharton School." *Chronicle of Higher Education,* March 6, 1991, p. A11.

O'Neil, C. and Wright, A. *Recording Teaching Accomplishment: A Dalhousie Guide to the Teaching Dossier.* Halifax, NS: Office of Instructional Development and Technology, Dalhousie University, Second Edition, 1992.

Seldin, P. "The Teaching Portfolio and It's Purposes: A Look at Current Practice." Paper presented at the AAHE National Conference on Higher Education, Chicago, IL, 1992.

Seldin, P. *The Teaching Portfolio: A Practical Guide to Improved Performance and Promotion/Tenure Decisions.* Bolton, MA: Anker Publishing, 1991.

Seldin, P. and Annis, L. "The Teaching Portfolio." *Journal of Staff, Program, and Organization Development* 8 (4): 197-201, 1990.

Seldin, P. "The Teaching Portfolio." Paper presented at the National Conference of the Professional and Organizational Development Network in Higher Education, Jekyll Island, GA, 1989.

Shore, M.B. and others. *The Teaching Dossier, Revised Edition.* Montreal: Canadian Association of University Teachers, 1986.

"10 Top Teachers Get Recognition (and a Surprise)." *The New York Times,* March 31, 1991, p. 29.

2

Preparing the Teaching Portfolio: A Firsthand Report

William L. Perry

I decided to develop a teaching portfolio for two reasons: to determine whether the process would improve my performance as a teacher and to determine whether teaching portfolios could provide valid data for promotion and tenure processes. While it is too soon to make inferences, my impressions so far have been very positive; my experiences in teaching calculus and overseeing the tenure and promotion processes in the 1992-93 academic year will allow firm conclusions. My experience has been so positive and the benefits already so apparent that I wish I had gone through the process many years ago so that my students could have benefited from better instruction on my part.

As faculty members we continually strive for improvement in teaching, scholarship, and all facets of our mission to provide the best possible educational experience for our students. Self-evaluation is the most powerful tool available for teaching improvement; preparation of a teaching portfolio focuses self-evaluation more effectively than any other process I have used. Rigorous self-imposed standards of quality in teaching and plans for personal development come together in the teaching portfolio to provide thorough evaluation of the past and a framework for the future.

Prior to developing my portfolio, some questions came to mind: Could I "summarize" twenty-one years of teaching? Would I gain insight as to my motives and methods in teaching? Would the process lead to a more critical self-examination of my teaching? Would the exercise be one that I could recommend to colleagues? Would teaching portfolios provide valid documentation for administrative deliberations on tenure, promotion and merit increases? Would I become a better teacher? Would my students benefit? Overall the answers have been very positive or, in the cases where the returns are not yet in, I believe the ultimate answers will be affirmative.

Luckily, as I developed my portfolio, I had the guidance of a mentor with experience in teaching portfolio preparation. My mentor keyed on the fact that, because of my administrative role, I teach the same course from semester to semester. He suggested that I develop a portfolio centered on improvement of that course. This approach made sense, saved me time (no twenty-one years to cover!) and provided tight focus. *Thus I learned that the advice of an experienced mentor is extremely helpful.* In my case the mentor's style was to let me write a draft and then suggest to me approaches to take, questions to ask myself, or supplementary material to provide in appendices. This interactive process (I recall three iterations) worked very well for me and led to a stronger portfolio. Overall I spent about ten hours of actual time in developing my current portfolio; of course, I will be revising and updating it each semester.

Prior to this first experience (June, 1992) with constructing a teaching portfolio, each semester I had analyzed my course/instructor evaluation completed by the students and made adjustments in my modes of instruction based on those evaluations. Yet, I had never conducted the depth of analysis required by teaching portfolio construction. In my administrative role as Associate Provost and Dean of Faculties, I had learned principles of strategic planning but had not yet applied them to my teaching. Construction of the portfolio brought new depth of analysis and important elements of planning to my efforts to always give the best to my students.

Construction of my teaching portfolio was an enjoyable experience. Guidance from colleagues was extremely helpful, just as it is in the other aspects of our academic endeavors. As I have said, a mentor is very helpful and the process takes time. Careful and rigorous introspection in asking oneself, "Why do I do what I do in my teaching function?" is essential. As I considered this question and others, I found my focus turning to the issue of student learning. That is, I found that my teaching was based on models I had constructed from observations of the best teachers from my past. My assumption was that if those modes of teaching were effective for my learning, those same modes would be effective for my students. That assumption was tested as I constructed the portfolio. This I believe is a most important outcome of teaching portfolio preparation: assumptions are tested and we can become better teachers as a result. In fact one of the most important functions of a mentor in the portfolio preparation process is to continually remind the preparer to challenge implicit assumptions that have developed over many years of teaching.

The teaching portfolio also serves an evaluation and planning function. Although thorough preparation of the teaching portfolio requires a substantial investment of time and effort, updates will require less time than the initial construction. Yet the process will never be routine—just as teaching itself is (ideally) never routine. In my updates I will be held to the expectations created by my plans and objectives stated in the existing portfolio. My progress will be measured against standards imposed by me, my colleagues and my students.

Reactions of my colleagues who have constructed portfolios have been uniformly positive. They have remarked that the time was well spent. They experienced a sense of renewal; they realized clearly for the first time to what extent they had (or had not, as the case may be) taken specific actions or utilized university or extramural resources to improve their teaching; and they had become much more critical of their teaching performance. Some colleagues remarked, as in fact I did, that they wished they had gone through this intense a self-examination of teaching years ago.

Based on firsthand experience, I heartily recommend teaching portfolio development. The portfolio provides focus for improvement of teaching and furnishes documentation that may be required in annual reviews or tenure and promotion dossiers. Properly done, the portfolio will provide an accurate picture of a faculty member's current accomplishments and status, as well as plans for improvement. An important lesson anyone will learn from portfolio construction is that the portfolio is not window dressing. The quality of thought and effort one brings to the teaching enterprise will be revealed. The questions that you are asked in developing a portfolio require documentable answers.

The teaching portfolio serves two extremely useful purposes for me in my role as an administrator who teaches mathematics: 1) it provides a mechanism for improvement of my teaching of calculus; and 2) it provides a mechanism for improvement of the processes of promotion, tenure and annual review, as teaching quality is documented. The portfolio preparation process reaps benefits for our students and our universities because of the focus provided and the rigor of self-evaluation driven by the value system of the faculty, for in the final analysis the quality of a university is determined by the quality of its faculty. The quality of instruction is influenced by many factors, but the most important is our colleagues' expectations of excellence in our teaching. When our colleagues expect excellence, we strive to deliver. The teaching portfolio allows us to plan for, measure progress toward, and finally achieve that level of excellence that our students deserve.

3

THE KEY ROLE OF THE MENTOR

Linda F. Annis

I have been extensively involved with the teaching portfolio concept. I have served as an administrator at my own university, acted as a consultant at other institutions, written on the concept, prepared my own portfolio, and worked with numerous faculty as a mentor while they prepared their individual teaching portfolios. In truth, my most personally rewarding role has been in serving as a mentor to my colleagues.

It is from that viewpoint that this chapter is written. I will discuss the importance of the teaching portfolio mentor and then describe the three-meetings process for helping faculty prepare portfolios that my teaching portfolio colleagues and I (Seldin and Annis, 1990) have found to be the most effective. Finally, I will offer suggestions about how an institution can best "grow" their own on-campus teaching portfolio mentors.

THE IMPORTANCE OF THE MENTOR

The use of a mentor is one of the main characteristics distinguishing teaching portfolios from the usual kind of documents prepared formally by faculty for personnel decisions or more informally to assist in teaching improvement activities. My experience has been that the teaching portfolio is best prepared by working in collaboration with a mentor.

The mentor can be a faculty colleague, a department chairperson, or a faculty development specialist. According to Seldin (1991, p.5), the mentor can discuss with the professor such important questions as: 1) why they are preparing the portfolio; 2) what they hope to learn from it; 3) which areas of the teaching-learning process they expect to examine; 4) what kinds of information they expect to collect; and 5) how the information can be analyzed and presented.

A good portfolio mentor must have wide knowledge of evaluation instruments and procedures. This enables the faculty member to avoid having to reinvent the wheel in documenting teaching effectiveness. For example, the competent mentor will be aware that there are many forms already available for utilizing peer evaluation of teaching in a portfolio, should the professor decide to include this data source.

Mentors also need to be aware of, and be able to provide examples of, different approaches and techniques for demonstrating effective teaching. One professor may find it useful to videotape a class in which there is a lot of student interaction. Another may profit from help in brainstorming options for documenting products of student learning, such as pre-testing and post-testing as applied to their discipline.

It is very important for the mentor to convey the notion that a portfolio is not just a "gathering" of all the "stuff" that a professor might have hanging around in their desk drawers and file cabinets. Instead, preparation of a good portfolio involves an analysis, a prioritizing, and then a *valuing* of exactly what we do in the classroom and why it is so important. The portfolio mentor can help the professor select and use the most valid teaching records for accomplishing this.

In actual practice, I have found that it is *not* necessary for the mentor to be in the same discipline as the mentee. In fact, it has been my experience that I may actually be more effective as a mentor when working in a field very different from mine. Why? Because when I am interacting with a professor in my own area, it is often difficult to avoid focusing on the content rather than the teaching activities. As a result, it may be more difficult to offer fresh approaches to documenting teaching.

Another important role for the mentor is to serve as a source of steady support and encouragement as the portfolio is prepared. It can be an uncomfortable experience for the mentee to reveal themselves so intimately as a teacher to another person. The mentor needs to be able to provide positive reinforcement for the strengths found in the various drafts of the portfolio while, at the same time, serving as a source of suggestions for improvement. This is a delicate balance. It requires a skilled mentor who really enjoys working with people, who believes passionately that our students deserve the very best teaching possible, and who is convinced that the teaching portfolio can serve as a springboard to achieving that teaching excellence.

I also discuss with my mentees the idea that the portfolio is a living, growing document. By dedicating a drawer in their file cabinets to "Teaching Portfolio," they can begin collecting over time relevant materials they might want to use later in revising their portfolios. Any new material relating to their teaching should automatically go into this drawer.

Mentees are also encouraged to think of the various headings in their portfolio such as "Student Evaluations of Teaching" or "Goals for Teaching Improvement" as modules. Because portfolios prepared for the purposes of personnel decisions and teaching improvement can be very different from each other, professors can pick and choose the modules to use based on the purpose behind revising the portfolio.

THE THREE-MEETINGS PROCESS

The most effective way that I have found to mentor a faculty colleague as they prepare a portfolio is to meet with them three times in scheduled, spaced appointments. The purpose of the first meeting is to plan the content of the portfolio, while the second is used to discuss the initial rough draft. The final meeting is used to polish the second draft. This series of three meetings is especially important when faculty come to the preparation of a teaching portfolio, as most do, with no prior experience with the process.

Before meeting with a faculty member, I ask them to complete a form entitled "Getting Started on Your Teaching Portfolio" and send it to me prior to our first meeting. This form has been designed to help the faculty member start writing the important narrative part of the teaching portfolio by *describing* accomplishments and giving *examples* where possible. Sample questions from this form include:

Please describe your teaching methods and explain why you teach as you do. (Particular attention should be given to strategy and implementation.) Give examples.

If you overheard your students talking about you and your teaching in the cafeteria, what would they likely be saying? What would you like them to say? Why is that important to you?

Mentees are provided in advance with a copy of *The Teaching Portfolio* (Seldin, 1991), a book which introduces the concept and contains model portfolios. They are asked to read it before our first meeting.

The first appointment lasts 20–30 minutes and is basically a planning session. Because I have read the "Getting Started" form *prior* to the appointment, I am better able to discuss with the faculty member their purpose in preparing the portfolio, what they teach, and why they teach as they do. We then consider the sources of information that would best document their teaching effectiveness.

It is crucial at this first meeting to consider the issue of *balance* among the three areas of "products of good teaching," "materials from oneself," and "materials from others." A good portfolio has an approximately equal amount of information from each of the three areas. A common problem is that most faculty have far more already available "materials from others" (e.g., course evaluations and department chairperson statements about teaching) and "materials from oneself" (e.g., personal statement of teaching goals and representative course syllabi) than they have on the "products of good teaching" (e.g., examples of student work with their comments and pre-test/post-test student scores). One of the major challenges for the mentor, then, is to brainstorm with the mentee about various ways for providing *evidence* that their students have learned as a result of their teaching.

For example, I have worked with many faculty to plan a way to pre-test their students at the beginning of the course on certain aspects of learning and then to retest them at the end of the course. This information provides concrete evidence about how students have changed as a result of their course. Since many times faculty do not have these data currently available, I suggest that they describe their plans for gathering this information in the future as a short-term goal in their portfolio.

As I work with my mentee in this session, I use a sheet of paper with three blank columns labeled "products of good teaching," "materials from oneself," and "materials from others" and fill in the information my mentee is planning to provide in each of these areas. This approach makes it easy to just glance at the columns and compare their relative length. If any one of the columns is significantly shorter than the others, then it is clear we need to talk more about ways to expand the list of sources. This list also goes in the file I prepare for each faculty member I work with to jog my memory about what we have planned for their portfolio when we meet again. Mentees, too, usually take notes at our meetings.

Once the basic list of sources for their portfolio is planned, I answer any questions the mentee might have. Then we schedule the second meeting of 30–45 minutes to go over the rough draft, as well as the third and final meeting of 20–30 minutes to polish the portfolio second draft.

I have found that it is important to offer considerable positive reinforcement at this first meeting. Faculty members are leaving this appointment to embark upon what is for most of them a new idea and they need to feel that they are on the right track.

The mentee sends me two copies of the rough draft of their portfolio prior to our second meeting so I can review it in advance. It seems to work best if I use one copy of the portfolio to write notes for my later use while the mentee takes their own notes on the second copy.

One of the best times for me as a mentor comes when I look at the first rough draft. The portfolio is like a still-wet piece of clay with only the rough outline formed. It is up to the mentor then to assist the faculty member in molding the best evidence of their teaching effectiveness without putting too much of the mentor's imprint on it. The balance is not easy to achieve but it is important. The portfolio must belong to the mentee.

Below are some guidelines the mentor may want to convey to the person preparing the portfolio at the initial meeting (Shackelford, 1992):

1. Be clear in communicating to the reader what you teach, how you teach it, why you teach it in that manner, and with or to whom.
2. Every portfolio should include a descriptive table of contents. Appendices should be specifically cited in the body of the portfolio as well as listed in the table of contents.
3. Because readers of portfolios are busy people, you cannot assume that

all appendices will be completely read. Therefore, selected examples of items (e.g., average student evaluation scores or sample student comments) should be included in the body.

4. All material in the portfolio does not need to be in prose form. For example, graphs can be used to summarize student evaluations. Photos of student work or videotapes of teaching can be included in the appendices.

5. Remember that many of the acronyms for professional organizations, instructional strategies, committees and conferences which are very familiar to you may need to be described to your portfolio reader so they can understand the significance to your teaching.

6. Be sure that your teaching strengths are *clearly* established in the teaching portfolio. You may want to address concerns or future goals in a section on teaching improvement.

The second meeting between mentor and mentee must address the issue of balance among the three categories of sources of information on teaching effectiveness. I mark off the items that we planned to include at our first meeting on my checklist as I find them. The faculty member and I then discuss anything that was omitted from the original list and why, as well as any new ideas for sources to document teaching that have emerged. We then consider the overall balance of the portfolio. The mentee should leave this meeting with a clear idea of the strengths in their rough draft and with definite ideas for further improvement.

The final meeting is the shortest. Once again, the faculty member submits two copies of their portfolio to me in advance so they can be reviewed before our meeting. New sections that have been added or rewritten since the rough draft need to be particularly considered and the overall balance of information from the three sources reviewed again.

The basic question I ask my mentee at this session is, "Are you satisfied that this document adequately describes and documents your teaching?" If not, we talk about ways to address these concerns. I also like to discuss future ways to revise the portfolio after new information, such as more on the products of good teaching, is obtained.

By this time, we are both usually so proud of the newly-developed teaching portfolio that it is not difficult to be very positive and reinforcing about the mentee's effort. But I think it is very important that the mentee leave the final meeting pleased with what they have produced and planning to continually update their teaching portfolio as an essential part of their ongoing professional development.

HOW TO "GROW" YOUR OWN MENTORS

Because money for faculty development efforts is scarce at many institutions, providing mentors from "outside" to implement a teaching portfolio project on your campus may be difficult. One of the best ways that I have seen to produce mentors is to "grow" your own on your campus.

Once a faculty development specialist or department chairperson or other such person on a campus becomes familiar with the teaching portfolio concept through reading the Seldin book (1991), attending a conference presentation or workshop on the topic, and, very importantly, preparing their own personal teaching portfolio, they can introduce the concept on their campus. My strong advice here is to start small.

Begin by inviting three to five faculty who have good reputations as teachers and who work well with others to meet with you, either as a group or individually, to develop their own teaching portfolios. The three-meetings approach should be used.

Once this initial cohort is trained, then they can return to their departments or colleges to work with others in an "each one, teach one" model. This pattern can be repeated many times until the desired number of mentors is locally available.

It is my strong belief that no faculty member should be dragooned into preparing a portfolio. It is far better to present the teaching portfolio as an attractive, useful teaching improvement activity. The best way to encourage faculty to participate is for them to hear positive comments about the benefits from their colleagues who have already prepared teaching portfolios.

In summary, I want to mention again how personally rewarding serving as a mentor in the preparation of teaching portfolios has been to me. Not only do I get personal pleasure in helping a colleague improve their teaching (and often make a new friend), but I also get new ideas that I can incorporate into my own teaching.

Perhaps one mentee who participated in a week-long teaching portfolio workshop said it best:

> "The rewards have been numerous and quite surprising. The consultant's knowledgeable and caring appraisal—the fine-tooth-comb—is perceived as coming from the university. This is what a university is. We do this for our students but rarely for each other. This project renewed my faith in myself, the accomplishments of the past, and the need to focus on the future.
> Thank you!"

The beauty of the teaching portfolio process is that I have found all of this to be just as true for the mentor.

BIBLIOGRAPHY

Seldin, P. *The Teaching Portfolio*. Bolton, MA: Anker Publishing Company, 1991.

Seldin, P. and Annis, L.F. "The Teaching Portfolio." *The Journal of Staff, Program, and Organization Development 8,* 197-201, 1990.

Shackelford, R. "General Guidelines for Preparing a Teaching Portfolio." Unpublished guidelines, Ball State University, 1992.

4

HOW PORTFOLIOS ARE USED
IN NINE INSTITUTIONS

This chapter describes in detail how nine institutions—large, small, public, and private—have implemented portfolios. The institutions are Columbia College (South Carolina), Dalhousie University (Canada), Gordon College (Massachusetts), Harvard University (Massachusetts), Miami-Dade Community College (Florida), Murray State University (Kentucky), St. Norbert College (Wisconsin), the University of Maryland's University College, and the University of Nebraska's Department of English.

The reports are arranged in alphabetical order by institution. Because each college or university is unique, varying purposes and practices are described. Some institutions use portfolios for teaching improvement, others for personnel decisions or for teaching awards, still others for a combination of purposes.

A cautionary note: the full range of portfolio use can best be understood and appreciated by reading many institutional reports.

Columbia College

Dalhousie University

Gordon College

Harvard University

Miami-Dade Community College

Murray State University

St. Norbert College

University of Maryland University College

University of Nebraska, Department of English

COLUMBIA COLLEGE
Jerold J. Savory

PORTFOLIO PROJECT: BACKGROUND AND OVERVIEW

With increasing demands for accountability brought into clear focus during an institutional self-study, Columbia College has reaffirmed teaching excellence and faculty professional development as the two highest priorities in the college's revised mission statement and strategic plan. Faculty and administrators have accepted joint commitment to backing these priorities with institutional resources, and the faculty has accepted responsibility for developing a plan for enhancing and assessing teaching performance.

During the 1991–92 academic year, forty-four members of the college's faculty of seventy-five participated in teaching portfolio workshops, seminars and individual conferences led by an outside consultant. This response from over half of the total faculty, while larger than expected since participation was strictly voluntary, resulted partly from three factors: 1) the college's renewed commitment to effective and innovative teaching, 2) the fact that the decision to experiment with portfolios was faculty-initiated, and 3) the shared enthusiasm from those who completed first drafts and found the experience personally rewarding.

STRATEGIES

Since faculty development through both scholarship and teaching has been our combined purpose from the start, our next steps were to set strategies for implementing a faculty evaluation process appropriate to the needs of our college. As Dean of the Faculty, my role is to serve as faculty advocate and as a facilitator of faculty projects. Since I also teach and serve on faculty committees, I have been actively involved in the following process as a collaborator with colleagues, including preparation of my own portfolio. This brings me to three recommended strategies for building a successful teaching portfolio program.

1. Begin with an existing faculty committee, or a faculty-appointed task force.

In our case, we decided to give primary responsibility for faculty evaluation to our Instruction Committee, with close cooperation from the Faculty Development Committee. The former deals with instructional needs, resources, and performance evaluation; the latter provides grant assistance for professional growth through research, travel to meetings, and participation in workshops and seminars. While this combination works for us, it may vary in other colleges. The most important point is that *faculty must be in charge of their own professional development and evaluation procedures.*

2. Review available faculty development models.

There are several good faculty evaluation models available, some more appropriate for one institution than for another. At Columbia College, we had been using two instruments: 1) a student evaluation form and 2) a combination self-evaluation/department chair's evaluation form, both of which need either revising or replacing. It became clear to us that *student evaluations, while important, are not enough; peer evaluation, also important, was rarely used; and our self-evaluation instrument did very little to document actual teaching performance.*

We agreed that we needed a more adequate process and tool, and Peter Seldin's teaching portfolio model was selected, primarily because of its comprehensiveness, flexibility, adaptability to individual faculty differences, and especially because of its strong focus upon the need for hard evidence and specific data for documenting good teaching with combined materials from oneself and others, especially students and colleagues.

3. Participation in a teaching portfolio project must be voluntary and not mandated.

Once we had decided on experimenting with the teaching portfolio model, those of us on the Instruction and Faculty Development committees agreed to be a pilot group in a two-day workshop led by an outside consultant. We invited academic department chairs to join us, making it clear that this would be strictly voluntary and for information only. Ten of our fifteen chairs joined us.

The initial workshop was successful in building base support for the project, even though only twelve of the twenty-one participants actually completed first drafts of portfolios during the two months following the workshop. In retrospect, we see this as a good beginning because those who completed them did so voluntarily and enthusiastically; and most of the other nine saw the value of portfolios, even if they were slow in getting started compiling one. We now had a core group of colleagues, including five department chairs, strongly committed to the teaching portfolio concept. It was clear to us that we should move ahead to encourage others to join us. However, before implementing the project with further workshops and seminars, we had a few tough decisions to make.

THREE TOUGH DECISIONS

1. Should we seek official faculty endorsement?

We decided *not* to do so, at least not in the early stages. We were convinced that the process of doing a portfolio carries its own endorsement and that voluntary participation works best with the core group serving as catalysts for encouraging others to attend future workshops and information sessions.

2. **Should we encourage using portfolios for tenure/promotion professional files?**

We agreed that well-documented successful teaching had a place in personnel decisions, especially in a college that values good teaching, along with productive scholarship and other professional activity. In fact, several of us in the pilot group decided to place sections of our portfolios in our files. However, we concluded that the primary purpose of the project would be improvement of teaching performance and not personnel decisions. Therefore, we decided to continue with this purpose until at least half of the faculty had completed portfolios and were better prepared to share in further decisions about uses. We were discovering that doing portfolios was stimulating serious discussion about our teaching goals and strategies, and we did not want to squelch the increasing momentum of this valuable exchange.

3. **Should administrators be invited into the portfolio project?**

Our first response was negative because of our caution that this might lead to mandating portfolio uses for personnel decisions. However, we decided that *open communication of the portfolio process must be presented not just to faculty but also to administrators*, especially the President, the Vice President for Academic Affairs, and academic department chairs. This would inform them not only of the nature and value of portfolios but also of the potential uses *and misuses* of them. We also sought continued administrative support for the project and agreed that openness would foster this support. Therefore, we decided to build an informational seminar into our plans for further faculty workshops and open sessions.

IMPLEMENTATION

Once our guidelines and strategies were in place, we set the following steps for implementation. As Dean of the Faculty, I have found this process especially effective and rewarding in my goals to involve faculty in self-directed professional growth as scholar-teachers, as initiators of innovative teaching, and as evaluators of their own and their colleagues' classroom performances.

1. The pilot group from the Instruction and Faculty Development committees invited other faculty to an open meeting on teaching portfolios. This was led by the outside consultant with "testimonials" from the pilot group. Over thirty-five (half of the entire faculty) were present, and twenty-four signed up for a second workshop which was held in May, 1992.
2. In addition to the twenty-four faculty attending the second workshop, the Academic Dean and Business Officer also showed up. This may have been because they, along with all faculty, had been mailed a copy of Peter Seldin's book *The Teaching Portfolio*, together with a statement of the portfolio's potentials and limitations. Like the first, the workshop

was successful. *We now had well over half of the faculty informed about the teaching portfolio process.*

3. Our next step was a session for administrators. We included top-level and full-time administrators, as well as department chairs. Thanks to an informative and provocative discussion led by the outside consultant, this led to a productive response on *the creation of teaching-support portfolios for administrators.* These might include departmental teaching-improvement programs, college-wide mentoring for new faculty, inviting visiting consultants and lecturers on teaching excellence, and special departmental and college rewards for good teaching. Six full-time or part-time administrators have now begun their own portfolios.

4. We now have a substantial core of faculty and administrators committed to the portfolio concept. This is a modest beginning, but *it is a solid one because it has remained voluntary, and it has involved faculty initiation and administrative support.* This may not work in all institutions, but it has been effective in this liberal arts college. The process has had a major impact upon us and we are grateful for the teaching portfolio, an idea whose time has come, especially for us.

SOME FUTURE PLANS

Because of the success of the workshops and informational sessions of the first year of the experimental project, sixteen others have joined the original twelve in compiling portfolios and at least ten additional ones have indicated plans to begin theirs also. Thus, we may realistically expect that over half of the faculty will have completed first or second drafts and will have started assembling portfolio files by the end of the second year.

This does not mean that we should expect full-faculty embracing of the use of teaching portfolios within two years. However, it clearly suggests that their use has stimulated sufficient support and enthusiasm to encourage us to set some plans for the future.

1. We will plan for at least two faculty-conducted portfolio workshops each year.

Thanks to the outside consultant's workshop model, we now have a well-trained cadre of faculty ready to train colleagues. Since this cadre includes both junior and senior faculty, we hope to attract both among our colleagues. We believe that new faculty will be especially receptive.

2. We plan to set up a mentoring and peer-evaluation program.

Each new faculty member will be assigned a senior faculty mentor, beginning in 1992–93. In addition to helping orient the new member to college procedures, the mentor will also encourage the use of teaching portfolios as a way of sharing ideas about teaching. We will also encourage peer-evaluation of teaching among established faculty. In some departments, this is already practiced. In others, it will be a new, and probably cautiously-received, idea. However, the teaching portfolio concept encourages it as a way of documenting teaching strengths and needs for improvement.

3. We will establish a faculty resource center for teaching improvement and evaluation.

This center, an adjunct to our newly-established Collaborative Learning Center, will contain files of faculty teaching portfolios, periodicals and other information on teaching, and will be a place where faculty can come for meetings with mentors and other faculty teaching discussions, seminars, and workshops.

4. We will continue to encourage portfolio preparation among colleagues.

We will continue to experiment with portfolios for at least one or two more years before deciding whether some type of standardized section of them might be used appropriately for documenting teaching effectiveness in tenure and promotion matters. In the meantime, it is obvious that the process of preparing a teaching portfolio carries its own value as a vehicle for stimulating thoughtful reflection and productive exchange with one another on what has become an increasingly lively topic, the challenges and rewards of good teaching.

5. We will commission the Faculty Instruction Committee to conduct research on the impact of the teaching portfolio on decision-making for both teaching improvement and personnel matters.

We need to know just how reliable teaching portfolios are in comparison to other teaching assessment methods we have been using. Our initial response is that the portfolio approach offers a far more comprehensive and concrete body of evidence of good teaching, but we need to test this over the next year or two. Just as a good portfolio requires continual updating, so does its use on the campus require continual and systematic evaluation.

DALHOUSIE UNIVERSITY
W. Alan Wright and Carol O'Neil

Two premises underlie this piece on the teaching portfolio. The first is that the evolution of the teaching portfolio at Dalhousie University (Canada) and perhaps at any university, is best understood by taking into account the characteristics of the local academic environment. The second is that there can be suggestions and advice, but no universal blueprint for the introduction of the teaching portfolio concept at the institutional level.

The story of the development and implementation of the teaching portfolio at Dalhousie is closely associated with the establishment of the Office of Instructional Development and Technology (OIDT) and an overall institutional effort to place a greater emphasis on excellence in teaching. At our university, recent interest in the teaching portfolio is bound up with the culture of the institution, the evolution of faculty development activity, and the dynamics of academic leadership.

Founded in 1818, Dalhousie is one of the oldest and most respected research universities in Canada. It has the highest percentage of graduate students in the country and several highly-regarded professional schools. In 1988, under the leadership of its newly-appointed president, the university expressed its renewed commitment to teaching and learning by initiating a variety of programs and policies aimed at providing an undergraduate program unsurpassed in Canada (Clark, 1988). The university organized a Symposium on Undergraduate Education (a valuable forum for over 700 members of the academic community to discuss teaching and learning issues), created a standing Senate Committee on Instructional Development (SCID), and established an instructional development office.

Efforts to implement the teaching portfolio as an integral part of an overall instructional development program here have focused on policy development, workshop activity, and the acquisition and development of print resources.

POLICY

With the new structures in place, the challenging work of mounting an instructional development program was undertaken. Aware of tensions remaining after a faculty union strike in the fall of 1988, planners recognized that it was important that the program be non-threatening and supportive of faculty teaching efforts, yet push for implementation of policies and practices which would promote improvement and change. To that end, the OIDT worked with the Senate Committee on Instructional Development to devise the *Focus on Teaching* plan which identified three areas of initiative to draw attention to the quality of teaching, encourage and support effort and improvement in teaching effectiveness, and increase reward and recognition for successful teaching (SCID, 1990). The three elements forming the basis of the instructional development program were: student ratings of instruction, peer cooperation, and the teaching portfolio (or the teaching dossier as it is called in Canada). The teaching portfolio was described as having two purposes: to present information which most fairly and fully reflects teaching activities and accomplishments [and to] allow the professor an opportunity for reflection with a view to improving instruction (SCID, 1990).

The policy development represented by the *Focus on Teaching* plan was supported by policies articulated by the university president, who announced in 1988 that he would be prepared to recommend promotion or tenure to the Board of Governors only in cases in which there was clearly documented evidence of teaching ability. With the policies and structures for promoting the use of the teaching portfolio firmly established, by 1991 the president was able to report "impressive progress" in the area of recording teaching accomplishments:

> "Most departments now have in place well-developed processes for providing documented evidence of teaching abilities and some of them are doing a remarkably fine job in assessing teaching...[making] a mockery of the view...that teaching cannot be fairly assessed" (Clark, in O'Neil and Wright, 1991, p. 1).

Adoption of policy statements by appropriate university bodies provided a solid foundation on which to build when implementing the portfolio concept on campus.

WORKSHOPS AND CONSULTATIONS

The second phase involved devising appropriate mechanisms to introduce and promote the use of the teaching portfolio. Ongoing efforts to keep in touch with attitudes and practices on campus provided information useful in deciding how best to proceed. A survey of departmental practices regarding the teaching portfolio found high interest and support for the concept; confirmed the need for guidance; and provided suggestions for implementation from twenty-seven responding departments (Wright and O'Neil, 1990). Subsequent investigations indicated considerable faculty interest in learning more about documenting and evaluating teaching accomplishments. *From our experience, we know that it is crucial that the expressed needs and concerns of the faculty guide activities which encourage the use of the teaching portfolio and improved methods of evaluating teaching.*

The OIDT adopted a variety of workshop strategies to meet various conditions and needs. The staff developed materials for a comprehensive three-hour session dealing with all aspects of the portfolio concept: origin, purpose, content, format, length, compilation, credibility, ethics and implementation. This format is used when the facilitators take the initiative to organize and publicize a portfolio workshop for target groups such as teaching assistants or new faculty as well as for interested academics in other institutions. However, it is also important to be able to fit into departmental time slots and formats, so faculty developers here provide brief presentations and otherwise adapt to the requirements of a given academic unit. For example, sessions have been offered, upon request, as part of the Department of Medicine's seminar series held late in the afternoon, and at midday for the Biology Department in the best tradition of the "brown bag lunch."

The OIDT also responds to requests for guidance from individual faculty members compiling their teaching portfolios. Very often, the early drafts of teaching portfolios consist of lists of teaching duties with some student ratings data or course outlines appended. Faculty members are encouraged to build on this basic information by adding statements on their teaching philosophy, goals, methods and evidence of effective teaching. *In doing so, they not only produce a more meaningful and comprehensive record of their teaching accomplishments, but also systematically examine the how and why of their pedagogical practices—the first step in improving instruction.* In addition to meeting with an instructional development specialist, faculty members can also consult a file of sample portfolios and a variety of books and articles on the teaching portfolio.

Our experience has been that a mix of cross-campus workshops, departmental seminars and individual consultations is essential if the portfolio is to enjoy acceptance which is both deep and widespread. The spirit of the sessions on the teaching portfolio must be in keeping with the overall approach to instructional development on campus: facilitators offer faculty suggestions which they are convinced are in the best interests of the teaching professor, but the decision—to participate, to adopt a technique, to implement an idea—remains essentially in the hands of the professor.

PRINT DOCUMENTATION

Having established a foundation in policy, and having developed materials and formats for workshops and presentations, the next step was to address the need for more substantial print documentation to support efforts to implement the teaching portfolio. Faculty had numerous questions concerning the portfolio. Some had misconceptions. Others lacked insight into the process of compiling a portfolio. Most needed to see examples of portfolio entries to fully understand the concept.

An institutional guide to the portfolio was needed to provide all faculty with an accessible resource, a handy reference to turn to during the process of putting together a portfolio. The development of this guide was undertaken as a major project by the OIDT. The result was *Recording Teaching Accomplishment: A Dalhousie Guide to the Teaching Dossier,* a 100 page document which includes excerpts from twenty-five portfolios of outstanding university professors from across Canada. The development of the *Guide,* and its dissemination both on campus and beyond, has been a stimulus for further dialogue about the portfolio. In addition, the availability of a variety of recently published print resources on the portfolio has lent still more credibility to the approach and facilitates its adoption in the academic milieu.

IMPACT OF THE TEACHING PORTFOLIO

At this stage in the introduction and implementation of the teaching portfolio on campus, we are encouraged by evidence of its utility within a broader effort to enhance and improve university teaching. There has been a discernable sea change at Dalhousie: teaching is now at the forefront of the academic community's agenda. The portfolio has proven to be a valuable organizational tool used to provide structure in the evaluation of teaching. It has also proven to be a valuable means of focusing attention on teaching and stimulating discussion on the pedagogical process. The growing use of the teaching portfolio on campus has also resulted in:

1. the development and presentation of better evidence of the quality of teaching;
2. greater recognition and reward for teaching;
3. better procedures and criteria for the evaluation of teaching; and
4. more "action research" by professors who engage in systematic inquiry into the teaching and learning process in their own classrooms.

We have found that the teaching portfolio supports and facilitates the professional career goals of individual faculty members striving for tenure and promotion. While the confidential nature of the personnel decision-making process makes it difficult to establish with precision the impact of the teaching portfolio on career outcomes, faculty members report that they find the teaching portfolio an invaluable means of documenting their work as teachers for this purpose. At OIDT, we encourage individual professors to adopt the teaching portfolio as the vehicle for describing this aspect of their responsibilities as part of the annual report process.

RECOMMENDATIONS AND CONCLUSIONS

Experience suggests that those interested in introducing the teaching portfolio in a particular setting should:

+ take into account the institutional culture;
+ involve faculty in decision-making at every level—policy and planning committees, personnel and review committees, faculty unions, and so on;
+ provide examples of methods of evaluating teaching to departments and relevant committees;
+ encourage departments and faculties to formally adopt a set of criteria for the evaluation of teaching and to make this information available to faculty members as a reference for teaching portfolio development;

✦ develop workshop materials and other resources and be prepared to respond to the differing needs within the institution through flexible and varied approaches;

✦ provide examples of teaching portfolios to individual faculty and discuss strategies for using the portfolio in the context of particular departments and faculties;

✦ obtain multiple copies of books and articles on the portfolio for faculty development resource centers; and

✦ circulate some form of guide to the portfolio to all faculty.

The strong tradition of decentralization on campus ruled out the possibility of imposing a uniform plan for implementation of the portfolio in all academic departments. Faculty developers pushing for change carefully avoided giving professors the feeling that they were *being* pushed. Institutional contexts must be considered when implementing the portfolio concept, keeping in mind Christopher Knapper's caution:

"The teaching [portfolio] is not a universal panacea and in itself can do little to alter the fact that the evaluation of teaching is a tricky business. The effectiveness of the [portfolio] will ultimately depend upon the amount of effort an instructor is prepared to put into documenting [his/her] case as well as the acceptability of such a procedure in the university itself" (1978, p. 8).

In order to increase the likelihood that the teaching portfolio will be accepted, it must be part of a larger overall plan to improve and enhance the teaching function. Links should be made with instructional development initiatives on campus. Faculty and administrative support is crucial. Only then can policy, workshop activity, and support documentation be developed to make widespread institutional adoption of the portfolio a reality.

Our very positive experience with portfolios at Dalhousie University leads us to predict that the concept will enjoy broad-based recognition and acceptance in the academy.

BIBLIOGRAPHY

Clark, H. C. Address to the Symposium on Undergraduate Education, Dalhousie University, Halifax, NS, March 1988.

Knapper, C. K. "Evaluation and Teaching: Beyond Lip-Service," Paper presented at the Fourth International Conference on Improving University Teaching, Aachen, July 1978.

O'Neil, M. C. and Wright, W. A. *Recording Teaching Accomplishment: A Dalhousie Guide to the Teaching Dossier*. Halifax, NS: Office of Instructional Development and Technology, Dalhousie University, 1991.

Wright, W. A. and O'Neil, M. C. "The Teaching Dossier at Dalhousie University: Departmental Responses," A Report to the Senate Committee on Instructional Development (SCID), Dalhousie University, Halifax, NS, October, 1990.

GORDON COLLEGE
Jonathan S. Raymond

For many years Gordon College has maintained a strong faculty development program with an emphasis on both teaching and scholarship. The faculty development program has served to keep faculty fresh in the classroom and productive in their scholarship and writing. It has been one of the major contributors to high faculty morale and high faculty retention. Teaching has been the primary task and focused passion of the faculty. Over the years, faculty evaluation for tenure and promotion have weighed teaching performance and quality highest among the evaluative criteria. In short, teaching is a very serious enterprise at Gordon College.

FROM EVALUATION TO DEVELOPMENT

In this context, the faculty development program more recently has embraced the use of teaching portfolios as a way to bring additional emphasis to the importance of teaching. Prior to the introduction of teaching portfolios, the college maintained a strong evaluation program in which student, peer, and administrative evaluations of the faculty are carried out on a regular basis. The college engages in three-year (pre-tenure), tenure, promotion, and six-year (post-tenure) evaluations. A comprehensive file including examples of syllabi, diverse forms of evaluations, and other teaching related materials have routinely been on file for use in the evaluation process. This substantial data base for the evaluation of teaching performance has been foundational to the introduction of teaching portfolios. In a way, the college has been engaged for many years in the use of portfolios by way of the extensive approach to the evaluation of teaching. More recently, however, a deliberate effort has been made to develop teaching portfolios to serve the evaluation process and, as importantly, to promote the ongoing development of the faculty in their capacity to teach.

Portfolios are customarily used to organize a data base of information on teaching for the purpose of faculty evaluation. Here, a faculty member presents his or her "best works" for evaluation by peer faculty and administrators toward tenure or promotion. Gordon College is beginning to use teaching portfolios for a different purpose. Rather than using them for faculty evaluation, as a presentation of best works, we are using portfolios as a part of the faculty development program. The college's faculty development program for the last seventeen years has encouraged faculty to set goals and pursue personal development of their teaching skills. Teaching portfolios are viewed as an ideal innovation for this purpose. The purpose of this approach is to document "lessons learned" in the classroom. The portfolio captures these lessons learned, permitting faculty to reflect on their own future planning for personal and professional development and to inform colleagues for their development in the area of teaching as well.

Gordon is a college of liberal arts and sciences. While it is not directly church related, nevertheless it is a Christian liberal arts college with a distinct world view. Faculty raise questions for their students regarding the relationship of faith to learning along with issues of ethics and morality as related to multiculturalism, gender, and life in general. The faculty are relatively mature. That is to say they are generally older than the faculty at many institutions. Approximately one third of the Gordon College faculty will likely retire in the next seven years. The college, then, has the challenge of replacing those faculty and recruiting and retaining new faculty of equally high quality. *Teaching portfolios are viewed as helpful in this undertaking of faculty renewal.*

STRATEGY FOR IMPLEMENTATION

In the implementation of teaching portfolios into the faculty development program, portfolios are viewed as an innovation to be adopted by a population. The strategy for implementation acknowledges that innovations are adopted by populations over time with some individuals characterized as early adopters and others as late adopters. Since participation in the faculty development program is voluntary, participation in the use of teaching portfolios is likewise voluntary. Initially, four senior faculty agreed to develop a teaching portfolio on one of their courses. As an encouragement, a modest stipend was awarded to each faculty member as part of the funding of their faculty development plan. These four senior faculty were initially recruited by the dean of the faculty because of their profiles: highly respected by other faculty, seasoned in the classroom, and representing a cross section of the faculty of the college (physics, elementary education, psychology, and history).

The centerpiece of the initial portfolios was a reflective piece of writing which discussed progress and problems in the development of a single course. An emphasis was placed on issues, challenges, problems, and successes in three areas related to their teaching: integration of faith in learning, multicultural and gender issues, and pedagogy. Four fascinating yet different portfolios were developed. Some faculty chose to focus on a core curriculum course. Others focused on an upper division course within their discipline. All four faculty expressed how powerful and positive the experience of completing a teaching portfolio was for them. It seemed to focus them more clearly on their present teaching experience and strengthen a desire for continuing to improve their performance in the classroom. This may be viewed as a rather remarkable outcome particularly for senior faculty who are already regarded by their peers as highly capable.

Each year the academic season begins with a faculty retreat. At the fall faculty retreat in the second year of implementation, a workshop was held for all faculty on the use of teaching portfolios for faculty development. The four faculty who developed portfolios in the previous year served on a panel sharing their experiences and perceptions of benefits of developing a teaching portfolio. Since then, ten additional faculty have begun to develop portfolios on a single course with a similar framework engaged by the original four faculty members. Among the ten faculty developing teaching portfolios are both senior (full professor) as well as junior faculty. *Of particular interest to the college is the development of portfolios on courses taught by senior faculty who will inevitably be retiring in the next few years. Now, lessons learned by senior faculty may be captured and passed on to younger faculty who will inherit those courses in the future.*

FUTURE APPLICATIONS

It is our hope that within two years there will be twenty-five to thirty portfolios on file for review by all faculty. The Gordon College approach is to use teaching portfolios as part of faculty development to garner lessons learned in the classroom. Nevertheless, some faculty are choosing to use their portfolio, of their own volition, as information to be shared with the personnel committee of the faculty senate. The portfolio then becomes helpful in the senate's review of the candidate for tenure and/or promotion. It is likely this will become a more common practice by many faculty in the future. However, our primary emphasis and purpose for the use of portfolios will remain that of faculty development. Likewise, it is possible that the technology of a teaching portfolio will be used in some modified fashion to recruit future faculty. Candidates for faculty positions in the future may be required to submit a modified, mini-portfolio which communicates their capacity and enthusiasm for teaching. At a college where teaching is a primary concern, teaching portfolios may prove very helpful in recruiting faculty who have a love and a capacity for high quality teaching.

The Gordon College approach began with the voluntary participation of a few highly regarded, senior faculty. More recently, there has been an effort to share their experience and stimulate interest among a larger number of faculty. The gradual, careful, and deliberate escalation of faculty participation is being pursued. It is not likely that there will be a 100% participation in the use of teaching portfolios. The faculty development program at the college, while well integrated into faculty governance, and having large faculty ownership, nevertheless has less than 100% participation. It has ranged from 75%–86% participation in the past. Teaching portfolios are likely to be utilized by some percentage less than the overall participation in the faculty development program. However, we are optimistic that portfolios will become an integral part of faculty development in the future; and that the lessons learned and shared will have a positive impact on the quality of what students experience in the Gordon College classroom.

HARVARD UNIVERSITY
James Wilkinson

In the fall of 1990, Harvard's president, Derek Bok, convened a faculty-administration committee to consider introducing teaching portfolios for graduate students in the Faculty of Arts and Sciences. By a stroke of good fortune, his initiative coincided with AAHE's 1990 portfolio conference, arranged by Russ Edgerton and Pat Hutchings, which we attended. There we learned a great deal from Peter Seldin and others about ongoing efforts to develop teaching portfolios at other institutions. The upshot of these two converging efforts was a pilot program, now several years old, which has registered both successes and setbacks. What follows is an attempt to outline our aims, experiences and some lessons we have learned in a manner that may be helpful to others engaged in putting the concept of teaching portfolios to work.

From the start, Harvard's portfolio focus has been on graduate students. Faculty portfolios may come later. For now, however, we have our hands full with the challenge of implementing a first step with graduate Teaching Fellows (as teaching assistants are called at Harvard). It seemed, and seems, a logical place to start. Since most graduate students teach in sections or labs for at least a year, we felt it important that they be able to use this experience to bolster their credentials when entering the job market. Simply saying "I taught in Professor Jones's course" is not nearly as informative or persuasive as demonstrating what that teaching involved, and offering some evidence of how well one taught. Indeed, from the prospective employer's point of view, Harvard's willingness to put its graduate students into the classroom on the teacher's side of the desk can be seen as a plus, since it offers significant on-the-job training. In competition with graduates of other Ph.D. programs, the argument went, our students should be provided with a portfolio that would give their greater teaching experience some weight with colleges and universities interested in hiring them.

But there was another reason as well to create a teaching portfolio for graduate students. With increasing frequency, Harvard faculty had requested more information about the teaching skills of the graduate TFs whom they proposed to hire as discussion section leaders or lab supervisors. In the "good old days," of course, they would have found their teaching fellows within their own departments—individuals known to them, or at least to their colleagues, so that an informal process of selection could occur at a leisurely pace. But alas, if they ever existed, those days are now gone. In large courses, such as those given in the Harvard Core Program, Teaching Fellows now must often be recruited from other departments or even from other faculties such as the Harvard Law School, Divinity School, or Kennedy School of Government. Since there is no preregistration at Harvard, course size is often difficult to project, especially when the course is new or courses are unexpectedly cancelled, thereby boosting the number of students in courses that remain in that particular field. The result of these factors is that instructors must often hire a number of Teaching Fellows at the last minute, with scant opportunity to delve into their backgrounds. The best have been hired months before. Course heads are pleased simply to find *anyone* once the semester has begun.

Thus the aims pushing toward the adoption of teaching portfolios led us to suggest two different portfolio models: one for external and one for internal consumption. The external model included more material, and allowed greater freedom of choice for the graduate student in selecting those materials. We felt that it was important for the graduate students to treat this aspect of the portfolio like an extension of their CV: *they* would decide what to include, just as they already decided what names to propose as references. The internal model, on the other hand, offered less scope for choice. It was centered on previous student evaluation scores and letters of recommendation from all previous course heads, not simply on those the TF chose to include. However, we felt that it was important to allow graduate students to comment on these elements of their internal portfolio. While they could not keep information out, they could still offer their own interpretation of what scores or faculty evaluations "really" meant.

Our hope in developing both types of teaching portfolios for graduate TFs was that they might serve as incentives for Teaching Fellows to pay attention to (and, when possible, improve) their teaching. There are plenty of incentives pushing in the opposite direction. Research is still rewarded at Harvard over teaching. And the particular kind of teaching that we ask graduate students to do is, by any measure, difficult to do well. Leading a discussion section or an honors tutorial requires indirect leadership, exercised through astute questioning rather than through statements delivered from the lecture podium. Yet we ask the least experienced teachers to deliver the most difficult sort of instruction. In a research university where many demands compete for graduate students' time, those of us on the portfolio committee felt that this performance should be recognized and rewarded. Furthermore, we wanted graduate students to gain a sense of learning to teach as part of their graduate course of study. Just as they were adding to their store of knowledge in their chosen field, so we wished them to consider their successive teaching assignments as an opportunity to progress in a set of skills which would form part of their claim to professional expertise once they sought employment in the job market after graduation.

A final hope was that faculty interest in making teaching part of the graduate curriculum would also receive a boost from a formal portfolio. Having to make statements about graduate students' teaching performance requires doing some homework. Faculty, being a busy group, often need a specific reason to pay attention to what is going on in their TFs' classrooms—and here it was. At another institution some years ago, I suggested that each department in the College of Liberal Arts award a $100 book prize to its best graduate TA.

When the plan was accepted and put into effect, a number of colleagues reported that their departments had no way of knowing who the best TA was. So they began to investigate. We hoped that the same might prove true at Harvard.

STRATEGIES AND HURDLES

By common consent, the Harvard portfolio project remains purely voluntary. We believed that it was far more important at the outset for users to have a positive experience than it was to obtain any sort of uniform "coverage" of a department or area. Numbers also played a role in leading us to make the process voluntary. Since there are over 1,000 graduate Teaching Fellows in the classroom in any one semester, it was clearly impossible for us to document the teaching of all of them at once. Therefore, our principal strategy has been to recruit willing participants. This means in practice that we have emphasized the "external model" of the portfolio, where it served the purposes of graduate students preparing for the job market, rather than the "internal model," aimed at giving faculty more information about their prospective Teaching Fellows.

Another reason to begin with the "external model" was that an institutional structure already existed to give it support. The Office of Career Services has offered a dossier service to both undergraduates and graduate students in the Faculty of Arts and Sciences for at least thirty years. Adding a teaching portfolio element to the dossier seemed like a natural extension of their activities. The content of the portfolio would be decided in consultation with the Office of Career Services and with the Derek Bok Center for Teaching, which could offer specific advice concerning which elements of a candidate's teaching record were most likely to impress future employers, and which elements the graduate students might wish to work on further. Given its extensive experience with videotaping teaching, the Bok Center was also a natural partner if students wished to include a short video of their teaching in the portfolio.

Our plan has been to move from a purely "external model" to both external and internal once we were able to establish a structure equivalent to the Office of Career Services. That structure was to be a Teaching Fellow Office, placed under the wing of the Graduate School of Arts and Sciences, with the express mandate to record Teaching Fellow evaluations and to make information concerning TFs available to any faculty who wished to hire them. The Teaching Fellow Office would make the final judgment in those cases where a TF appeared to be unable to teach effectively, and would have the power to require remedial work before the TF could return for another semester in the classroom. All in all, the Teaching Fellow Office would function in a way that acknowledged that graduate TFs were employees of the university as well as students, and that they therefore should be judged by professional standards of competence in their job performance.

IMPLEMENTATION

Even in its modest, first-phase form, Harvard's teaching portfolio project has been slow to gather momentum. We have scored some individual successes, but are still far behind where we had planned to be at this time. There are a number of reasons for this. One is the fact that several key administrators—all of them original participants in the plan—have since left the scene for reasons quite unconnected with the project. President Derek Bok retired in the summer of 1991, as did Acting Dean Rosovsky; a new president and new dean of the Faculty of Arts and Sciences assumed office in the fall. One year later, the Dean of the Graduate School and the Dean for Undergraduate Education also left their posts to make way for a new team. The discussions that led to the original program therefore have had to be started up again, so as to bring these new players on board. Given their busy schedules at the outset of their terms of office, it has often been difficult to get the teaching portfolio concept placed high enough on their several agendas to get rapid action.

We have, however, begun to assemble portfolios for and with some graduate students about to enter the job market. Here we have found, as Peter Seldin and others predicted, that *the consultations that go into selecting material for the portfolio are perhaps the most valuable part of the process.* Graduate students become far more aware of the choices they are making in the classroom when they have to justify those choices, and far more sensitive to student views on their teaching when they have to ask those students for letters of recommendation. Only a few have asked for videotapes of their teaching. More TFs, however, have asked the Bok Center to videotape and give critiques of their upcoming job interview presentations—seminars or (in some instances) guest lectures, which are often the first lectures that they have ever delivered in their lives. So far the volume of these requests is tolerable; but at some point we will have to decide whether this is a service best performed by a teaching center, or whether it could better be taken over by the Office of Career Services.

The elements which most often go into a Teaching Fellow portfolio at Harvard do not differ substantially from those in other portfolios. Student evaluations, a letter from the course head, samples of corrected written work, a syllabus (especially one showing section or lab topics), a self-evaluation, and (occasionally) a short videotape constitute the primary ingredients. We have tried to keep the materials brief, so as not to tax the time of search committees. A more extended version of the portfolio is available for such committees to consult once a candidate has made the short list.

LESSONS

It is perhaps a bit soon to be drawing lessons from a program that has been in existence for such a relatively short time. However, one immediate conclusion is that starting small is a good idea. Had we elected to put both our "models" into practice at once, we would have lacked the administrative support required to create and sustain a fully-featured Teaching Fellow Office. (We, of course, had no idea there would be so much change at the top so soon when our initial strategy was being crafted.) Therefore, beginning with a program that could be integrated into an existing office retrospectively makes good sense. Making the program voluntary also seems a good idea. Word-of-mouth information about the program has already brought us a number of recruits. "Do a good job with a few people" seems an appropriate lesson to draw from this aspect of the project.

Among the problems we have encountered, most are predictable. A number of faculty and graduate students are skeptical about the value of something that takes even *more* of their time. There is a sense in some quarters that the university is trying to intrude on the relationship between faculty advisor and graduate student, and would do better to keep away. That sense is often accompanied by a suspicion that the teaching portfolio constitutes an indirect criticism of the job performance of dissertation advisors or directors of graduate studies. These are, we believe, largely perceptual problems, which will tend to diminish once the merits of the teaching portfolio are more widely recognized, especially by graduate students themselves. But for now, in our start-up phase, they require a fair amount of attention to diplomacy.

Another problem is one of coordination. Even for those loyal to the project, the number of groups involved is daunting. The President's Office, the Faculty of Arts and Sciences, the Graduate School of Arts and Sciences, the Office of Career Services, the Derek Bok Center for Teaching and Learning, and the Graduate Student Council all have some interest in the outcome, and all want to be consulted. When one adds to that list the individual department chairs, directors of graduate studies, and dissertation directors, the possibility for confusion and missed signals increases almost exponentially.

The real test will come when we attempt to move from phase one to phase two, and implement the "internal model" of the portfolio. One difficulty which we anticipate here is the need to keep the formative and summative aspects of the portfolio separate. This is, of course, a problem not just for graduate students, but for teachers at all levels. However, the fact that graduate Teaching Fellows are simultaneously students *and* teachers compounds this common problem. Most faculty who depend on Teaching Fellows to staff their courses, but are not involved with them as students, naturally will wish for summative evaluations; they will want to know whether these TFs will be any good as teachers in *their* classroom. How willing they may be to help weak TFs improve, once those weaknesses are clearly documented in the student's record, remains to be seen.

It would be unfair to end on a note of caution, however. My strong sense is that the potential of the teaching portfolio to "professionalize" Teaching Fellow performance will outweigh the difficulties of implementation, and that we will all be glad of its effects once it is in place. In the meantime, we continue to work on portfolios as part of the graduate students' job dossiers, which is a worthwhile project in itself, and to lobby for a renewed institutional commitment to the portfolio concept as a whole.

MIAMI-DADE COMMUNITY COLLEGE
Mardee Jenrette

PURPOSE

The production of performance portfolios by faculty is an integral part of a new set of policies and procedures at Miami-Dade Community College that is collectively called Faculty Advancement. Designed to encourage and support the professional development of faculty members and to align the college's reward system with professional performance, Faculty Advancement encompasses a performance review process and the award of tenure, promotion in academic rank, and Endowed Teaching Chairs.

The portfolio is the principal vehicle through which faculty members (teachers, counselors or librarians) express their professional philosophy and goals, chronicle professional development activities, and attest to accomplishments over a period of several years. The content of the portfolio focuses on criteria drawn from the college's *Statement of Faculty Excellence.* That *Statement* includes twenty-nine qualities that have been identified as significant faculty contributors to student success.

THE MIAMI-DADE PORTFOLIO

The portfolio is compiled from a variety of sources. It contains input from the faculty member's chairperson, students, and self. Faculty may choose to include evidence from peers or other sources. Guidelines for the portfolio include: 1) a narrative of no more than twenty pages which describes how the criteria for the desired outcome (i.e., tenure, promotion, endowed chair) have been met; 2) a documentation section that supports the narrative; and 3) performance reviews, student feedback reports, and self-assessments for the previous three years.

If willingness to participate in a program is an indicator of approval, the faculty at Miami-Dade Community College have accepted the new Faculty Advancement policies and procedures. In the first year of the program, more than 300 of the 950 full-time faculty developed portfolios as part of the application process for tenure, promotion or an Endowed Chair.

PREPARATION AND IMPLEMENTATION

Five years of preparation preceded the launching of the program. During the development years (1987-1991) there was a systematic progression. First, there was articulation and communication of the goal of ensuring that the institutional reward system would recognize performance in accordance with a universally accepted set of teaching/learning values and a definition of excellent performance. Second, research and initial drafts of a program were prepared. Third, feedback on the draft was collected. Fourth, re-draft and re-cycle of input and feedback was performed. And finally, formal adoption of policy and procedure by a referendum of the faculty, the College Executive Committee, and the Board of Trustees was established.

By the time we were ready to implement, we felt assured of widespread buy-in to the new program. Buy-in does not automatically bring with it understanding, however, nor does it mean that individuals who would be participating would be clear on the specifics of their respective roles and responsibilities. Accordingly, it was agreed that once the new policies and procedures were adopted, the college would *not* immediately move into the new system. Instead, there would be "business as usual" until there had been sufficient time to prepare people to behave in what would amount to radically different ways.

How did we prepare people to behave in new ways? The Faculty Advancement Procedures were formally adopted in October, 1990. The first portfolios were not submitted for review until February, 1992. In the intervening period, activity proceeded at a rapid pace. Targeted for training were the following groups:

1. Faculty (in the preparation of portfolios),
2. Chairpersons (in their roles as faculty "coaches" and developers, and ultimately as performance evaluators),
3. Upper-level administrators (in their roles as facilitators of the process and evaluators), and
4. Promotion, Tenure, and Endowed Chair committee members (in their roles as evaluators).

STRATEGIES

A series of workshops was begun on each of the five Miami-Dade campuses in the spring of 1991 with an overview of Faculty Advancement. Early fall brought portfolio *development* sessions. In the winter portfolio *evaluation* was the topic. Enrollment built slowly. Fifty percent of the targeted groups attended overview sessions. By the time we were ready for portfolio preparation, attendance had leapt to 90%.

The training progressed under something of a handicap. Workshop participants wanted "real" examples of portfolios. But we had none. As a partial solution to the problem, samples representing a wide range of teaching situations (arts and occupations, for example) and non-teaching roles (counselor, librarian, department chair) in which Miami-Dade faculty find themselves were produced. These samples were used in portfolio development sessions and for Promotion, Tenure, and Endowed Chair committee training.

LOOKING BACK

At the year's end, the Faculty Advancement Monitoring Committee reported that, although there was some anxiety and frustration and the progress still requires fine-tuning, *the new Faculty Advancement program works.* Some observations:

1. Time and opportunity were provided for "buy-in" but it wasn't until portfolios actually touched lives that people began to *really* try to understand how to prepare or evaluate one. In retrospect, it might have been wiser to have tried to implement on a smaller scale, involving fewer people, and thus creating less overall institutional disturbance.

2. The training, so critical to a successful implementation, was weakened by the lack of experience on which to build. This was expected and anticipated. What was not anticipated, however, was the degree to which a solid training program can (and for Miami-Dade by the second year *will*) help manage a change process. Based on the experiences of portfolio preparers and portfolio evaluators in the program's first year, the second generation training series will be able to address critical questions like: What are the best types of documentation to provide evidence? How do you document *substantive involvement* in professional activities? How much is enough?

3. While workshops are necessary, they are only helpful up to a point. After a general session it is very important that faculty have someone who can work with them as they prepare their portfolios to answer a question like, "Does this make my case to you?"

4. There needs to be some limit imposed on the size of the portfolio. Because there was a twenty page limit on the narrative, most faculty wrote twenty pages. Probably ten would have sufficed. No limit was imposed on documentation except that it was to be placed in a three inch, white, three-ring binder. A number of faculty submitted many more than one binder. Most faculty over-made their cases and all expressed fears about whether they had enough material. As a consequence, anxiety was high.

5. Work must be done to prepare chairpersons to play a coaching role with faculty to help them set and pursue appropriate professional goals and prepare good portfolios. Expertise needs to be diffused throughout the college. Right now a few individuals are seen as "authorities" on how to negotiate the new Faculty Advancement program.

6. Looking back, we've learned that if the portfolio is to be made critical to the professional advancement of faculty members, it is essential that: 1)*faculty and administrators* support the basic concept of the use of the portfolio; 2) *faculty* have a significant say in the policies and procedures that govern the use of the portfolio; 3) clear *guidelines* be given for portfolio construction and evaluation; and 4) sufficient *training* be provided to all individuals involved prior to implementation.

THE FUTURE

We enter the second Faculty Advancement "cycle" certain that we *can* use portfolios as a significant component in the decision-making process as faculty members present themselves for tenure, promotion, or an endowed chair. But we must help faculty and administrators better understand the intent of the program and their roles and responsibilities within it. We must also study the portfolio itself to determine what is most effective (and, conversely, least effective) in making the portfolio an accurate representation of a real person so that sound personnel judgments can be made.

We know we are on the right track. Using multiple sources of information is right. Putting responsibility and initiative into the hands of the faculty member is right. Providing for corroboration from other sources is right. Building on a set of locally developed criteria is right. Our adjustments will be primarily a fine-tuning of the system.

MURRAY STATE UNIVERSITY
Marian Posey

In the academic year 1991-92 Murray State University put into place a completely new teaching evaluation system which requires that all faculty develop teaching portfolios. These portfolios will be used to make decisions about teaching quality for purposes of awarding tenure, promotion, and merit pay.

While the elements of this teaching evaluation system are new to Murray State, evaluation of teaching has been standard practice for over fifteen years. All faculty have had regular student ratings of their teaching which, for the most part, constituted the sole basis for evaluations of teaching quality. Each of the six colleges used a different, locally-developed rating instrument. The results of these student ratings were used in tenure, promotion, and merit pay decisions.

NEED FOR CHANGE

By 1990, dissatisfaction with the limitations of this system led the provost to appoint a Task Force on Teaching Evaluation. He charged them with the responsibility of developing a complete system for evaluating teaching that would provide campus-wide consistency in procedures and criteria for teaching evaluation as well as flexibility to accommodate diversity among disciplines and instructional goals.

The goal of the Task Force members was to develop a system of teaching evaluation which would aid faculty in instructional development as well as fulfill the provost's requirement of a comprehensive system for personnel decision making. They were convinced that the process of teaching evaluation should engage faculty in a healthy discussion of what constitutes effective teaching. Task Force members were moved by Ernest Boyer's call for a redefinition of scholarship to include the scholarship of teaching, and they worked to develop a system which would recognize and reward the scholarly aspects of teaching. They determined early in their work that multiple sources of information are essential for comprehensive evaluation of teaching effectiveness.

STRUCTURE OF NEW EVALUATION SYSTEM

Drawing on the work of Raoul Arreola, who served as a consultant to the Task Force, they decided to evaluate four components of teaching: 1) instructional delivery (largely based on student ratings); 2) instructional design; 3) content expertise (including the scholarship of teaching); and 4) course management. Once these components were identified, faculty were surveyed in a series of college meetings held by the Task Force, to determine the relative values of the components. The values that emerged represent a consensus of the campus community.

Choosing a standard student rating instrument that would provide consistency as well as flexibility for assessing instructional delivery proved a relatively easy task. The University of Washington's Instructional Assessment System was selected, in large part because it provides nine different versions of its rating form to accommodate a variety of different teaching situations. Finding means for collecting information about instructional design and content expertise presented a more difficult challenge. Peter Seldin's work on teaching portfolios provided a model for collecting this information and for giving faculty an active role in the evaluation of their teaching. Since some departments had already been using a variation of this method for tenure and promotion files, asking faculty to provide documentation in support of their teaching was not an entirely foreign concept.

CONTENTS OF PORTFOLIOS

The structure of the new teaching evaluation system focuses on a set of core items which all faculty are expected to include in their portfolios: 1) a reflective statement; 2) course syllabi; 3) examinations; 4) graded assignments; and 5) student rating reports. The table below, copies of which were distributed to all faculty, outlines the elements of the portfolio and the relative weightings of the four components of teaching to be evaluated.

The Teaching Portfolio
A collection of documents and material which together suggest
scope and quality of a professor's teaching performance

Core Items	Reflective Statement

• Professor's Reflective Statement
 	
• Course Syllabi
 	
• Examinations
 	
• Graded Assignments/Term Paper
 	
or Term Project (example)
 	
• Summary of Student Ratings
	Reflective Statement of Teaching (3–5 pages) to include:
	1. Teaching Responsibilities
	2. Teaching Philosophies, Strategies and Objectives
	3. Efforts to Improve Teaching
	  a. Workshops, conferences
	  b. Readings
	  c. Course development
	  d. New course materials
	4. Relationship of Teaching/Research
	5. Direction of Student Research
	6. Course Constraints

Rating Form — Teaching Evaluation

Component	Weight	Rating	Weighted Rating
1. Instructional Delivery	.30	_____	_____
2. Instructional Design	.30	_____	_____
3. Content Expertise	.30	_____	_____
4. Course Management	.10	_____	_____
		Total	_____

Ratings based on a scale of 0–5 in which
5 = excellent, 4 = very good, 3 = good, 2 = fair, 1 = poor, 0 = very poor.

The reflective statement provides a framework for judgments about the appropriateness of instructional design and about an instructor's scholarship and currency in their field as they relate to instruction. Course materials (syllabi, examinations, etc.) provide documentation in support of the reflective statement. These core items are expected in all portfolios; departments or colleges, at their discretion, may choose to request the inclusion of additional information as needed to meet unique needs.

Evaluation of portfolios is the task of department committees composed of two elected faculty members and the chair. This structure is designed to bring collective professional judgment to the evaluation process and to encourage an active discussion of what constitutes effective teaching.

IMPLEMENTATION OF PORTFOLIO SYSTEM

Designing a teaching evaluation system is one thing; making it work is quite another. The decision to abandon an existing method of teaching evaluation, whatever its shortcomings, and to implement a new, more comprehensive one is a high-risk undertaking. Faculty are naturally apprehensive about how they will fare under a new evaluation system used for personnel decisions. They have concerns about the amount of time that preparation of portfolios will take and they want guidance as they develop their portfolios. Faculty and administrators want assurances that portfolio materials will accurately reflect what takes place in the classroom and that portfolio evaluation will not degenerate into an evaluation of portfolios for their own sake. Some faculty resist any sort of evaluation and view portfolios as an affront to their professionalism. Coupled with these apprehensions are questions about how to evaluate the quality of portfolios. How does one assign a rating to a colleague's "instructional design" or "content expertise?"

The Task Force members anticipated these concerns and recommended two mechanisms for addressing them. First, the Task Force provided for an oversight committee appointed by the provost to monitor the implementation of the evaluation system, receive questions and concerns from faculty and administrators, and make recommendations to the provost for modifications in the system as needed. This committee, the Teaching Evaluation Review Committee, was appointed in the first semester of implementation (Fall, 1991) and has already made a number of recommendations for modification or clarification in the evaluation process. The work of this committee will help assure that the teaching evaluation system will evolve to meet needs that become apparent with experience.

The second mechanism was the recommendation that the Faculty Resource Center, Murray State's faculty development unit, be given major responsibility for coordinating the evaluation system and for providing development activities linked to the evaluation process. At the direction of the provost, the Faculty Resource Center (FRC) coordinates ordering and distributing student rating forms campus-wide. Prior to the first administration of the rating forms, the FRC conducted training sessions on the use, administration, and interpretation of the Instructional Assessment System student ratings for deans, chairs, and department secretaries. This aspect of the new evaluation system has been implemented with few problems in spite of the fact that centralized coordination of student ratings is a new procedure.

The provost wisely directed that full-blown use of portfolios should be phased in after use of the new student ratings was firmly established. Therefore, faculty were advised to begin developing portfolios in January, 1992, for evaluation in the spring of 1993. In the interim, the FRC developed training sessions for deans and chairs in evaluation of portfolios and for faculty in the development of portfolios. These sessions took place in the summer and fall of 1992.

EXPECTATIONS FOR THE FUTURE

Murray State is just beginning an undertaking which will require a great deal of patience and flexibility from both faculty and administrators. While training in portfolio development and evaluation will be helpful in establishing some general criteria and guidelines, experience with the processes will be necessary before faculty and administrators can begin to feel confident about the value of portfolios. In one college the dean required all faculty to develop portfolios in the spring of 1992 to provide the essential experience so that the processes could be refined before the 1993 portfolio evaluation. The results of this exercise revealed some of the difficulties of portfolio development and evaluation, but also showed means of improving the processes. Although this first attempt was difficult, *faculty* reported that they were pleased that information in addition to student ratings would be used in the evaluation of their teaching. They welcomed the opportunity to describe their teaching and to show how their scholarship informs instruction. *Chairs* reported that portfolios gave them broader and deeper bases for decisions about teaching effectiveness.

Use of teaching portfolios holds the promise of giving the teaching-learning process a more prominent position in the overall evaluation of faculty. Open discussion of what constitutes effective teaching and how that effectiveness can best be illustrated will serve development as well as evaluation purposes. Though the challenge of implementing an entirely new evaluation system is great, the rewards are well worth the struggle. Fortunately, the provost and the deans strongly support the use of teaching portfolios and are firmly committed to making the system work.

ST. NORBERT COLLEGE
Kenneth J. Zahorski

GENESIS

The teaching portfolio and St. Norbert College (SNC) are old friends. The friendship began in 1978 when newly-appointed Academic Dean Robert L. Horn introduced the portfolio concept as a means of making the college's approach to evaluation more open, comprehensive, consistent, and constructive.

Noting that the existing system of evaluation offered neither a regular assessment of faculty, nor a means of building a broad base of documentation, Dean Horn set out to improve it. Blending ideas he brought with him from his experience as Academic Dean at Stonehill College with input he received from a broad array of SNC faculty leaders, Dr. Horn drafted a set of procedural guidelines for a more comprehensive program of evaluation. These guidelines, incorporated into the "Procedures and Information" section of *The Faculty Handbook*, have served the college well for the past fourteen years.

The new system was elegant in its simplicity. It required the division chairs to evaluate faculty according to specific guidelines on a periodic basis: every year for non-tenured faculty, every five years for tenured faculty. The evaluation addressed the faculty member's professional strengths and achievements as well as those areas which could be improved. The approach was to be constructive: to give more credit where credit was due and to help the faculty member focus his or her future efforts at professional self-development. Further, the evaluation process was designed to be individualized and non-quantitative; in no sense was it an attempt to rank faculty members.

The three primary goals set forth in 1978 remain the same today. The St. Norbert College system of evaluation is to: 1) keep faculty members regularly informed of their progress toward tenure and promotion; 2) assist individual faculty to grow and develop professionally as teachers, scholars, and collegial citizens; and 3) maintain a concrete and meaningful record of that progress and development by means of a portfolio. Undergirding all of these goals is the understanding that they are to be reached through a humane and open process not meant to be punitive, but rather supportive and constructive.

IMPLEMENTATION

Two characteristics of St. Norbert College's evaluation/portfolio program deserve special attention: 1) its integrative nature and 2) its interactive approach. By looking closely at each of these defining traits we can gain an understanding of the system as a whole, including its basic components, its key players, and its primary strengths.

One of the most attractive features of the SNC portfolio approach is its organic nature. Over the course of its fourteen-year history the concept of the portfolio has become an intrinsic feature of the faculty mindset and an integral part of the college's academic lifestyle. Let us look more closely at how the portfolio thread weaves its way through the SNC academic tapestry.

To begin with, special steps are taken to familiarize new faculty with the portfolio system. Key to this process is the college's New Faculty Orientation and Mentor Program. The Orientation Program, designed to acclimate both full- and part-time new faculty to the SNC community, has three primary components: 1) a late summer orientation session designed to acquaint new faculty with key academic programs and administrative offices, to outline institutional expectations and faculty responsibilities, to supply information about college facilities and services, and to provide a forum for exchanging ideas about teaching and advising; 2) a series of fall semester workshops exploring topics of particular concern to new faculty; and 3) a Mentor Program in which experienced instructors work with new faculty during their first year at the college, offering them opportunities to discuss professional and personal concerns.

The portfolio concept is introduced in all three components of the Orientation and Mentor Program. During the two-day orientation session, for example, the division chairs define the concept when describing the instructional, collegial, and professional responsibilities of new faculty. One of the principal goals of this initial discussion is to take the mystery out of the evaluative process and to ease possible apprehensiveness about it by stressing its open, human, and helpful nature.

This brief introductory presentation is followed by a fall semester workshop on the teaching portfolio. Planned and facilitated by the Director of Faculty Development, the workshop focuses on three areas pertaining to the portfolio: its nature and function, its preparation, and its benefits. Each new faculty member is provided with a copy of Peter Seldin's *The Teaching Portfolio* (1991) before the workshop, and care is taken to schedule the session early in the semester so that new faculty can get an early start at preparing their portfolios.

Complementing these activities are those connected with the Mentor Program. Since mentors and new faculty are matched in the preceding spring semester, the mentors are in a position to help their new colleagues with work on the portfolio and other teaching-learning matters early in a new colleague's career. As a service for mentors, the Director of Faculty Development schedules a "Mentor Informational Session" the first week in September which is designed to help mentors review the kinds of help they can provide their new colleagues, including assistance with the teaching portfolio.

While the Orientation and Mentor Programs are key vehicles in familiarizing faculty with the portfolio concept, they are not the only ones. Still another is *The Beacon*, a faculty development newsletter published six times a year as a service to St. Norbert College faculty. Within its pages faculty can share ideas not only about the concept of the teaching portfolio, but about a wide range of teaching-learning topics. In addition, the Director of Faculty Development regularly routes teaching-learning materials to all faculty and academic administrators.

Further, when full-length works on the teaching portfolio are published, the Director of Faculty Development orders multiple copies and makes them readily available for faculty use by placing them on the shelves of the Faculty Development Resource Center, a repository of teaching-learning materials housing an extensive collection of books, journals, monographs, pamphlets, software, and videotapes. Currently in the Center are copies of Seldin's *The Teaching Portfolio* (1991); Russell Edgerton, Patricia Hutchings, and Kathleen Quinlan's *The Teaching Portfolio: Capturing the Scholarship in Teaching* (1991); and several articles dealing with the portfolio and related topics.

Finally, each year the Office of Faculty Development sponsors a number of topical sessions which lend themselves to the discussion of teaching-learning topics. One of the most noteworthy is "Food for Thought," a series of informal noon-hour discussion sessions designed to provide a forum for the exchange of ideas about teaching and scholarship. A guest presenter begins each session with a brief description of some teaching strategy or scholarly project and then invites questions and comments.

The second distinguishing feature of the St. Norbert College evaluation/portfolio system, its interactive approach, was part of the system's initial design. Believing that the portfolio approach would work best through a process of interaction and mentoring, Dr. Horn made second-party assistance central to the system. A step-by-step description of the procedures used in the SNC evaluation of faculty system will reveal just how integral consultation and corroboration are to the entire process.

STEP ONE: INITIATING THE PROCESS

The division chair initiates the formal evaluation process for non-tenured faculty early in the second semester by writing a letter concretely describing its fundamental procedures. More specifically, this letter: 1) explains the philosophical tenets underlying the process; 2) describes the procedures to be used; 3) outlines the steps the faculty member should take in preparing for the evaluation; 4) identifies the teaching, scholarly, and collegial areas upon which the faculty member should reflect; and 5) invites the faculty member to compose a self-evaluation essay according to *The Faculty Handbook's* "Evaluation Guidelines" and to submit the essay to the division chair by a specified date. The "Guidelines" are divided into three categories: Teaching Effectiveness; Collegial Activities; and Scholarly, Creative, and Professional Activities.

STEP TWO: PREPARING THE PORTFOLIO

Once the process has been explained and the objectives agreed upon, *both* the division chair *and* faculty member begin the process of collecting and reflecting. Based upon the "Guidelines," the faculty member is asked to consider such matters as: 1) teaching philosophy, objectives, and strategies; 2) steps taken to assess and enhance one's teaching; 3) judicious interpretation of the data yielded by the Student Opinion of Teaching questionnaire; 4) updating of the content and/or pedagogy of courses in response to changes or new knowledge in the discipline; 5) flexibility in responding to student needs, concerns, and rights; 6) conscientiousness in carrying out obligations to students; and 7) short- and long-term goals.

The division chairs also have homework. In preparing for the meeting with the faculty member, the chair gathers input from other *appropriate* sources including: 1) Student Opinion of Teaching surveys; 2) syllabi and other classroom materials; 3) current students (usually at least three students, one from each class, are interviewed); 4) colleagues within the discipline, the division, the college, and the wider academic community; and 5) previous evaluations. It is important to stress the term "appropriate." The chairs must use their judgment on the kinds of input which are necessary to assess the faculty member's performance in a fair, comprehensive, and consistent manner. Also, it is neither necessary nor desirable for either the faculty member or the chair to address every item on the list of guidelines. Prudential judgment on the most important areas of emphasis for the evaluation of the individual faculty member is paramount.

During this important preparatory stage, faculty do not work in isolation. Rather, they are encouraged to work closely with the division chairs, their mentors (in the case of new faculty), and the Director of Faculty Development. The Director can help colleagues find appropriate instruments and procedures for documenting, analyzing, and assessing teaching-learning methods and strategies. Faculty seek counsel from the Director of Faculty Development not only during the time they are preparing for their meetings with the division chairs, but also when they are preparing applications for promotion, tenure, and sabbatical leave.

STEP THREE: DISCUSSING THE PORTFOLIO

Using the faculty member's reflective essay as a basis, the division chair and faculty member meet to discuss the faculty member's professional achievements, growth, areas in need of improvement, and his or her professional priorities for the future. This conference is of the utmost importance to the evaluative process and both parties must carefully prepare for it.

The faculty member's preparation manifests itself primarily through the self-evaluation essay. In order to serve the purpose for which it is designed, the essay must be concrete, well organized, and genuinely reflective. These essays average about five pages, and vary in form, texture, and style, reflecting the individuality of the author. However there are standard components, including: 1) an overview of teaching responsibilities; 2) a statement of teaching philosophy and approach; 3) a description of steps taken to enhance the teaching-learning process; 4) a self-critique; and 5) a statement of short- and long-term goals. In addition, faculty are encouraged to include pertinent documentation, such as syllabi, teaching-learning exercises, student and colleague testimonials, and classroom videotapes.

The division chairs also carefully prepare for the conference. They see the interview as the linchpin of the process and make sure they bring to the meeting their own portfolio of materials. Each chair uses an approach most congenial to his or her interactive style. In the case of one chair, this involves writing out two to three pages of notes before the conference and then going over the notes with the faculty member, modifying preliminary conclusions. Thus, the faculty member is given an opportunity to respond to each point in the chair's "tentative evaluation." This division chair has "many times changed in major ways conclusions based upon the insight faculty members have shed on various data."

STEP FOUR: REFLECTING UPON THE EVALUATION REPORT

Following the conference, the division chair writes a concrete formal report (usually about 2–4 pages) which is sent to the faculty member. The report contains an assessment of the faculty member's strengths and achievements, as well as recommendations for helping the faculty member improve in any area(s) of perceived weakness. The faculty member either initials the report or responds in writing to any aspect of the chair's report which he or she feels to be incomplete or inaccurate. Perhaps most importantly, faculty are encouraged to discuss the written evaluation with their division chair. Faculty regularly avail themselves of this opportunity. Finally, the division chair forwards the self-evaluation essay, the chair's report, and any commentaries by the faculty member to the Dean's Office. In cases of substantial disagreement between a faculty member and the division chair, the dean interviews both to resolve the differences.

On the surface this step seems to involve a fairly cut-and-dry procedure, but in reality it, too, offers important opportunities for further reflection—and at a crucial juncture in the evaluation process. Frequently, some of the most stimulating, substantive, and productive dialogue goes on after the faculty member studies the evaluation report. Indeed, this stage of the evaluative process generates not only deep reflection, but some real soul searching.

STEP FIVE: FILING THE EVALUATION REPORT

The self-evaluation essay, the chair's report, and any commentaries are placed in the faculty evaluation files. The intent of the evaluation process dictates that this information be held in confidence and release of the evaluative documents must be requested by the faculty member in writing.

While this step may have the ring of finality, it would be a mistake to view it in terms of closure. In fact, the SNC evaluation system is decidedly more circular than linear. While the process is systematic and may be divided into distinctive stages, an artist's rendering would probably take the form of a Midgard Serpent, tail in mouth, never ending. The collecting and reflecting which begin the process continue beyond the filing of the report, and perhaps even in a more thoughtful and ruminative fashion.

FUTURE PLANS

Although the evaluation/portfolio system has been working very well at St. Norbert College, faculty and academic administrators are constantly seeking ways to improve it. At the time of this writing, for example, the Academic Dean, Division Chairs, and Director of Faculty Development were in the process of reassessing the system in light of the most recent literature on the teaching portfolio. In short, this case study describes *process*, not *product*: it describes a dynamic system that is regularly modified to meet the changing needs of the SNC academic community. The ultimate goal of this system is to help all St. Norbert College faculty become "reflective practitioners" of one of humankind's most sophisticated and challenging crafts.

BIBLIOGRAPHY

Edgerton, Russell, Hutchings, Patricia, and Quinlan, Kathleen. *The Teaching Portfolio: Capturing the Scholarship in Teaching.* (A publication of The AAHE Teaching Initiative.) Washington, DC: American Association for Higher Education, 1991.

Seldin, Peter. *The Teaching Portfolio: A Practical Guide to Improved Performance and Promotion/Tenure Decisions.* Bolton, MA: Anker Publishing Co., 1991.

THE UNIVERSITY OF MARYLAND
UNIVERSITY COLLEGE
Barbara J. Millis

Since 1987, the University of Maryland University College (UMUC) has used a modified version of teaching portfolios as the selection criterion for its Excellence in Teaching Awards. Initially, the Office of Faculty Development (OFD) asked each nominee to provide a statement of teaching philosophy, current syllabi and examinations, and a summary of community activities related to teaching. The OFD then duplicated from faculty files evidence of good teaching, including computerized summaries of student evaluations, peer classroom observation reports, thank-you letters for attending workshops, faculty meetings or commencement, and other teaching-related materials. Approximately two years ago, when the teaching portfolio movement became more widely known in the United States, UMUC decided to request portfolios from the nominees, resulting in faculty "ownership" of the selection process. This decision also eliminated the wholesale duplication of over sixty-five faculty files for the seven committee members, a labor intensive, environmentally destructive practice that overwhelmed the committee with undifferentiated paper.

This initiative dovetailed with overall faculty development efforts to enhance teaching and learning at an institution whose mission is to provide a quality education for adult learners. Thus, the teaching portfolio became a viable way to focus attention on successful teaching and learning. In 1991, UMUC began a systematic effort, through the OFD, to inform faculty about the opportunities provided by teaching portfolios and to motivate them to invest the time and emotional commitment into initiating them. Because our faculty are primarily working professionals with advanced degrees, they tend to be intrinsically motivated individuals who consider teaching an avocation; they also tend, like faculty on traditional campuses, to have many conflicting demands on their time.

Our efforts to encourage portfolio preparation include all faculty, but we have specifically targeted the Excellence in Teaching Award nominees because: 1) they already have a vested interest in preparing portfolios as part of the selection process for the award, and 2) as UMUC's "best and brightest" faculty, they provide positive role models for their teaching colleagues.

Now when we notify faculty of their nomination for the Excellence in Teaching Award, we also explain the teaching portfolio concept and invite faculty to request an information packet, "Developing a Teaching Portfolio," containing various articles and UMUC-specific examples. To make the portfolio process as easy as possible, we also offer to duplicate for them the "evidence of good teaching" from their files that prompts the reflective part of the portfolio. We also tie the portfolio process to an important component of our faculty development efforts, the partially FIPSE-sponsored Peer Visit Program. We arrange—except in the rare case when nominees decline—for a peer visitor to observe their class and document in a formal report their teaching expertise. The report then becomes part of the evolving portfolio, and the visitor sometimes becomes a coach or mentor who helps the faculty member prepare the portfolio.

We find that focused, collegial dialogue about the teaching portfolio almost invariably contributes to the improvement process. In fact, we encourage all faculty to work in pairs. These peer partners can heighten their awareness of the complexities of the instructional process and forge new ideas and understandings. They can inspire one another to try new ideas and then provide comfort or congratulations as they explore teaching options and document successes in the evolving portfolio. Reciprocal classroom visits by trusted peers build confidence and create a detailed record of faculty initiatives. Faculty are also encouraged to consult the Assistant Dean, Faculty Development or key faculty who have already completed portfolios.

Our targeted attempts to convince our "best and brightest" that the portfolio effort is worthwhile have been fairly successful—of the thirty-two finalists nominated for the Excellence in Teaching Award, twenty completed teaching portfolios. They were encouraged to do so by a series of letters outlining the process and offering assistance, including one summarizing the reasons for preparing a portfolio and another relating the portfolio process to UMUC's teaching mission. Another informative letter, sent to over 100 faculty with the "Developing Teaching Portfolios" packet, contains a key summary intended to focus attention on the reflective nature of the portfolio:

> "The portfolio itself consists of two distinct parts: 1) the reflective 'body' in which you comment on what appears in 2) the appendices containing the 'raw' data—the supporting documents—which prompted the reflection. Thus, the body of your portfolio might contain a paragraph or two about why you developed your syllabus as you did; the appendices would contain the actual syllabus."

We also offer in this letter two organizational strategies. The first one, advocated by Peter Seldin and the Canadian Association of University Teachers, suggests that faculty arrange entries in three categories: 1) material from oneself, 2) information from others, and 3) products of good teaching. The second, a model endorsed by AAHE and based on work done by the Stanford Teacher Assessment Project, recommends a format based on the "core tasks" of teaching: 1) course planning and preparation, 2) actual teaching, 3) evaluating student learning and providing feedback, and 4) keeping up with the professional field in areas related to teaching performance.

To encourage uniform components, we also give faculty a copy of the Excellence in Teaching Award Committee Rating Sheet which identifies the specific categories of information the committee will evaluate: the student nomination letter(s), the statement of teaching philosophy, peer visit report(s), syllabi and examinations, student evaluations, recommendations from the staffing individuals, evidence of participation in faculty development activities, evidence of community service, and grade distributions.

Besides the practices already described, we have attempted to make the teaching portfolio concept more visible. In the fall of 1991, for example, twenty-six faculty attended a workshop on "Creating a Portfolio To Enhance Teaching." As a follow-up, during a Faculty Showcase held in conjunction with the fall all-day "Faculty Opportunities Day," a computer science faculty member gave a presentation on his experiences in preparing a portfolio. Later, at the spring "Faculty Opportunities Day," the keynote speaker, Patricia Hutchings of the AAHE Teaching Initiative, highlighted the portfolio as a viable way to enhance teaching and learning. A general article on teaching portfolios and one containing excerpts from faculty portfolios, entitled "Reflections on Teaching," have been written for *Faculty Focus*, UMUC's teaching newsletter.

During each mandatory New Faculty Orientation, we tell faculty that a premise underlying the faculty development program is that a "professor is never a finished product." Similarly, we tell faculty preparing portfolios that they should update and refine their reflections and supporting materials as they grow professionally. (One instructor describes his portfolio as an historical document that is always evolving!) Thus, the OFD also believes that we need to improve continuously our efforts to help faculty understand and accept the challenge of creating a portfolio to enhance teaching. The following initiatives are planned for the coming academic year:

1. A two-to-three page summary, tentatively called "The Teaching Portfolio at UMUC," will be included in the Faculty Survival Kit, a folder of teaching-oriented and logistical information given to all new faculty at the three-hour required orientations offered four times a year.
2. The packet, "Developing a Teaching Portfolio," will be revised to include more UMUC examples.
3. Three-hour training workshops, "Creating a Portfolio To Enhance Teaching," will be offered each fall semester.
4. Each issue of the teaching newsletter, *Faculty Focus*, will contain articles on the teaching portfolio.
5. A Teaching Excellence Award subcommittee will attempt to develop a more systematic approach to the selection process, so that teaching portfolios can be evaluated more effectively, based on specified criteria of excellence. As a result, we hope to be reasonably certain that the selection committee members are interpreting and weighing uniform data in the same way.
6. We will investigate the desirability and feasibility of using teaching portfolios for summative purposes by requiring them for faculty advancement.

7. If a grant proposal is funded by the Maryland Association of Higher Education (MAHE), UMUC and the University of Maryland at College Park (UMCP) will initiate a joint research project to investigate whether the teaching portfolio is valuable for both sets of faculty: the traditional, full-time, research-oriented faculty at UMCP, and the nontraditional, primarily part-time teaching-oriented faculty at UMUC. We plan to use interviews, document analysis, and observations to record the similarities and dissimilarities: a) in the way our faculty members go about compiling portfolios, b) in the finished teaching portfolios, and c) in the faculty's and administration's perception of the program's value and worth. Disparate as our faculties are, this research project would be a test of the teaching portfolio's viability and flexibility.

It is difficult to determine exactly what factors influence faculty participation in any teaching improvement initiative, but we can summarize some of the reasons for the success of the current program:

+ We continually focus attention on the value of the teaching portfolio process to enhance teaching and learning.
+ We tie the teaching portfolio process to other faculty development efforts, including the Excellence in Teaching Award, the workshop series, the Peer Visit Program, the teaching newsletter, and the "Faculty Opportunities Day."
+ We encourage Excellence in Teaching Award nominees, some of UMUC's most effective teachers, to complete portfolios, so that other faculty have positive role models and sterling examples from a variety of disciplines.
+ We make it easy for faculty to succeed by: 1) duplicating the "evidence of good teaching" from faculty files, so that they don't have to initiate their own paper chase; 2) providing lots of written material, including the packet, "Developing a Teaching Portfolio," with examples of portfolios prepared by UMUC colleagues and focused letters which highlight the reflective nature of portfolios and several organizational options; and 3) offering a good deal of support, such as peer partners to help in the teaching portfolio preparation process or consultations with the Assistant Dean, Faculty Development.

We plan to build on the past successes of our program by expanding and improving our teaching portfolio initiatives because, just as with our professors, "a teaching portfolio is never a finished product."

UNIVERSITY OF NEBRASKA-LINCOLN
DEPARTMENT OF ENGLISH
Robert D. Narveson

Whereas, not long ago, faculty members in the English Department at the University of Nebraska-Lincoln were expected to submit only a bare bones report of their teaching, consisting mostly of numbers, they are now invited to submit a portfolio of materials that give a much fuller picture of what they have done. The changes are affecting teaching and the reward structure in the department in complex ways.

The introduction of a portfolio-style annual report of teaching performance is intended, in part, to provide more adequate documentation than has been the case, and therefore a closer correlation of reward to performance. While less often cited as an intention, preparing portfolios has had the effect, in the UN-L English Department, of focusing attention in a more searching way on classroom practices, on interactions with colleagues, and, in short, on a wide range of other aspects of teaching that formerly were silently taken for granted. The change may have lessened but has not eliminated dissatisfaction with the evaluation and reward of teaching. A recent survey of faculty in the department found nearly 50% questioning the relationship between their performance as teachers and their reward.

Experience in the English Department relates to its context in a public research university. The University of Nebraska, "an AAU land-grant institution" (as it proudly identifies itself), faces the same problem as other institutions of its type in balancing its emphasis among its different missions that include teaching at baccalaureate, masters, and doctoral levels, a major commitment to research, and a variety of services in education, arts, humanities, agriculture, and industry. For well-known reasons, faculty members at UN-L perceive that recognition and reward come to them preeminently from their specialized research and the publications that result from it. A survey of faculty in departments participating in a UN-L project on reward of teaching found a majority of faculty agreeing that effective teaching effort was not as well assessed or rewarded as research activity. Nevertheless, there is, in general, a strong commitment to teaching, and most faculty members participating in the survey indicated that they would like to see teaching more effectively assessed and rewarded. In this desire, they were at one with administrators at all levels. A university such as UN-L encompasses a bewildering array of enterprises, and each unit evolves forms and practices suited to its missions. The wide range of structures, norms, and values in the diverse departments and colleges leads to differing practices in assessing and rewarding faculty performance. Upper echelon university administrators establish general policies, but successful means of carrying them out must be worked out by departments to satisfy their special needs and desires.

Officials at The Fund for the Improvement of Post Secondary Education (FIPSE) were impressed by the institution-wide interest in effective teaching at UN-L, and approved a project to examine and improve the institutional processes of documenting, evaluating, and rewarding teaching. Assisted by a grant from FIPSE, twenty-seven departments in five colleges of the university participated over a three year period.

When the FIPSE project started, the English Department had already adopted most of the elements of a portfolio approach for the assessment of teaching. The departmental plan called for student evaluation of each course and teacher, for submission by the teacher of the course syllabus and schedule, for the teacher to write a brief assessment of his or her performance and the performance of the students, and for an assessment of the student evaluations. It invited an optional letter, with supporting exhibits, describing and illustrating unusual successes, revisions in course content and teaching method, and plans for the future. A personnel subcommittee read the files and assigned separate ratings from one to five in teaching, research, and service. These ratings were then given weights in proportion to an individual's assignment, typically 50% teaching, 40% research, and 10% service. Theoretically, then, at least half of the typical teacher's overall rating was based on assessment of teaching, and was therefore the major influence on recommendations for tenure, for promotion, and for salary increases based on merit. But in actuality, as everyone knew, this was not so for many reasons: because variations in ratings tended to be narrow for teaching and wide for research, because many on the faculty regard research as the activity that distinguished UN-L as an institution, because reputation within the disciplines depends on one's publications, because research records receive the most critical scrutiny in recommendations for tenure and promotion, and because the administration smiles upon projects that bring support money to the institution. In economic terms, the FIPSE project, by emphasizing reward for teaching, threatened to bring the "real value" of the teaching rating closer to the "book value." This threat focused faculty interest on the questions of what really counted in the ratings game as played by faculty who put together the files, and by the personnel subcommittee that read them and assigned numerical weights.

Two intertwined rationales for requesting teaching portfolios are commonly enunciated by University of Nebraska faculty and administrators during their discussions of teaching, its encouragement, and its appropriate emphasis in the reward system. The first is to enable administrators to determine appropriate reward for past performance (summative use). The second is to assist individual teachers in analyzing past performance in order to identify opportunities to improve future performance (formative use). The summative rationale, fostered by the need for better documentation of teaching performance, has been the chief motivator for administrators, including department chairs, at UN-L in moving toward the use of teaching portfolios.

Motivations among individual faculty members are more complex. The present Chair of the English Department has remarked, in good humor, that chairing English is like herding cats: "you can expect a lot of hissing and many tiny scars"—an abundance of them stemming from assessments of teaching. An emphasis on summative uses of portfolios arouses opposition in some faculty members who question the pay-off. Their attitude: "Convince us that the work of putting together a detailed portfolio will make any real difference in our pay checks." The English Department is not finding it easy to demonstrate that a faculty member receives a greater reward for submitting a detailed, thoughtful portfolio than would have otherwise been the case. And besides, faculty members are probably correct in thinking that equal effort devoted to their research has a greater financial payoff.

Others of the faculty argue that a departmental request for a portfolio of evidence on teaching in itself motivates teachers to do reportable and documentable things about their teaching. Such activity, in their opinion, has the effect of raising the level of performance for the whole department. In their eyes, those who provide portfolio materials are making a greater contribution to the teaching mission than those who do not, and this in itself should be recognized and rewarded. It can sometimes seem to the former that the sole question of interest to the personnel subcommittee is "What is your comparative ranking on student evaluations?"

For some faculty members, the formative uses of information about teaching are more significant than the summative. If "teaching performance" is interpreted by the personnel subcommittee as including the faculty member's personal growth as a teacher—if it is also asking "What are you doing to improve your teaching?"—and this is how most members of the personnel subcommittee claim they interpret it—then faculty members persuaded that questions of this nature influence committee decisions have another strong motive for documenting teaching performance in a broad sense. No doubt, say members of the committee, but should faculty members long recognized as effective teachers, who win outstanding comments and ratings on student evaluations, be penalized for not submitting portfolios that would only confirm what is already evident? Another source of perplexity to the committee is the frequent lack of correlation between the effort some faculty members devote to their teaching and any effect these efforts have on their ratings by students. This is a seriously unsettling problem that can quickly undermine morale and cast doubt on the value of the portfolio approach.

This mere sampling of issues indicates that the dust from the department's participation in the FIPSE project is far from completely settled.

Because the Department of English was already requiring some and inviting others of the components of a teaching portfolio, its experience during the three years of the FIPSE project is probably not typical. Participating departments, twenty-seven in all, were a heterogeneous group, belonging to five colleges ranging from undergraduate arts and sciences to graduate professional.

Eight departments participated during the second year and fifteen during the third year. Each produced a plan appropriate to its situation. Most adopted some version of the portfolio approach. English perhaps changed less than most in the amount and nature of the materials requested from teachers for their annual report.

What about the future? Demands for accountability of teachers and departments are unlikely to decrease. The portfolio approach is a way that goes beyond numbers in giving an account of teaching activities. In the English Department, as throughout the University of Nebraska, support for the portfolio approach is strong and seems to increase with experience. There will undoubtedly be continued soul-searching as more irritants in the process are identified. The personnel subcommittee will have to find ways of "counting" and perhaps giving weights to the variety of materials professors are including in their portfolios, though in keeping with their humanistic bent, committee members are reluctant to depart from a holistic approach.

The department in general will need to move toward consensus about the quantity and form of portfolios. There will need to be discussion of productive ways for individual faculty members to use their portfolios as a resource for improvement. The evolutionary approach that has characterized the department in the past will no doubt continue. The focus upon teaching produced by this evolving process may itself be the most important outcome. It will be increasingly difficult for entering faculty members to attain tenure, promotion, or merit adjustments without solid records of successful teaching. It is unrealistic to expect, however, that an institution such as UN-L will quickly shift its major rewards from research effort and accomplishment, to effort and accomplishment in teaching.

The author wishes to thank his colleagues G. Brookes, S. Hilliard, K. Ronald and L. Whipp for their helpful suggestions.

Evaluating Teaching Portfolios for Personnel Decisions

Peter Seldin

In an earlier chapter, the writer answered some common questions raised by professors or administrators about the teaching portfolio concept. One perennial question was, "What should personnel committees be looking for when they evaluate teaching performance from a portfolio?" This chapter addresses that question in greater depth.

When you get down to it, the evaluation of teaching performance, from portfolios or any other instruments, is an exercise in subjective judgment. It is unavoidable. Of course, tenure, promotion, retention, and merit award decisions should be based on objective data. But the purpose of objective data is to help shape a subjective decision. This does not suggest, of course, that the judgments cannot be systematized and sanitized. On the contrary, if the evaluation process meets key requirements, the likelihood of making more accurate personnel decisions is greatly enhanced.

KEY REQUIREMENTS

Seldin (1988) cites certain key requirements in the evaluation of academic administrator performance that are readily adaptable to the evaluation of teaching through portfolios:

Relevance. There must be a clear link between the crucial elements in teaching and the elements selected for evaluation. Put another way, relevance can be determined by answering one question, "What really makes the difference between effective and ineffective teachers in a particular discipline?"

Reliability. As used here, the word refers to consistency of judgment. Appraisals of a professor as teacher by ten different committee members may not coincide exactly, but they should be in general agreement. Certainly evaluators from different vantage points will perceive the teaching performance differently. But there is every reason to believe that together they will paint as complete a picture of the professor as teacher as they do of the professor as researcher/scholar.

Practicality. Portfolios should be readily understood and easily put to use by personnel committees. They should not demand an inordinate amount of time or energy to read and evaluate. One way to assure this is to put a page limit on the length of portfolios. Whatever the limit—five, ten, even twenty pages—the figure should be clearly known by professors and personnel committee members.

Acceptability. This is perhaps the most important requirement. Unless the portfolio program has won the unqualified support of the evaluators and of those being evaluated, it will be on very shaky ground. That means that academic administrators and faculty leaders must build support for the program by focusing attention not on the technical soundness of the portfolio concept but on its attitudinal and interpersonal aspects. They must engage in frank and open discussions in order to garner active support for the portfolio on campus.

THE IMPORTANCE OF MANDATED PORTFOLIO ITEMS

Because each portfolio is unique, the content and organization will differ from one professor to another. This can create possible difficulty in using portfolios for personnel decisions. As discussed in the opening chapter, one way around this problem is to require portfolios used for tenure and promotion decisions, or for teaching excellence awards, to include certain mandated items along with the elective ones. By standardizing some items, comparison of teaching performance (for example, of six faculty members from different teaching contexts seeking promotion to associate professor) becomes possible. Not surprisingly, this approach has been adopted by a great many colleges and universities using portfolios for personnel decisions.

Although such mandated items vary somewhat from one institution to another, they often include: a reflective statement on the professor's teaching, summaries of student ratings on core questions for the past three years, course syllabi for all courses taught within the past three years, innovative course materials, and evidence of efforts to improve one's teaching.

Professors preparing portfolios are urged to pay close attention to any items required by their department or institution. As previously suggested, it is urgently recommended that discussions between department chair and professor address teaching responsibilities and expectations, and how teaching performance is to be reported. Such information should be available to members of the personnel committee as part of their review of a professor's portfolio.

CHECKLIST OF GENERAL ITEMS FOR EVALUATING PORTFOLIOS

The following suggested checklist of general items was developed from a review of the current literature on evaluating teaching portfolios and from discussions with more than 100 members of personnel committees at colleges and universities of varying sizes, shapes, and missions:

1. If an institution requires core items, they must *all* be included in the portfolio.
2. Evidence must be presented to show that academic institutional goals (for example, development of critical thinking skills or group presentation skills) are met in the classroom.
3. Evidence of accomplishment, not just a reflective statement, must be present in the portfolio.
4. The reflective statement of what and why professors teach as they do must be consistent with the syllabus and with student and peer evaluations of their teaching.
5. There must be evidence of student learning, not just material from others and material from one's self.
6. The degree of documentation in the three areas of student learning, material from others, and material from one's self must be in general balance and several sources should be used as documentation in each area.
7. Efforts of improved performance over time must be reflected in the evaluation reports.
8. The ratings on all common core questions on student rating forms from several courses and several years must be included in the portfolio.
9. Some evidence of peer evaluation through classroom visitation or review of instructional materials must be presented, unless this would be inconsistent with the institution's culture.
10. The teaching responsibilities section must be consistent with the department chair's statement of the professor's responsibilities.
11. Including selected information from years ago is permissible, but the vast majority of data must be current or from the recent past.
12. Data on scholarly research or publication must be considered in a teaching portfolio *only* if it relates directly to teaching, or student learning, in one's discipline.
13. The portfolio must reflect consistency between a professor's reflective statement of teaching philosophy and his or her teaching actions in the classroom.
14. All claims made in the portfolio must be supported by evidence in the appendices.
15. Evaluators must focus attention on the *evidence* supporting teaching effectiveness, and ignore an elegant cover, or attractive printer's font, or other such packaging.

SUGGESTED MODELS FOR EVALUATING PORTFOLIOS

Ordinarily, when an institution decides to evaluate teaching from portfolios, a committee is named to develop an appropriate draft model. Then administrative and faculty feedback is obtained and the draft model is redrafted and tested for reliability and validity. If this time-consuming approach increases acceptability, the lengthy developmental process may be justified. But instead of creating an original model, most institutions can benefit from the experience and models already developed and available elsewhere.

Obviously, the model must be congenial in nature and content with the goals of a particular college or university. And the selection of the criteria and their ultimate appraisal will depend on local conditions as well as institutional and department objectives. In general, therefore, it is better to adapt—not adopt—an already existing model and reshape it to meet local conditions and needs.

Several administrators and faculty can be enlisted to adapt the model so that the final instrument actually measures what it is supposed to measure and fits local goals.

Four models for evaluating teaching from portfolios are presented in the Appendix to this chapter. They should not be considered as the definitive word, but as a starting point for campus discussion intended to mold and reshape the model for a better fit with institutional or department needs.

A general model (see Exhibit 1 in this chapter's Appendix) patterned after one developed at the University of Nebraska-Lincoln School of Music, is used at Murray State University (Kentucky), where it is adapted to department needs.

Another model (see Exhibit 2) is in use at a Texas community college. During a one-year field test, this college trained a small group of portfolio readers from across disciplines. Specializing in types of entries, the readers, as an evaluative team, are now responsible for rating complete portfolios.

Most forms designed to evaluate teaching from portfolios run several pages, but a shorter version, running less than two pages, (see Exhibit 3) has been developed by a California liberal arts college. The short form includes questions requiring completion of a rating scale plus a narrative response.

The Department of English at a New York university has taken a different approach to evaluating portfolios. It requires the personnel committee to respond to short-answer questions about a professor's teaching performance (see Exhibit 4).

AVOIDING PITFALLS IN THE EVALUATION OF PORTFOLIOS

Equipped with hindsight and the benefit of experience, we have learned a good deal about some common pitfalls in evaluating portfolios for personnel decisions. They are offered as four "don'ts:"

1. *Don't Use the Portfolio Alone for Personnel Decisions.* The professor's role is multifaceted and the teaching portfolio covers only one, although very important, facet. When placed in a professor's curriculum vitae, it provides a record of teaching accomplishments so that they can be accorded their proper weight in the professor's overall assessment.
2. *Don't Rely Heavily on Any One Source of Evidence.* No personnel decision—for promotion, tenure, teaching excellence award, retention, or merit pay—should be made on the basis of a single rating or other source of evidence. Such decisions should rest on a holistic examination of the professor's teaching portfolio. The focus should be not on a single stone but rather on the mosaic formed by all of the stones.
3. *Don't Assume that Standards and Ratings Will be the Same Across Disciplines and Institutions.* Standards and ratings are mercurial and tend to fluctuate, sometimes widely, even unfairly. Some raters are strict, others are lenient. This may give momentary pause to an institution about to introduce portfolios for personnel decisions. But it is no solution to decide not to institute such a program. Off-the-cuff appraisals of teaching based almost exclusively on student ratings, while currently popular, are hardly the answer. It is better to instill the teaching portfolio which has the advantage of documenting both the complexity and individuality of teaching, and work on refining portfolio appraisal so that it is more accurate, more fair, and more complete.
4. *Don't Assume that Everyone Must Teach the Same Way.* In truth, it is neither possible nor desirable. It is better to allow for individual differences in teaching styles and techniques so long as they can be tolerated by departmental and institutional goals. In general it is best to develop criteria within the smallest practical unit. At times, it will be the entire institution. More often, it will be a department or group of departments with dominant similarities.

GETTING STARTED

Perhaps the best way to get started is for a group of faculty to develop general standards of good teaching. Guiding the group should be the emphasis on teaching in the institution's strategic plan, and the need to develop an institution-wide system with common elements and procedures, yet have enough flexibility to accommodate diverse approaches to teaching and its evaluation (Cartwright, 1991). Among the institutions using this approach successfully are Murray State University (Kentucky), Miami-Dade Community College (Florida), and Dalhousie University (Canada).

It is important to allow a year, even two years, for the process of acceptance and implementation. During this period, draft documents should be carefully prepared, freely discussed, modified as needed. And always keep in mind that all details of the program need not be in place before implementation. Start the program incrementally and be flexible to modification as it develops. Remember that the quest for perfection is endless. Don't stall the program in a futile search for the perfect approach. The goal is improvement, not perfection.

President John F. Kennedy was fond of telling a story about the French Marshall Louis Lyautey. When the marshall announced that he wished to plant a tree, his gardener responded that the tree would not reach full growth for more than one hundred years. "In that case," Lyautey replied, "we have no time to lose. We must start to plant this afternoon."

Colleges and universities thinking of using portfolios for personnel decisions have no time to lose. They must get started now.

BIBLIOGRAPHY

Cartwright, J. "Report of the Task Force on Teaching Evaluation." Interoffice Communication to the Provost, Murray State University, September 6, 1991.

Seldin, P. *Evaluating and Developing Administrative Performance.* San Francisco, CA: Jossey-Bass, 1988.

APPENDIX TO CHAPTER FIVE
SELECTED FORMS TO EVALUATE TEACHING PORTFOLIOS

EXHIBIT 1

The general model in Exhibit 1, patterned after one developed at the University of Nebraska-Lincoln, School of Music, is used at Murray State University (Kentucky), where it is adapted to department needs.

I. Focus: Instructional Delivery (30% Weight)
Suggested Portfolio Materials
+ Student ratings summary.
+ Information about course loads, number of preparations, special circumstances that may have affected teaching, whether course was required or elective.
+ Grade reports (optional).
+ Other departmental data if collected, i.e. chair or peer observations.

Suggested Focus in Examining Portfolio Materials
+ How do this faculty member's ratings compare with other faculty in the department/college teaching similar courses?
+ What are this faculty member's teaching strengths? Weaknesses?
+ What trends or tendencies are apparent across courses? Across time?
+ What evidence is there of change?
+ Other questions relevant to your department or college.

Rating: 0   1   2   3   4   5

II. Focus: Instructional Design (30% Weight)
Suggested Portfolio Materials
+ Instructor's statement of goals and objectives.
+ Instructor's statement of teaching responsibilities.
+ Syllabi.
+ Examinations.
+ Graded assignments/term papers or projects.
+ Handouts (reading list, study guides).
+ Student ratings summary.

Suggested Focus in Examining Portfolio Materials
+ Is there a clear relationship between stated goals and objectives and teaching?
+ Are materials and course content appropriately thorough? Appropriately challenging?
+ What level of performance is achieved by students?
+ Are student tasks consistent with the course's expected contribution to the department curriculum?
+ Do requirements appropriately address critical skills development?

Rating: 0   1   2   3   4   5

III. Content Expertise (30% Weight)
Suggested Portfolio Materials
+ Evidence in teaching materials.
+ Record of attendance at conferences, symposia, and workshops resulting in presentations to faculty, or application to classroom, as reflected in course materials.
+ Participation in faculty colloquia.
+ Development of new courses or course materials.
+ Participation in programs that require use of expertise, i.e. workshops, consulting, reviews of scholarly/creative work, participating in international activities, residence hall programming, and ad hoc assignments.
+ Record of student research directed.

Suggested Focus in Examining Portfolio Materials
+ Are these materials current?
+ Is the best work in the field represented?
+ Does this faculty member take an active role in the improvement of instruction in the department?
+ Does this faculty member demonstrate a willingness to direct efforts toward the instructional needs of the department or college?
+ Does this faculty member seek opportunities to increase knowledge of subject? To use expertise in settings outside the classroom?
+ Is there evidence that this faculty member's efforts produce improvement in student performance?
+ Does this faculty member actively involve students in scholarship?
+ Other questions relevant to your department or college.

Rating: 0   1   2   3   4   5

IV. Course Management (10% Weight)
Suggested Portfolio Materials
+ Syllabi.
+ Student ratings summary.
+ Evidence presented by chair.

Suggested Focus in Examining Portfolio Materials
+ Are students adequately informed of course requirements and deadlines? The basis of their grades?
+ Are student assignments and examinations returned in a timely fashion?
+ Does the faculty member maintain regular office hours? Adequately maintain student records? Complete requested tasks in a timely manner?

Rating: 0   1   2   3   4   5

Component	Weight		Rating		Weighted Rating
1. Instructional Delivery	.30	(x)	_____	=	_____
2. Instructional Design	.30	(x)	_____	=	_____
3. Content Expertise	.30	(x)	_____	=	_____
4. Course Management	.10	(x)	_____	=	_____

Total _____

Ratings based on a scale of 0–5 in which
5 = excellent, 4 = very good, 3 = good, 2 = fair, 1 = poor, 0 = very poor.

_____

Source: Murray State University. Used by permission.

EXHIBIT 2

The model in Exhibit 2 is in use at a Texas community college. During a one-year field-test, this college trained a small group of portfolio readers from across disciplines. Specializing in types of entries, the readers, as an evaluative team, are now responsible for rating complete portfolios.

Instructions: In reviewing portfolios, evaluators are asked to please bear in mind two thoughts. First, some instructors achieve excellence through skillful presentations, others through stimulating high student involvement. There is no one right way to teach. Second, in rating a professor on each item, please reserve the highest score for unusually effective performance.

I. Knowledge of Subject and of How Students Learn
Key Portfolio Items
1. Classroom materials, course syllabi, assignments.
2. Participation as instructor or student in workshops, conferences, symposia designed to enhance subject expertise or knowledge of how students learn.
3. New course or curricular material developed.
4. Evidence about direction/supervision of honors and student research group activities.

Questions to Consider in Reviewing Portfolios

Highest			Average		Lowest
6	5	4	3	2	1

_____ Are teaching materials current? Relevant? At an appropriate level of difficulty?

_____ Does this professor seek to increase personal knowledge of subject matter?

_____ Does this professor seek to increase personal knowledge of how students learn?

_____ Does the content knowledge reflect contemporary views and the weight of evidence in the subject?

_____ Is there evidence that the efforts of this professor produce improvements in student learning?

_____ Does this professor work toward the instructional needs of the department?

*_____Overall, how would you rate this professor's content knowledge and knowledge of how students learn?

II. Instructional Design
Key Portfolio Items
1. Course syllabi.
2. Statement of teaching responsibilities.
3. Statement describing personal teaching philosophy, strategies, objectives.

4. Curricular revisions, including new course material, projects, assignments.
5. Teaching materials and graded assignments/examinations.
6. Student rating summary.

Questions to Consider in Reviewing Portfolios

Highest			Average		Lowest
6	5	4	3	2	1

_____ Is there a clear relationship between stated goals and objectives and the course design?

_____ Are the teaching materials/examinations appropriate to the course level?

_____ Are the curricular revisions appropriate? Challenging?

_____ Is the level of student performance sufficient?

_____ Is organization and design of this professor's courses appropriate for this department/college?

*___Overall, how would you rate the instructional design of this professor's courses?

III. Pedagogical Skill

Key Portfolio Items

1. Student rating summaries.
2. Peer or department chair observations.
3. Information about any special circumstances that may have affected teaching performance.
4. Teaching goals for the next three to five years.

Questions to Consider in Reviewing Portfolios

Highest			Average		Lowest
6	5	4	3	2	1

_____ Does this professor appear to have stimulated student interest or curiosity in the subject?

_____ Is there evidence of high-level performance over time?

_____ Is there evidence of improvement over time?

_____ Does the professor take an active role in improving instruction in the department/college?

*___Overall, how would you rate the pedagogical skill of this professor?

IV. Course Management

Key Portfolio Items

1. Student rating summaries.
2. Syllabi.
3. Peer and/or chair report.

Questions to Consider in Reviewing Portfolios

Highest			Average		Lowest
6	5	4	3	2	1

____ Are students adequately informed of course goals, requirements, deadlines?

____ Are students adequately informed of the basis of their grades?

____ Are examinations and assignments returned promptly to students?

____ Is appropriate feedback on performance given to students?

____ Does the professor post and maintain regular office hours?

*__Overall, how would you rate the course management of this professor?

Composite Rating: Write your rating here for each of the items above marked with an asterisk:

1. ____ Knowledge of Subject and of How Students Learn.

2. ____ Pedagogical Skill.

3. ____ Instructional Design.

4. ____ Course Management.

____ Total Score as a Teacher.

EXHIBIT 3

The model in Exhibit 3 has been developed by a California liberal arts college. The short form includes questions requiring completion of a rating scale plus a narrative response.

Instructions: Please rate each item using the scale of 1 (low) to 7 (high).

I. *Instructional Delivery and Design (60% Weight)*

	low 1	2	3	4	5	6	high 7
1. Student Ratings	—	—	—	—	—	—	—
2. Syllabi	—	—	—	—	—	—	—
3. Graded Assignments or Tests	—	—	—	—	—	—	—
4. Class Exercises	—	—	—	—	—	—	—
5. Course Handouts	—	—	—	—	—	—	—
6. New Pedagogy	—	—	—	—	—	—	—
7. Overall Instruction Delivery & Design	—	—	—	—	—	—	—

II. *Content Expertise and Course Management (40% Weight)*

1. Attendance at Conferences Relating to Teaching	—	—	—	—	—	—	—
2. Develop New Course Content	—	—	—	—	—	—	—
3. Direct Student Research	—	—	—	—	—	—	—
4. Other Scholarly/ Creative Activity	—	—	—	—	—	—	—
5. Student Ratings	—	—	—	—	—	—	—
6. Information From Chair or Dean	—	—	—	—	—	—	—
7. Overall Content Expertise & Course Mgmt.	—	—	—	—	—	—	—

Overall Instructional Delivery
and Design (from above) ____ (X) Wt. of .60 = ____

Overall Content Expertise and
Course Management (from above) ____ (X) Wt. of .40 = ____

TOTAL: ____

III. Overall Performance Rating

After reviewing your responses in Parts I and II, please comment on your overall rating of this professor's performance as a teacher.

EXHIBIT 4

The Department of English at a New York university has taken a different approach to evaluating portfolios, as shown in Exhibit 4. It requires the personnel committee to respond to short-answer questions about a professor's teaching performance.

Directions. In evaluating a professor on each item, please do not let timidity prevent you from being explicit about a candidate's assets. Equally important, try to be just as candid about the candidate's shortcomings. This assessment should be based only on information and evidence presented in the professor's teaching portfolio. As a reminder, all of us who teach—even in the same discipline—have varying concentrations of knowledge in the field and varying familiarity with teaching approaches.

Broad Teaching Skills. Within the discipline of English, which area do you regard as this professor's strongest? Which teaching method does he or she use most effectively?

Course Organization and Planning. How effectively does this professor use class time? Develop presentations that are well-planned and organized?

Feedback to Students. How does this professor inform students of their performance? Review tests and assignments with them?

Instructor-Student Rapport. How would you describe the atmosphere in this professor's classroom? How does this professor encourage students to seek help when necessary?

Knowledge of Discipline. How would you judge the professor's mastery of content in the courses currently taught? Efforts to stay current in the field?

Personal Beliefs About Teaching. How would you describe this professor's attitude to teaching? Has it changed in recent years? In what ways?

Overall Evaluation of Teaching. Considering the previous items, how would you rate the teaching performance of this professor?

ANSWERS TO COMMON QUESTIONS ABOUT THE TEACHING PORTFOLIO

Peter Seldin

Since 1989, the writer has discussed the teaching portfolio concept at scores of colleges and universities of differing sizes, shapes, and missions. I've talked with countless faculty groups and administrators about the portfolio and its place in the evaluation of teaching. And I've served as mentor to more than two hundred professors across disciplines as they prepared their portfolios.

In the course of this activity, certain questions were raised by professors or administrators with much greater frequency than others. This chapter is devoted to answering those questions.

1. **How does the teaching portfolio differ from the usual faculty report to administrators at the end of each academic year?**
   First, the portfolio empowers faculty to include the documents and material that, in their judgment, best reflects their performance in the classroom, and is not limited just to items posed by administrators. Second, the portfolio is based on collaboration and mentoring, rather than being prepared by faculty in isolation. Third, the purpose of the portfolio determines what material is included and how it is arranged. Fourth, in the very preparation of the portfolio professors are often stimulated to be reflective about *why* they do *what* they do in the classroom, and produces for many faculty, almost as a by-product, an improvement in teaching performance.

2. **If professors design their own portfolios, how can they be sure they are producing what administrators are really looking for?**
   From mounting experience, we know that portfolios are best prepared collaboratively. The reason is that portfolios prepared by professors working in splendid isolation lack the control or corroboration of evidence essential to sustain personnel decisions. As a collateral point, since most

professors prepare portfolios with someone other than their department chair, it is of special importance to have a periodic, written exchange of views between chair and professor about such items as teaching responsibilities, the general content and structure of the portfolio, and how teaching performance is to be reported. In this way, professors can be more sure they are in sync with administrative expectations and preferences.

3. **Who "owns" the portfolio?**
   No question about it, the portfolio is owned by the faculty. Decisions about what goes into the portfolio are generally cooperative decisions between mentor and professor. But the last word, the final decision on what to include, its ultimate use, and retention of the final product, all rest with the professor.

4. **How time consuming is preparation of a portfolio?**
   Preparing and maintaining a portfolio is not a burden. Although it may appear that putting together a portfolio would steal too much time, in practice, this has not proved to be the case. Experience has taught that most professors can complete their portfolios in about a single day. They already have much of the material on hand, such as departmental annual reports, student ratings, and letters of invitation or thanks. These items represent the basics of the portfolio. Updating the material demands no more than keeping files of everything relating to teaching, in the same way that files are kept of everything relating to the professor's research or publication. When those sections of a CV are updated, so too is the teaching section. Soon the faculty gain experience and confidence, the preparation of the portfolio becomes routine and simple, and the portfolio wins an accepted place in institutional life.

5. **Don't all portfolios look alike?**
   Not at all. The only similarity is that all of them are called teaching portfolios. In truth, the portfolio is a highly personalized product and no two are exactly alike. Both content and organization differ widely from one professor to another. (See the seventeen sample portfolios, this volume.) Different fields and courses cater to different types of documentation. For instance, an introductory freshman biology course is world's apart from a senior seminar in landscape design. And a graduate studio art class is far removed from an undergraduate lecture course in history. It should be added that individual differences in portfolio content and organization should be encouraged so long as they are allowed by the department and institution.

6. **Can an impressive portfolio gloss over weak teaching?**
   That's a contradiction in terms because the weak teacher cannot document effective teaching performance. The evidence is just not there. To invent it presents too many insurmountable obstacles. An elegant cover and layout

and fancy typeface cannot disguise weak performance in the classroom. The portfolio is an evidence-based document. Support material must be available for every claim made.

7. **Should administrators develop the portfolio program and then tell faculty to prepare their portfolios?**
   Experience tells us that imposing a portfolio program on faculty is almost certain to lead to strenuous faculty resistance. Faculty need to be involved both in developing and running the program. It makes no difference if portfolios are used for improving teaching or for personnel decisions. Either way, the program must be faculty-driven.

8. **Why are portfolio models and mentors so important to professors preparing their own portfolios?**
   The models enable them to see how others—in different disciplines—have combined documents and materials into a cohesive whole. Some institutions have found it helpful to make available portfolio models of exemplary, satisfactory, and unsatisfactory quality. In a similar way, most faculty come to the portfolio process with no prior experience with the concept. That is why the resources of a mentor are so very important. The mentor—who is comparable to a dissertation advisor—makes suggestions, provides resources, and offers steady support during the portfolio's development.

9. **Should the mentor be from the same discipline as the professor who is preparing the portfolio?**
   The process of collaboration is *not* subject-matter specific. In fact, it is often advantageous for the mentor not to know the details of the teaching content. In that way, the mentor can concentrate on documenting teaching effectiveness instead of how the professor teaches a particular subject. Incidentally, an agreeable by-product of working with a colleague from a different discipline is that the mentor learns something about a new field.

10. **What guidelines would you suggest for getting started with portfolios?**
    You have to build a climate of acceptance at the institution. To do this, you should follow the seven guidelines: 1) start small; 2) field-test the portfolio process at the institution; 3) find faculty volunteers but don't force anyone to participate; 4) encourage some high-visibility professors to take part; 5) include faculty who are new to teaching and others who are new to the institution; 6) use the carrot not the stick approach; 7) keep everyone fully informed every step of the way about what is going on.

11. **How can student learning be documented?**
    Evidence of student learning can be gleaned from such sources as student scores on standardized tests before and after the course; student publications or conference presentations on course-related work; and student

field-work reports and laboratory workbooks. Some professors use examples of graded student essays showing excellent, average, and poor work along with comments as to why they were so graded, and specific suggestions on how to improve them. (Of course, permission must be obtained from students to include evidence of their work in the portfolio.) Such evidence is intended to demonstrate the professor's tangible contributions to meeting course and/or departmental learning objectives, and to student development.

12. **Is the syllabus actually inserted into the portfolio? Are student ratings? Peer observations? Letters of invitation?**
These normally appear as appendices. But specific references to them are made in the body of the portfolio. An example: "Appendix A includes copies of my current syllabi for all courses now taught. Each syllabus includes course goals and objectives, a daily breakdown of course content, the dates for major papers and tests, and information on grading, attendance, and general classroom management." For student ratings, peer observations, and letters of invitation, a slightly different approach is recommended: place the actual material in the appendices but include some highlights of that material in the body of the portfolio. This is particularly important if the portfolio is being prepared for purposes of tenure or promotion. What would such highlights look like? Here is one example:

My student rating scores are consistently higher than the department average. For the Fall, 1992 semester, the twenty-five students in my history course on the British Empire (Hist. 290) rated my teaching as follows:

	My Score	Dept. Average
✦ Motivates Best Student Work	4.65	4.05
✦ Explains Clearly	4.50	3.95
✦ Interesting Assignments	4.15	3.68
✦ Best Course in Department	4.30	4.00
✦ Best Instructor in Department	4.65	3.80

Scale: one is low and five is high.

Why include highlights of selected sources of information in the body of the portfolio? Because promotion and tenure committee members are often overworked, frequently tired, and usually pressed for time. They may tend to skim the appendices. Highlights, like peaks of mountains, cannot be easily overlooked.

13. **What should committees be looking for in evaluating teaching performance from a portfolio?**
They should scrutinize the portfolio for answers to such questions as: Is there evidence that institutional goals (for example encouraging students

to engage in critical thinking) are met in the classroom? Is real evidence of teaching accomplishment presented, not just a reflective statement? Is the reflective statement of why and what is done in the classroom consistent with the syllabi and student or peer evaluations of performance? (For details on how to evaluate portfolios, see Chapter 5, this volume.)

14. How do teaching portfolios improve teaching?

Wide experience with portfolio preparation tells us that implicit in the process of assembling the portfolio is a learning experience for the professor. The process offers the opportunity to step back and reflect on one's teaching. Following are some guiding questions to help structure that reflection:

◆ What kind of activities take place in my classroom? Why?
◆ Which courses do I teach most effectively? Why?
◆ How has my teaching changed in the last five years, and are these changes for the better? Why or why not?
◆ Would it help to introduce more contemporary or real-world material into the course?
◆ How heavy a workload can I reasonably impose?
◆ What is the underlying value of the course and my way of teaching it?
◆ Do my students really learn by preparing for tests or merely prepare themselves to survive them?
◆ Should I encourage collaborative effort in class and/or on homework assignments?
◆ How promptly do I grade and return assignments?
◆ Where do I draw the line between acceptable student absenteeism and abuse?
◆ Am I easy for students to talk to, easy to make a mistake in front of?
◆ What have I learned about myself as a teacher, or about the course, that needs changing this year?

15. How important is strong administrative backing?

It is crucial. Unflinching administrative support is key in persuading faculty to invest time and energy in preparing high-quality portfolios. Administrators must vigorously and publicly commit themselves to the portfolio concept and provide the necessary financial support. And the concept must be presented candidly, clearly, and completely to faculty and department chairs before its implementation. It must also be made crystal clear that the portfolio is viewed as an additional, not replacement, source of information on teaching.

16. What seems to surprise faculty as they put together their portfolios?

Following are some comments from a group of professors who developed their portfolios during an intensive, week-long summer workshop:

- ✦ "I began to recognize a need to improve my teaching."
- ✦ "I guess I haven't given much thought to why I teach the way I do."
- ✦ "It wasn't bad at all, and it took much less time than I thought."
- ✦ "Well, there are many things I could, and should, be doing in the classroom."
- ✦ "I knew I was a good teacher. Now I have the proof."
- ✦ "It upsets me to think of the evidence that I have *not* kept."
- ✦ "It will help document my teaching for tenure."

17. Who can best introduce the portfolio at an institution?

Faculty development specialists are especially well-qualified to introduce the concept *and* to serve as mentors. Why? Because they are trained in multiple approaches and techniques to demonstrate teaching effectiveness and are experienced in working with faculty to improve teaching performance. Assuming they have the training, academic deans, department chairs, and teaching enhancement committee members can fill the same role.

18. Any final words?

We are still learning about teaching portfolios. This makes for difficulty in giving more than tentative advice. But equipped with hindsight and the benefit of research, we know many more things about portfolios today than we did even two or three years ago. We know, for example, that:

1. Portfolios can be fitted into current evaluation practices with virtually no disruption.
2. As preparation of portfolios becomes routine, and tenure and promotion committees become familiar with them and learn how to evaluate them, portfolios earn an accepted place in personnel decisions.
3. Knowing that their teaching portfolios will be scrutinized by tenure and promotion committees, professors take greater pains to collect material along the way and develop portfolios in the months, even years, prior to personnel judgments.
4. Although portfolios provide evidence from which to make judgments about teaching performance, it is very important to remember that the primary purpose of the portfolio is to improve teaching performance.
5. The portfolio can be an especially effective tool for instructional improvement because it is grounded in discipline-related pedagogy; that is, the focus is on teaching a particular subject to a particular set of students at a particular point in time.
6. The cornerstone of the portfolio program is its acceptance by the faculty, which depends in turn on the faculty's confidence in the program's relevance, utility, integrity.
7. Portfolios are best prepared not by professors working alone but instead by collaborating with colleagues who serve as mentors.

8. Portfolios must be selective in content. They are not intended to be a catch-basin compilation of all the documents and materials that relate to a professor's teaching performance. For most professors, six to eight pages plus appendix material seems to be sufficient. But bear in mind that portfolios are always unfinished documents in the sense that, from time to time, old items are deleted and new ones added.

9. The portfolio program must be cost-and-time efficient and administratively manageable.

10. Think of the teaching portfolio as an imperfect system striving for perfection which is unobtainable. By definition, evaluation and improvement of teaching is an art involving value judgments. But living itself is imperfect which is no argument against it. The teaching portfolio has proved its merit.

7

A Roundtable Discussion of the Portfolio and its Results

Ray Shackelford

During the past three years, I have worked one-on-one with scores of faculty during the preparation of their portfolios and have made presentations on the teaching portfolio concept at conferences and faculty meetings. From these efforts and interviews with faculty, administrators, and other practitioners, a clear picture is starting to emerge in my mind as to the portfolio's value and use. This chapter will address two questions: 1) "How are teaching portfolios being used in the educational community?" and 2) "What effect does the 'teaching portfolio process' have on faculty?"

Information from faculty and administrators points to four major uses of teaching portfolios in the educational community (Figure 1). These uses include documenting teaching accomplishments for enhancing personnel, salary, and career decisions; and teaching practices. Note that the focus is on *accomplishments*. This entails focusing on and describing teaching achievements, qualities, results, performance, skills, and practices.

Uses of the Teaching Portfolio

Personnel Decisions	Salary Decisions	Teaching Practices	Career Decisions
Promotion	Market	Teaching Enhancement	Position Searches
Tenure	Merit	Introspection	Grant Applications
Annual Report		Professional Planning	
Teaching Awards		Revitalization	
		Constructive Feedback/ Interaction	

Figure 1. Examples of how teaching portfolios are being used.

Faculty develop teaching portfolios for different reasons. Some do it to prove to others that they are a good teacher. Others develop portfolios because a mentor or administrator supports the concept. Still others do so because portfolios are an opportunity to investigate and document the teaching/learning process. But most faculty enter the teaching portfolio process with one primary objective—to communicate to others their teaching effectiveness. Yet, at the same time, this objective may actually be secondary to the "process." In other words, the *process* of developing a teaching portfolio can be more beneficial than the resulting portfolio, itself. This is not to say that the teaching portfolio is not an extremely valuable document for supporting personnel, salary, and career decisions—it is! But, its fundamental value may actually be in the arena of teaching practices.

THE IMPACT OF PORTFOLIOS ON FACULTY

In my experience, the process of developing a portfolio has a substantial impact on faculty attitudes toward teaching and the process of student learning. The "teaching portfolio process" (e.g., that extended period of introspection and self-reflection, focus on the teaching/learning process, interdisciplinary dialogue about teaching, etc.) supports enhanced teaching, revitalizes faculty, and sharpens their interest in teaching.

How do individual faculty describe the values of portfolios and the "portfolio process?" To seek answers to these questions, I interviewed faculty and administrators from different universities and asked them the following questions:

1. Why did you develop a portfolio?
2. Have you kept your portfolio updated?
3. How have you used your portfolio?
4. How has the teaching portfolio process affected your teaching?

From this group, I have selected three representative faculty interviews. They include: a contract (non-tenure track) faculty member, a tenure-track faculty member, and a full professor/departmental chair. I included these individuals because of their diversity in positions, reasons for doing a portfolio, and different ways in which they have used their portfolios. The names are fictional, but their sentiments and responses (presented in dialogue form) are accurate and based upon interviews with them.

Dick is a contract faculty member in the department of biology at a public university in the East. Because he does not have an advanced degree in biology, Dick has no hope of moving into a tenure track position. He has no formal training in teaching. Yet, in 1992, students and a university committee identified him as one of the outstanding teachers in his university.

Mary is a tenure-track faculty member in the department of mathematics at a large private southern university. She is making good progress toward promotion and tenure, but her peers have cautioned her not to spend too much time on teaching.

John is a full professor and chair of the department of psychology at a public university in the Midwest. As chair, he teaches one class a semester. He is a past recipient of the university's outstanding teaching award.

INTERVIEWER: **"Each of you developed your original teaching portfolio two or three years ago. Why did you develop a portfolio?"**

DICK: I felt I was in a state of stagnation and wasn't sure I was accomplishing my teaching objectives. I wanted to know more about my teaching but wasn't getting any departmental feedback. My colleagues didn't seem to care about teaching—but I did. I was getting good student evaluations but didn't know how to improve. I signed up for the teaching portfolio workshop offered by my university because it gave me an opportunity to talk to master teachers about teaching and provided me with a system for taking a hard look at my teaching.

MARY: As you know, I am working toward promotion and tenure. Being brand new, I wanted to check out anything my mentor, colleagues, and, in particular, the administration said was important. You know—jumping through hoops, getting my ticket punched, feathering my career, etc.! But once I learned the true purpose and value of the portfolio, I became committed.

JOHN: As a quasi administrator, I began the process of developing a teaching portfolio because I was chair. I believe that no administrator should ask faculty to do something that they are not willing to do themselves. But, like Mary, once I got into the process, I really started to see its value to my teaching practices.

INTERVIEWER: **"Have you kept your portfolio updated?"**

DICK: Oh yes! I update it at the end of each semester—after we get our student evaluations back. I use it for personal feedback and to check my progress toward my short- and long-term goals. I also use it to check the effectiveness of my teaching, guide changes in future instructional strategies, and establish a new, clear set of goals.

MARY: Can I say ditto to what Dick said? I update my portfolio two to three times a year. However, my portfolio is now an enormous electronic document because I constantly add material to each section. Remember, I have two portfolios. One is written for "my eyes only" (letting me focus on major ideas without the hassle of sentence structure, punctuation, etc.). The second is developed for others to read. I end up extracting material from my portfolio for one reason or another six to eight times a year.

JOHN: I wish I could say that I update mine every semester or year, but I don't. I do, however, maintain current files for future updates. I recommend that everyone keep portfolio materials (i.e., from oneself, information from others, and student products) on file for future purposes. I put a copy of appropriate "information from others" in my personnel file. This way, it is in there for the administration to see.

INTERVIEWER: **"How have you used your portfolio?"**

JOHN: Let me respond to this question in two ways—as a teacher and as an administrator. I like to think that I am a good teacher. But, during the "process" of developing my portfolio, I had myself videotaped for the first time. I found I was doing small distracting things—like clicking my ball point pen a thousand times during 30 minutes of tape. I also didn't like my tone of voice or the way I "teased" some students. I always thought I did it in a positive manner but it did not always appear that way on tape. And, when I went to find examples of student work, I looked at several of my students' graded papers and noticed that the majority of my feedback was negative—even on the A+ papers. I just didn't comment on what students were doing well. As a teacher, then, I have used the portfolio primarily to examine *my* teaching techniques.

   As an administrator, I use the portfolios of faculty in my department. How do I do so? First, the letters that I write to the dean supporting the retention of contract faculty and of other faculty toward tenure and promotion are now much stronger. Based on my observations and the information contained in their portfolios, I am able to be very specific about their teaching. In one case, I was able to determine that a particular teacher was actually more effective in larger classes than small ones. That helped me schedule classes more effectively to the benefit of the teacher and her students.

MARY: As I mentioned earlier, I use elements of my portfolio six to eight times a year. For things like annual reports, documenting progress toward promotion and tenure, and in grant applications. I have successfully used sections of the portfolio in my last three faculty development grants and I know of colleagues who have included major sections of their portfolios in successful research, travel abroad, and Fulbright grants. I am also slowly but surely expanding my original teaching portfolio into three portfolios—teaching, research, and service.

DICK: I want to stress again how important the teaching portfolio process has been in establishing a system for providing valuable feedback on my teaching performance. Like Mary, I also include it in my annual report to the dean. But, more important, because I now discuss my teaching with others from different disciplines, I have gotten involved in some inter-disciplinary activities and I am learning more everyday about this process we call "teaching." Oh yes! I also used a major por-tion of the portfolio in my acceptance speech for the university-wide teaching award.

INTERVIEWER: **"How has the teaching portfolio process affected your teaching?"**

JOHN: I don't believe in change for the sake of change. But doing a portfolio has really helped me fine-tune my teaching. I am working on the pos-itive and negative behaviors I saw in my videos, trying to make my teaching an even more positive learning experience for students. And, in grading papers, I am providing feedback on what students do cor-rectly as well as pointing out ways they can improve.

MARY: I'm using my portfolio to maximize my teaching efforts. The process helped me clarify why and how I teach. It helped me understand the value of clearly communicating the purposes of each class to students. I do this through discussion, complete syllabi, and clear learning objectives. Remember, I was not trained as a teacher. I taught as I was taught and used no other teaching methods. By working with a port-folio consultant and other teachers who had done portfolios, I became aware of how I was teaching and enhanced my instruction by adding a repertoire of instructional strategies plus the use of technology. My testing and evaluation procedures had no focus—I used to bust my students' "chops." Now my assessment system is used as a diagnostic tool for looking at my effectiveness and student learning based upon specific objectives and goals.

DICK: Mary, it sounds like we had the same syllabi. Mine were just infor-mation sheets with names, dates, etc. Now, they communicate class policies, major assignments, methods to be used, and why this class is important to the students' needs. Like you, I taught as I was taught. Now, I make sure that there is always a planned strategy for each thing I do in class and that, given my understanding of the teach-ing/learning process, it is the best one available.

   During a faculty development seminar, I ran across this saying: "I hear—I forget; I see—I understand; I do—I remember and can apply." Now, more than ever, based on insights developed through the teach-ing portfolio process my students hear, see, and do through discus-sions, cooperative activities, instructional technology, and hands-on learning experiences.

A FINAL POINT

Although space limited the reporting of these interviews to a dialogue with three faculty, the following statements summarize the responses of some others who were interviewed:

Why did you develop a teaching portfolio?
+ "I wanted to know more about my teaching."
+ "I didn't want to ask my faculty to do something that I wasn't willing to do myself."
+ "It was a tool to help me reflect upon my teaching practices and accomplishments."
+ "To document my teaching effectiveness."
+ "The administration supported the concept."

How have you used your portfolio?
+ "To clarify the teaching/learning process."
+ "It provides me with a system for analyzing my teaching."
+ "I use the process to check the effectiveness of my teaching."
+ "It helped me win my teaching award."
+ "It helps me establish a clear set of goals."
+ "My teaching video opened my eyes."
+ "Promotion, tenure; grant applications."
+ "Before the portfolio I didn't have a written philosophy. Now I measure my consistency against it."

Have you kept it updated?
+ "I update it each semester."
+ "It is now a large electronic document."
+ "I am constantly adding new materials."
+ "I now maintain teaching records for future updates."
+ "I keep it updated because I use parts of it six to eight times a year."

How has the teaching portfolio process affected your teaching?
+ "I have enhanced the verbal and written feedback I provide students."
+ "It helped me fine-tune my teaching."
+ "I no longer teach as I was taught!"
+ "I'm now a better teacher."
+ "My syllabi communicate!"
+ "I have progressed from 'just grading' to assessing and evaluating student learning and my teaching."
+ "I now consciously select the best instructional strategies for a given objective."

8

Sample Portfolios From Across Disciplines

This chapter is comprised of seventeen sample teaching portfolios from across disciplines. They have been prepared by faculty at Ball State University (Indiana), Columbia College (South Carolina), Miami-Dade Community College (Florida), Shenandoah University (Virginia), the University of Massachusetts at Amherst, and Texas A&M University.

The appendix material referred to, though part of the actual portfolios, is excluded because of its cumbersome nature.

The portfolios are arranged in alphabetical order, by discipline, in three sections. Because each portfolio is an individualized document, varying importance has been assigned by different professors to different items. Some professors discuss an item at length, others dismiss it with just a sentence or two, or even omit it.

IMPORTANT: *You are urged to bear in mind that reading sample portfolios not in your own discipline often provides helpful information and insights applicable to your own discipline.*

SECTION ONE

Agricultural Education
 Christine D. Townsend
 Texas A&M University

Biology
 Nina Caris
 Texas A&M University

Educational Psychology and Educational Curriculum & Instruction
 Patricia A. Alexander
 Texas A&M University

Elementary Education
 Clement A. Seldin
 University of Massachusetts-Amherst

English
 John Zubizarreta
 Columbia College

 Valerie M. Balester
 Texas A&M University

TEACHING PORTFOLIO
Christine D. Townsend
Department of Agricultural Education
Texas A&M University

Table of Contents
Teaching and Learning Philosophy
Teaching Responsibilities
Teaching Materials Developed
Student Products
Assessment of Teaching Effectiveness
Awards and Recognition
Future Teaching Program Goals
Teaching Improvement Activities
Appendices: Summary of Documentation

Teaching and Learning Philosophy

My goal in teaching is to directly effect the learning of students. I believe all students should learn to solve problems, find the answers to their inquiry and think creatively. If students learn to apply theory to become better human beings or to improve the quality of life for others, my teaching is successful.

Additionally, my teaching/learning philosophy is intertwined with what I believe about students.

1. *Students are different.* Students are individuals and they learn in different ways. As a teacher, then, it is my responsibility to vary teaching approaches to "hit the learning buttons" of students.
2. *Students are 24 hour people.* The life of a student is dynamic and they have more happening in their lives than one particular learning situation. Effective learning occurs when I can understand the world of a student. Students have different motives for education, and as their teacher, I strive to adjust to individual motives in order to maximize learning.
3. *Behavior is caused.* I can change the behavior of students with my expectations of them. Quality, excellence, and depth are expected in all work of students.
4. *Students are the same.* All people have the need to feel important and a part of the situation. As a teacher, I have the responsibility to treat students as human beings. I will not demean, ridicule, or belittle them. All students have the educational right and all teachers have the responsibility to create a learning environment.

Teaching Responsibilities

My teaching responsibilities in Agricultural Education include two major programs—leadership studies and horticulture education. This combination of subjects finds me involved with both a social and a technical science in agriculture.

The typical undergraduate and graduate teaching assignment is a part of the leadership studies program and includes development, organization, and instruction of AGED 340 (Professional Leadership Development) and AGED 607 (Youth Leadership). The undergraduate course, AGED 340, has grown from approximately 30 students in 1984 to over 300 students in 1992. The undergraduate course is the basis for additional courses including the graduate course, AGED 607, and numerous student independent study projects. An honors section for AGED 340 has been incorporated into the program and is a highly successful component. I have incorporated various teaching methodologies into all of the leadership courses. Lecture is used to present content and specific information. Other methods are fused into the course to allow students the opportunity to demonstrate, practice, and simulate leadership theory. Discussion and case study analysis brings student experiences and reality to the courses. Students also role play leadership scenarios as a part of their learning experience. Numerous student activities are used to help students identify leadership skills and follower reactions. Additionally, students plan part of the courses by organizing guest speakers and panel discussions to add breadth and depth to our leadership studies. Other experts in leadership are incorporated into the course via videotapes which have been purchased from national leadership organizations. See Appendix A for sample lesson plans that illustrate the variety of methods used in the course.

Various motivational strategies are used in AGED 340. On all assignments, I write comments. Students are permitted to write rebuttals to examination questions so they will "hunt" for why they think my answer is wrong. In class, discussion is encouraged, and I learn students' names, change the pace with various teaching methods, and surprise students with the unexpected. Students are motivated to learn by moving from ideas they know well to undiscovered knowledge.

The objectives for the students in AGED 340 are to define leadership knowledge, skills, and abilities, develop effective leadership techniques, and evaluate technical issues facing leaders. From these broad objectives, students have investigated subjects such as teaching leadership components to high school students, developing leadership case studies, and creating leadership training for agricultural organizations. My teaching program allows me to practice my teaching and learning philosophy. I am able to watch students learn human relations skills which they will use in their lives. One student wrote, after the course, "Thank you for sharing your time and knowledge with us this semester. I have learned so much from you—about leadership, communication, teaching, learning…it is all something I'll keep and apply to my life and career." See Appendix B for entire student letter and additional letters.

My second teaching responsibility is support for the secondary horticulture teachers of Texas. Each year, since 1984, I have planned at least two inservice workshops for these teachers. The workshops are very well attended with up to 140 teachers at a session. Teaching diversity is demonstrated in this program. The participants are more mature in their learning styles; they have different needs than undergraduate students. I develop programs, teach technical horticulture, create instructional materials, and respond to their teaching questions. One teacher wrote a thank you letter and stated, " The program represented a lot of preparation time. I appreciate the idea that, 'We must be ready to teach all students' expressed in the workshop." See Appendix B for additional comments. As a part of this teaching program segment, I developed two instructional videos for the teachers to use in their floral design classes. Appendix C contains the videos and additional evidence of my teaching program in horticulture education.

Teaching Materials Developed

Representative teaching materials developed for AGED 340, Professional Leadership Development, are found in Appendix D. The materials include a course syllabus complete with objectives, outline, assignments, evaluation criteria, and expectations. The course syllabus is a communication tool that contains information to aid students in their understanding of the concept requirements of the course. I format the syllabus to contain a daily outline of material so students may see what is presented in the course. Assignments, examinations, and readings are listed with due dates and relevance to course grade. I list my office address and telephone number so students may contact me when necessary. The teaching assistants' names and offices are listed also to help students keep in contact with the course personnel. At the bottom of the syllabus is my philosophy of attendance and assignment deadlines. By reading the syllabus, students can gain a quick understanding of my philosophy, requirements, and course content.

A major teaching tool developed in my teaching program is the "AGED 340 Packet" which is updated each semester and available to students at a local copy store. See Appendix E for representative pages of the packet. This packet is developed and revised to respond to student needs, industry trends, and educational changes and the packet format allows me to update materials each semester. In the packet are an additional copy of the syllabus, explanations of assignments, readings (both my writing and material obtained with permission), handouts, and copies of student activities to be used in class. The packet follows the course outline and is organized in a three ring binder so students may take notes and add material to it. This packet has been displayed to Agricultural Education peers at regional and national meetings. My professional peers have purchased the packet to use in their current or developing leadership programs.

Other teaching materials developed for AGED 340 are color overhead transparencies. These transparencies are used for two reasons. First, they outline key words from the lecture to help students follow along. Second, they are formatted to demonstrate a correct visual presentation so students can learn presentation techniques as a leadership skill. Appendix F contains sample overhead transparencies.

Student Products

Assignments are developed to assess students' progress and to allow them leadership skill practice. The assignments are organized so students build their leadership knowledge throughout the course. See Appendix G for copies of the assignments and a representative student's product. The first assignment, "Leadership Responsibilities," calls for students to forecast, without much theoretical background, their leadership tasks of the future. The next assignment, "Leadership in Action," has them analyze leadership demonstrations found in a popular film. The film analysis is a dramatic incorporation of leadership theory and what they viewed in the film. Since many students are not in leadership positions during the class, the film analysis is one way to allow them to "see" how leadership theory is used in practical situations. A third assignment, "Leadership Profile," requires students to investigate a leader and analyze the skills that person used to acquire success. The assignments used in AGED 340 are developed to help students bridge the gap from theory to reality.

The students in the honors section of AGED 340 developed, organized, and presented leadership workshops to various clientele in the university community. The students chose topics, researched the subject matter and instructional techniques, and presented a one-and-a-half hour workshop. This activity was highly valuable to the students and they learned leadership subject matter, practiced presentation skills and responded to reactions of their workshop groups. All of these results are critical to leadership development. See Appendix H for sample print material and a videotape of their presentations.

Assessment of Teaching Effectiveness

Each semester, since 1984, all of my classes have been evaluated by students. Because I have taught in both the Department of Horticultural Sciences and the Department of Agricultural Education, my teaching evaluations represent assessments of my teaching abilities in a technical field (horticulture) as well as social science (leadership development). Continually and with consistency students rate my teaching as effective. Regardless of the scale used, my teaching is rated in the top 10%. See Appendix I for copies of the assessment results.

During the course evaluation, students often expand their assessment by writing comments about the course and my teaching. Some students write letters after the course is completed. An honor leadership student remarked, "Dr. Townsend's course emerges as one of the top two or three (honors courses)." Horticulture seniors during exit interview said, "very good prof—knew how to teach; her approach to teaching and the subject matter were practical, realistic, and applicable; Townsend treated me with respect (and) she led me though my education by letting me find my way by asking questions to make me discover..." See Appendix J for sample student and peer comments and letters.

Peers have also recognized the effectiveness of my teaching. They have supported my expansion of AGED 340 to include an honors section and they have nominated me for several teaching awards. A colleague in another department wrote, "Dr. Townsend makes very significant time commitments to helping students...her dedication goes well beyond the teaching function in the classroom. She exhibits the qualities of teachers at A&M that students, parents, administrators and former students cherish." A former department head said of my teaching, "It is evident that she is an effective teacher when she receives her highest rating on the student evaluation form from the statement 'I would take another course from this professor.'" Additional statements are located in Appendix J.

Students' evaluations have been used to improve my teaching and courses. Due to students' comments, I have incorporated small group sessions into the AGED 340 class. Previously, the class was presented three days a week, one hour per day, to a room of 120 students. Following recommendations of students, today the class is structured in a lecture/small groups format. Two days a week, one hour per day, the 120 students meet together. Then one day a week for one hour, students meet in groups of twenty-five or less. With this format, lecture/discussion occurs in the 120 member session and student activities are used in the twenty-five member small groups. This innovation was initiated in Spring 1992, and has received positive response from students. Additionally, because of student evaluations, textbooks have been added to the course and teaching material has been added or deleted. Students' assessment of the course is a critical component of the evolution of AGED 340 or any other course I teach.

Other assessments of teaching are the statistical analysis available from the computer analysis of examinations. It is a part of my teaching concept that every test question is not always the best question. Therefore, in the large section of AGED 340, machine scored examinations have an advantage. I utilize Measurement and Testing Services at Texas A&M and analyze the questions for discrimination and difficulty. This effort has been effective in making better examinations since I eliminate poor questions as future tests are developed.

Awards and Recognition

Throughout my teaching career I have been recognized as a quality teacher. It is a tremendous honor to be elected by students or peers as recognition of success in one's profession. I have been honored by students in the College of Agriculture and Life Sciences as "Honor Professor." For this student-based award, students in each College of Agriculture club nominate outstanding professors. The list of nominees is then voted on by club representatives in the College of Agriculture Council.

Administrators in my college recognized my accomplishments by selecting me for the "Center for Teaching Excellence Scholar." This award was presented to one non-tenured, tenure track faculty in each of the colleges of Texas A&M University. I submitted a teaching proposal to the Executive Associate Dean, College of Agriculture and Life Sciences, and was selected as the recipient.

A combined group of students and peers recognized my teaching by presenting me the "Association of Former Students Distinguished Teaching Award." This award is an annual presentation to two or three faculty members of each college in the university. First, nominations were made by students in departmental clubs. Then student representatives of the College of Agriculture and Life Sciences Council voted on the nominations and selected several faculty member names to send to the next level. At that time, a committee of students, faculty, and administrators of the college selected the recipient for the award.

Another reaching award was presented by a departmental student organization, The Collegiate FFA. Students in this club nominated faculty, voted, and awarded me the "Outstanding Professor" honor.

Many citations have been written for these awards and are located in Appendix K. One of my former department heads wrote in a citation for an award, "In my fifteen years as a department head, I have never seen a faculty member have as great an impact on students and the teaching program." Continuing in this award statement, a colleague wrote, "(She) is the epitome of what a teacher should be." Recognition by students, peers, and administrators is very appreciated by me and shows support of my teaching by various groups.

Teaching Improvement Activities

Several teaching improvement activities have been completed or are in progress. I attended and participated in the "Teaching Portfolio Workshop" sponsored by the Center for Teaching Excellence at Texas A&M. This workshop was organized and produced by Dr. Peter Seldin of Pace University, an expert in developing teaching portfolios. During the Spring of 1992, I audited the AG*SAT course—"Advanced Methods of Teaching." This course was taught by Dr. L. H. Newcomb, Ohio State University. I wanted to experience the "student-response" of a tele-video course as well as update my teaching strategies. I videotaped each lesson for future reference. I also attend regional and national professional Agricultural Education conferences. At these conferences, teaching methodology and instructional research results are presented. Additionally, I visit with colleagues to discuss teaching innovations and learn new techniques for my classes. See Appendix L for documents of teaching improvement activities.

Future Teaching Program Goals

The future holds many possibilities for teaching. An overall goal is to continue to develop, update, and revise instructional strategies and subject matter to keep pace with the ever-changing world. Specifically, my goals are:

1. Complete a follow-up study of AGED 340 students. How is leadership theory used in their lives; does the course have an impact?
2. Develop the 340 packet on computer disk. The disk could be sold to students or the material could be presented as printed text.
3. Develop the leadership program to include "nontraditional" students found in Texas agricultural industries. The courses could be short seminars, continual programs, or for credit graduate courses.
4. Become a champion for development of leadership studies programs at Texas A&M and other campuses throughout the United States.

Appendices

Appendix A: Sample AGED 340 Lesson Plans
Appendix B: Student Comments on Teaching Responsibilities
Appendix C: Horticulture Education Teaching Products and Documentation
Appendix D: AGED 340 Teaching Materials
Appendix E: AGED 340 Packet—Representative Pages
Appendix F: AGED 340 Sample Overhead Transparencies
Appendix G: AGED 340 Assignments and Student Products
Appendix H: AGED 340 Honors Video of Student Workshops
Appendix I: Student Assessment Results
Appendix J: Student and Peer Comments and Letters
Appendix K: Awards and Peer Recognition
Appendix L: Teaching Improvement Activities
Appendix M: Evidence of Teaching Committees and Activities

TEACHING PORTFOLIO
Nina Caris
Department of Biology
Texas A&M University

Table of Contents
Statement of Teaching Responsibilities
Teaching Strategies and Methods
Syllabi and Objectives
Exams from Courses Taught
Future Directions
Efforts to Improve Teaching
Measures of Teaching Effectiveness
Teaching Awards
Other Teaching Initiatives
Appendices

Statement of Teaching Responsibilities

As Director of Freshman Programs, I am responsible for curriculum development and coordination of the large-enrollment introductory lecture and laboratory courses. I routinely teach Introductory Biology (BIOL 113/114) with approximately 300 students per semester. Additional teaching responsibilities include an undergraduate problems course (BIOL 485H) and a graduate level problems course (BIOL 685) that are preservice and inservice training for new teaching assistants. Brief course descriptions and past enrollments are included in Appendix A.

Teaching Strategies and Methods

Because of the large class size and great amount of material covered in Introductory Biology, the primary teaching method is lecture. Some of the strategies I use include:

1. *Advanced Organizers.* I always begin each lecture with an outline and a combination of useful analogies, models, metaphors or examples. This helps students integrate the subject matter with their outside experiences. Evidence is that these advanced organizers help students fix newly acquired knowledge in long-term memory.

2. *Lecture Outlines and Objectives.* I have written teaching objectives for the Introductory Biology course which are statements of measurable behavioral standards expected from students. A copy of these objectives is included in Appendix B. Lecture outlines are based upon these objectives to help focus lecture material on important concepts and to avoid overemphasis on the trivial—a common criticism of introductory biology

courses. Additionally, careful selection of behavioral objectives helps us strike a balance between knowledge level objectives and those requiring higher-order cognitive processes. Since comprehension and recall are strongly influenced by the structure and organization of material, I believe that a thoughtful organization of lecture material that uses behavioral objectives as a guide is an important aid to student learning.

3. *Questioning Strategies.* To encourage active participation in class, I design questioning strategies to be interspersed with the lecture content. This allows me to model the thinking process of students in addition to actively engaging them in class.

4. *Concept Mapping.* At the beginning of each semester, I teach my students how to construct a concept map. This is a hierarchical mapping of concepts and an explicit statement of their relationships. The reflective thinking required to create a map helps students learn meaningfully as they select and write key concepts, make an attribute list and spatially organize the concepts. Students examples are included in Appendix C. To encourage the students to use the strategy, I model it in class and require the students to construct at least one map on each test.

5. *Variety of Presentation Styles.* Because the student population in my classes is so diverse, I try to appeal to a variety of learning styles by giving an overview, providing detailed examples and then repeating the major points in a summary. For each major point, I orally present content and then follow it with a summary on an overhead transparency. Whenever appropriate, I supplement this with a diagram or photograph. Samples are included in Appendix D.

6. *Balanced Assessment That Reinforces Behavioral Objectives.* I use the behavioral objectives as a guide for both the content and cognitive level of exam questions. I also construct a table of specifications, so that even though the exam contains objective type questions, there will be an appropriate number of higher-order questions and an even coverage of material. I explain this to students at the beginning of the semester to motivate them beyond rote memorization as they study for exams. A sample table of specifications is included in Appendix E.

7. *Learning Strategies, Tutorial Program and Study Groups.* One of my primary teaching goals is to teach learning strategy with content so that students can become independent learners. At the beginning of the semester, we offer a learning strategies workshop designed to teach students how to put basic biological facts and knowledge into a conceptual framework that will enhance understanding and retention. As part of this program, students learn to go beyond passive listening and to analyze lecture content, seek organizational cues, identify key concepts, and establish the relationships among those concepts. Some of these strategies are modeled and reinforced in lecture, and students who wish to participate in small formalized study groups can practice these skills

further. In conjunction with the learning strategies training program, faculty and graduate students teaching Introductory Biology offer topical tutorials. Both lecture and tutorial content are the basis for small group work. A description of the tutorial program and fliers announcing topics are included in Appendix F.

8. *Cooperative Learning.* I have also been involved in curriculum development for the Introductory Biology Laboratory course. In the honors sections of the course, we are currently implementing a pilot project on cooperative learning among groups of four students. The intent is to enhance student learning by requiring students to take responsibility not only for their own learning, but for their group members' learning as well; structure opportunities for student/student interaction and articulation of ideas; and address diversity in the classroom by appealing to a variety of learning styles. A project description and photographs can be found in Appendix G.

Syllabi and Objectives

Syllabi and course objectives for lecture and laboratory courses are included in Appendix H. The syllabi are given to students during the first day of class and include a statement of course structure; required and optional materials; a description of hourly, make-up and final exams; how the course grade is computed; course outline; a description of the tutorial program; and a schedule of events including exam dates.

Exams from Courses Taught

Representative exams from both regular and honors sections of Introductory Biology are attached in Appendix I. These exams include a variety of question types including multiple-choice, concept map, short answer and essay questions. Each question is at or below the cognitive level of the behavioral objective it addresses.

The majority of questions for the large lecture course must, by necessity, be computer graded. Thus, these exams contain mostly objective questions. The way students prepare for an objective exam does not necessarily motivate them to develop the skills and strategies to achieve higher-order cognitive objectives. Consequently, I include a map or short essay on each test. Research evidence indicates that just *one* good essay question or map can make the difference in how students learn. Exams for the smaller honors sections include all question types, which gives greater flexibility in assessing student progress and provides students an opportunity to articulate their ideas.

Future Directions

A primary teaching goal is to learn more about cognitive science, especially current research on learning and critical thinking, in order to translate this newly acquired knowledge into practical applications in the large classroom and laboratory. This year I will attend a national meeting on critical thinking and will read recommended references and primary literature. By the end of the second year, I want to develop and test at least one exercise appropriate for the large enrollment lecture course that will enhance student comprehension of a complex process. A related goal is to improve the learning strategies workshops and to develop discipline related exercises for small study groups.

For the laboratory course, I want to develop new curricular materials such as simulations, lines of questioning, lab exercises with field and quantitative components, lab exercises for cooperative group work, lab exercises that are experimental and discovery-driven, and exercises that can be used as alternatives to dissection labs. This will be an ongoing project for at least the next five years proceeding at a pace of one or two exercises per year.

Efforts to Improve Teaching

In an effort to improve teaching, I have and will continue to refine my teaching skills and strategies based upon feedback from an ongoing evaluation process, which includes the results from a student evaluation of teaching questionnaire, peer evaluation including classroom observation, consultation with instructional specialists in the university's Center for Teaching Excellence, and subjective and cognitive interaction analyses from videotapes of lectures.

In addition to assigning concept maps for improved student comprehension, I also use the students' maps to improve the way I teach a particular topic. An advantage to using maps is that they can be diagnostic of common misconceptions and a measure of general student understanding.

I attend and participate in teaching related workshops, roundtables and inquiry seminars presented by the university's CTE and at national professional meetings. In the recent past, I have attended workshops on critical thinking, methods for teaching large classes, learning styles, learning strategies, multicultural diversity, biology laboratory education, computer-assisted learning, Sloan Foundation New Liberal Arts Program, using case studies in group work, TA training, and teaching portfolios.

Measures of Teaching Effectiveness

Indicators of teaching effectiveness include quantitative results and student comments from teacher evaluations. Detailed summary sheets of "Student Ratings of Faculty," representative student comments and letters from former students are included in Appendix J. Sample questions and mean responses are summarized in the following table.

Student Ratings of Faculty

Comparison of mean scores from Caris' lecture sections (B113/114) with the average mean scores of all lecturers' sections in Introductory Biology.

Sample Questions	Mean Fall 89		Mean Fall 90		Mean Spring 91		Mean Fall 91	
	Caris B113	All Sect.	Caris B113	All Sect.	Caris B114	All Sect.	Caris B113	All Sect.
1. The instructor was consistently well prepared and well organized for class sessions.	4.72	4.28	4.79	4.25	4.48	4.19	4.71	4.43
2. The instructor had the ability to explain difficult material clearly.	4.28	3.36	4.52	3.39	4.52	3.65	4.48	3.61
3. The instructor encouraged students' questions.	4.71	3.90	4.79	4.03	4.83	3.63	4.75	3.85
4. The instructor appeared to enjoy teaching this course.	4.77	3.94	4.84	3.88	4.86	3.91	4.84	3.90
5. The instructor has increased or improved my understanding of the subject.	4.24	3.67	4.44	3.79	4.45	3.83	4.43	3.85
6. For an overall rating, this is one of the best instructors I have had at TAMU.	4.22	3.03	4.36	3.05	4.05	3.03	4.26	3.19

Mean scores on a 5 point basis (SA=5, A=4, U=3, D=2, SD=1)
Comparison of individual classes (B113=Biol 113/B114=Biol 114 and
All=all Biol 113/144 sections)

Comments from Students. It is rewarding to end the semester by reading the unsolicited comments on the back of the teaching evaluations. Some excerpts follow:

"Dr. Caris was able to increase my understanding of the material as well as pique my interest."

"Dr. Caris is the most charismatic, enthusiastic and effective instructor I've *ever* had."

"Dr. Caris was very excited about the subject material and is a professor who really cares about her students."

Letters of support from graduate students and peers are also located in Appendix J.

Comments from Graduate Students. One of the most meaningful and rewarding letters of support I have ever received is a letter of recommendation signed by twenty-nine graduate students. Some quotes follow:

"Dr. Caris is without a doubt one of the most effective teachers on this campus. Working so closely with graduate teaching assistants, she has become somewhat of a role model."

"She wants to insure that the freshman biology student will have the best possible instruction, and she also wants to see that each incoming graduate student has a good base from which to build a teaching career."

Comments from faculty. A faculty member who teaches Introductory Biology writes:

> "Nina is an outstanding teacher. She has successfully led the Department of Biology's Introductory Biology Program through a period of substantial change and growth with the goal of improving the program in terms of how well it serves the academic needs of the students."

A former associate department head and faculty member with whom I have worked closely writes:

> "Each semester many of my advisees relate her many abilities as a teacher which include: organization skills, comfortable manner of speech, genuine concern for the students and their learning, high standards, and enthusiasm that is infectious."

The Head of the Department of Biology, who has been immensely supportive of my teaching efforts, writes the following:

> "Dr. Caris is continually rated by student evaluations as one of the best instructors in the department. She successfully combines the ability to provide a high quality, rigorous teaching style with a genuine concern for the student's well-being and ability to obtain knowledge."

> "Dr. Caris has earned the respect and admiration of students, teaching assistants, staff and peers due to her dedication, innovative techniques, and performance in the classroom."

Appendix K includes student outcomes that are a reflection of teaching effectiveness. I have attached examples of concept maps, student lab reports, exam responses and final problems course reports. Whenever possible I have included exemplary, satisfactory and poor work, in order to provide a frame of reference for comparison.

Teaching Awards

I am honored to have recently received the following awards in recognition for teaching:

Association of Former Students Distinguished Achievement Award, College-Level Teaching, Texas A&M University, 1991.

AMOCO Foundation Award for Distinguished Teaching, AMOCO Chemical Company, 1991.

Center for Teaching Excellence Scholar Award, Texas A&M University, 1991.

Other Teaching Initiatives

1. *Instructor's Guide.* I have coauthored the Instructor's Guide for Campbell's *Biology*. This extensive guide includes chapter outlines, course objectives, lecture notes and suggested references. We have received much positive feedback from faculty who use the notes and are currently working on the second edition. Sample pages are included in Appendix L.

2. *Teaching Assistant Training Course.* I developed and implemented a discipline-specific TA training course for new teaching assistants in the Department of Biology. Many of our teaching assistants are recent graduates with no prior teaching experience, so a training program has the immediate benefit of improving Introductory Biology and is a prime opportunity to train future biology faculty to be effective teachers. Major course objectives are to familiarize TAs with lesson design and varied teaching strategies including appropriate situations for their use. During the course, TAs witness effective teaching behavior with videotapes and practice teaching in front of peers with evaluative feedback on teaching effectiveness. A description of our program has recently been published as both a book chapter and monograph abstract. I have also given several invited presentations on our program at national professional meetings. A more detailed description of the program follows in Appendix M.

3. *Sea Grant.* We used a Sea Grant to enhance the teaching of Introductory Biology by setting up saltwater aquaria in five teaching laboratories and by adding a marine field trip to the Teaching Assistant Training Course. This allowed us to bring a diversity of living marine organisms into the lab for our landlocked students. In preparation to teach the diversity labs, TAs took a field trip to the University of Texas Marine Science Institute in Port Aransas, Texas. The purpose was both to educate and stimulate interest among the instructors in the hopes that they would pass that enthusiasm on to their students. The project has been quite successful and popular. Supporting documentation and photographs are included in Appendix N.

Appendices
Appendix A: Course Descriptions and Enrollments
Appendix B: Lecture Outlines and Objectives
Appendix C: Student Examples of Concept Maps
Appendix D: Sample Transparencies
Appendix E: Table of Specifications
Appendix F: Tutorial Program Description and Fliers
Appendix G: Cooperative Learning Project Description and Photographs
Appendix H: Course Syllabi
Appendix I: Exams from Introductory Biology
Appendix J: Summaries of "Student Ratings of Faculty" and Support Letters
Appendix K: Examples of Student Work
Appendix L: Instructor's Guide
Appendix M: Description of Teaching Assistant Training Course
Appendix N: Sea Grant Project Description and Photographs

TEACHING PORTFOLIO
Patricia A. Alexander
Departments of Educational Psychology and
Educational Curriculum & Instruction
Texas A & M University

Table of Contents
Statement of Teaching Responsibilities
Overview of Teaching Philosophy
Description of Instructional Practices
Evidence of Instructional Effectiveness
    Student evaluations and feedback
    Teaching honors and awards
    Research and service activities
Measures of Student Achievement
    Student placement
    Honors earned by former students
Future Goals and Agenda
Appendices

Statement of Teaching Responsibilities
    As a full professor with a joint appointment in the departments of Educational Psychology (EPSY) and Educational Curriculum and Instruction (EDCI), my primary teaching responsibilities are in the areas of Human Learning and Development (EPSY), and Language, Literacy, and Culture (EDCI). I teach an array of undergraduate and graduate courses in these areas. However, the majority of my instructional time is focused on the subjects of reading, general educational psychology, and gifted and talented education. Although enrollment in my courses generally ranges form twenty-five to thirty-five students, I recently have begun teaching the introductory course in Educational Psychology with typical enrollments between 250 and 300.

Overview of Teaching Philosophy
    I have come to realize how significantly my educational philosophy has colored the whats, hows, and whys of teaching. This philosophy holds that students learn best when (a) they are actively involved in and committed to what they are learning, (b) the subject matter has relevance, and (c) the teacher communicates important information clearly and in varied ways. Thus, I work to identify and acknowledge students' existing knowledge base, skills, and interests in my teaching, to offer them illustrations and examples that are meaningful and personal, and to change my instructional style according to students' ability levels and the specific content. I have also found

that involvement, commitment, and subject-matter knowledge are strongly correlated. In accordance with my philosophy, therefore, I must ensure that students acquire not only essential content but a love of learning and teaching as well.

Perhaps because I am in the enviable position of studying learning and instruction, I believe that teaching and research are inseparable components of scholarship within higher education. My research contributes to my teaching by giving me up-to-date information to share with my students and by freeing me from any overreliance on textbooks so that I can explore varied concepts and procedures. My teaching also serves to inform my research by posing new questions to be investigated. Further, as someone nationally recognized for research in learning and instruction, and as someone entrusted with the important responsibility of preparing tomorrow's teachers, I believe it is essential for me to be a very effective model of good teaching practices. In my classes, students will inevitably learn as much from what I do as what I say.

Finally, I do not believe that good teaching begins and ends at the doors of the classroom. Effective teaching is also effective mentoring and occurs as often outside the classroom as inside. Much of what I do as a full professor is to serve as a mentor to students (particularly graduate students) and colleagues—to guide and challenge them while providing them a supportive environment. To this end, I was recognized by the College of Education as the faculty member most helpful to junior faculty.

Description of Instructional Practices

In Appendix A, I have enclosed three syllabi that offer a glimpse at my teaching both at the undergraduate (RDNG 260) and the graduate levels (RDNG 650), and in the areas of primary responsibility (Reading, RDNG 260 & RDNG 650; Gifted and Talented, EDCI/EPSY 629). As evidenced in all three syllabi, students are alerted to the importance of active participation and required to build their knowledge base through outside reading, in-class activities, and outside projects. In addition, feedback is given in the form of extensive written comments that are shared on the attached evaluation forms. Students are encouraged to write back on this form. I believe this procedure not only enhances evaluation but also personalizes the instruction. Examples of several complete forms are presented in Appendix B.

In undergraduate courses, significantly more attention is given to the development of basic concepts and procedures than in graduate courses. In contrast, in graduate courses much more class time is devoted to debate and discussion of theoretical issues and practical concerns presented in the literature. In graduate courses, students contract for individual class projects that are particular to their educational goals, interests, and expertise (i.e., relevant). I often urge graduate students with career aspirations in higher education to consider preparation of manuscripts as projects. Well over 290 of these projects have resulted in publications and presentations. One such publication,

Alternatives for Assessing the Presence of Advanced Intellectual Abilities in Young Children, by C. S. White, is displayed in Appendix C, along with several other class projects. Further, course examinations are designed to elicit critical and creative thinking on the part of the students, as are the in-class activities. Sample tests from EDCI/EPSY 629 are provided in Appendix D along with one in-class activity from that particular course.

It is important to note that EDCI/EPSY 629 was a course that I developed upon my arrival at Texas A&M University. In the fall, I will be teaching yet another course that I am developing. That course, EPSY 698, will examine emerging theories of language learning and instruction, and will follow a similar instructional model to those previously described.

Evidence of Instructional Effectiveness
Student Evaluations and Feedback

Since I became a professor in 1981, I have received exceptional student ratings on every course taught. Sample items from these rating forms are displayed in the Table that follows.

Sample Items	Mean*
1. Overall, I think the instructor did an acceptable job in teaching this course	9.62
2. I think the instructor was well informed about the subject taught in the course	9.66
3. I think the instructor seemed interested in the subject of the course	9.88
4. I think the instructor had the ability to motivate others	9.77
5. I think the instructor encouraged me to use independent thought	9.67

*Maximum score of 10

The cumulative mean rating to the question of the instructor's overall effectiveness in these evaluations is 9.62 on a 10-point scale. Very high ratings have also been consistently received in response to inquiries about my subject matter knowledge (9.66), personal motivation and interest in the subject (9.88), ability to motivate others (9.77), and the encouragement of independent thought (9.67). In addition, students' written comments often describe the courses as "informative," "motivating," and "among the best they have ever taken." Student comments from one graduate course are reprinted in Appendix E.

Teaching Honors and Awards

My effectiveness as a teacher has been recognized by my students and colleagues through a number of honors and awards. In 1984, I was named the first recipient of the Outstanding New Faculty Award—an award that was created to recognize outstanding teaching and research productivity in junior faculty. I was nominated for the college-level Distinguished Teaching Award in 1985 and 1986, and received the university's Association of Former Students Distinguished Achievement Award in Teaching in 1987. This year (1992) I received the university's Association of Former Students Distinguished Achievement Award in Research. Even in the letters of support for this research award, former students and colleagues made reference to my teaching and mentoring abilities.

Research and Service Activities

As I have noted, my research agenda is directly aimed at the areas of learning and instruction. Much of this research has been directed toward the nature, development, and training of general learning and study strategies. Recently, my research has been concerned with understanding the relationship between subject matter knowledge and student interest. I believe that this research has significant implications for classroom instruction.

Further evidence of my teaching effectiveness comes from the fact that I am frequently called upon to provide workshops or to serve as a consultant to school districts and Educational Service Centers throughout the state of Texas. The topics of these presentations frequently center on (a) developing curriculum and instructional programs for special populations, (b) learning and study strategies, and (c) reading in the content areas. As with my course instruction, these presentations are intended to provide educators with the subject matter knowledge, pedagogical knowledge, and general strategies they need to teach effectively.

Measures of Student Achievement

One important measure of one's teaching effectiveness is found in the successes of students. In this section, several forms of my students' achievement will be presented.

Student Placement

As shown in Appendix F, many of my graduate students have found employment at major universities and major corporations. Among the universities where my students have begun their careers in higher education are the University of Georgia, the University of Connecticut, the University of Alabama, Syracuse University, and California Polytechnic Institute at Pomona. The corporations where these students have found employment include the Psychological Corporation and Digital. Several others have gone on to key instructional positions within school districts in Texas, Ohio, and North Carolina.

Honors Earned by Former Students

Not only have my former students succeeded in obtaining good jobs, but several have received various honors and awards, themselves, for both teaching and research. For example, my first doctoral student, Dr. C. Stephen White, University of Georgia, received Texas A&M University's Distinguished Achievement Award for Graduate Research for his dissertation work. One of my more recent graduates, Dr. Jonna Kulikowich, also had her dissertation research recognized by the College of Education. Just this year, Dr. P. Elizabeth Pate, a 1989 graduate and Assistant Professor at the University of Georgia, received two outstanding teaching awards from UGA. As noted in support letters from Drs. White and Kulikowich in Appendix G, these students attribute some portion of their academic success to my mentoring—an honor indeed.

Future Goals and Agenda

While I am very pleased with my teaching accomplishments to date, there are several goals I would like to pursue with regard to instruction over the next two years. These goals will form the basis of my agenda for future teaching efforts. Specifically, I intend to:

- ✦ Become more proficient at delivering instruction in large lecture classes (i.e., classes with enrollments exceeding 100);
- ✦ work toward greater infusion of computer technology in instruction;
- ✦ Include more activities and projects in undergraduate classes that give students opportunities to work with real learners in real classrooms;
- ✦ develop new undergraduate and graduate courses in my areas of expertise that provide these students with state-of-the-art content in learning and instruction.

Appendices

Appendix A: Sample Course Syllabi.

Appendix B: Examples of Teacher and Student Comments on Evaluation Forms.

Appendix C: Selected Outside Class Projects from EDCI/EPSY 629.

Appendix D: Sample In-Class Projects and Tests from EDCI/EPSY 629.

Appendix E: Student Comments from EDCI 650

Appendix F: Advisorships

Appendix G: Letters of Support from Former Students

TEACHING PORTFOLIO
Clement A. Seldin
Elementary Teacher Education Program
University of Massachusetts-Amherst

Table of Contents
Teaching Philosophy
Teaching Responsibilities and Strategies
Representative Course Syllabi Including Assignments, Examinations
   and Supplementary Reading
Evaluation of Teaching
Honors Relating to Teaching
Teaching Improvement Activities
Reflective Statement
Appendices

Teaching Philosophy
   The following eight statements provide fundamental structure for me as a teacher and learner. They support a strategic filter through which I place my courses, advising and supervision, writing and research, and other faculty activities. They help maintain my sense of balance and professional direction.

+ Growth is developmental and requires time and patience. We are the instruments of our own growth.
+ Teachers must focus on strengths and use feedback and support to help learners grow academically, socially, and emotionally.
+ Critical thinking helps students internalize learning.
+ Structure and shared decision making are significant to the learning process.
+ Success stimulates further success.
+ Teachers must strive to meet all learner needs and be keenly aware of social, emotional, and physical variables which affect the learning process.
+ Teachers and learners must appreciate and value diversity and seek unity in a multicultural nation.
+ All teachers must seek continuous renewal and growth.

Teaching Responsibilities and Strategies
   My teaching assignments are centered broadly on foundations of education and specifically within the Elementary Teacher Education Program (ETEP). Courses are framed on a vigorous knowledge/research base and I utilize a lecture, discussion, problem-solving approach. Students are systematically urged to actively contribute to class discussions and learning activities.

Substantial use of videotapes and slides serve to stimulate class discussion and analysis.

I teach the following undergraduate courses: Educ. 256, Life in Classrooms (two sections each semester); Educ. 282E Pre-Practicum I Field Experience (five sections); Educ. 256H Clashing Controversial Issues in Education; and Educ. 398 Advising Practicum. In previous years, I have taught Principles and Methods of Teaching Social Studies in the Elementary School and Developmental Education.

EDUC. 256, LIFE IN CLASSROOMS: AMERICAN EDUCATION. This introductory course on the American public school focuses on the elementary school environment. It enrolls twenty-five to twenty-seven students in each of two sections. The course explores the teaching/learning process, the sociology and history of public schooling, teacher roles, and philosophical and psychological aims of education. Importantly, I have designed the course to help students identify the degree to which their interests and strengths are consistent with those demanded by the teaching profession. During this course, students apply to either ETEP or the Early Childhood Program (ECE). Many hours are devoted to helping students prepare their application portfolios and position themselves for program interviews. In addition, substantial energy is devoted to helping non-accepted students regain emotional equilibrium and refocus their academic directions. (See Life in Classrooms syllabus in Appendix A, and Supplementary Reading Booklet in Appendix B).

EDUC. 282E PRE-PRACTICUM I FIELD EXPERIENCE. This course is designed for the fifty to sixty students enrolled in Educ. 256. Working with a team of two graduate student supervisors, I have constructed a comprehensive system to place the students with local teachers in elementary schools one morning each week for ten weeks. In weekly meetings with supervisors, I coordinate their directed student observations and three-way teacher/supervisor/cooperating teacher conferences. (See Pre-Practicum I Booklet in Appendix C).

EDUC. 256H CLASHING CONTROVERSIAL ISSUES IN EDUCATION. Designed for university honors students, this course explores fundamental educational issues and investigates multiple solutions. With a maximum enrollment of twelve, the course attracts honors students from many university disciplines and involves extensive readings, discussion, presentation and debate. (See Honors Course Syllabus in Appendix A.)

EDUC. 398 ADVISING PRACTICUM. Each semester, I select four to six undergraduate students from many applications to serve as members of the Student Advising Corps. I help train the student advisors who serve as ETEP and ECE academic advisors for the school's several hundred undergraduate students. Meeting regularly with student advisors, I focus on accuracy, organization, and professionalism. This advising program has been an integral part of the School of Education since I designed it in fall 1988. (See Student Advising Corps Booklet and Application in Appendix D).

Representative Course Syllabi including Assignments, Examinations, and Supplementary Reading

My comprehensive syllabi include course descriptions, specific academic requirements and expectations regarding course organization, examinations and papers as well as a precise outline of how final grades will be awarded. Required and recommended readings are identified. A detailed weekly breakdown of topics and readings is presented (See Course Syllabi in Appendix A).

It is my belief that a comprehensive syllabus is a fundamental teaching tool. For students, it provides essential information and expectations about the course on the first day. For the teacher, it is a formal vehicle which conveys a blueprint for the course and expectations for student learning and academic performance. For the academic department, comprehensive syllabi collectively describe the department's curriculum, its scope and focus, and its academic rigor and standards.

Evaluation of Teaching

Student evaluations are vital to my efforts to improve courses. I have used a two-pronged approach to gaining student perceptions. I have regularly administered the Center for Instructional Improvement (CIRI) evaluations since my initial part-time faculty appointment thirteen years ago and I routinely request detailed written student assessments at the conclusion of courses. Therefore, I have longitudinal statistical and descriptive data focused on both presentation and content areas. CIRI evaluations are consistently at the highest levels in all categories (see Appendix E). Illustrative of the positive student evaluations are the following student ratings by 425 undergraduate students in courses (256H and two sections of 256) during the past five-year period. Mean student ratings on a scale from 1 (*hopelessly inadequate*) to 7 (*unusually effective*) follow:

- ✦ 6.66   Instructor is sensitive to response of class, encourages student participation and welcomes questions and discussions.
- ✦ 6.52   Instructor is clear, states objectives, summarizes major points, presents material in an organized manner, and provides emphasis.
- ✦ 6.70   Instructor enjoys teaching, is enthusiastic about the subject, makes the course stimulating.
- ✦ 6.57   This course has given me extensive knowledge and skills which I expect to be able to put to practical or professional use, and/or to help me deal with and comprehend day-to-day events or phenomena.

Anonymous student evaluation narratives reveal significant strengths of my courses and instruction (see Appendix F). Representative examples from different classes in the past five-year period are as follows:

> *I cannot speak highly enough about what you have given to the class and myself. I love to learn, and Life in Classrooms has been the best experience I have ever had incorporating topics I love in an atmosphere where I felt genuinely at home.*

What struck me as the most important aspect in this professor's personality was his belief in all his students. He successfully demonstrated his belief that we were all learning human beings who each had something powerful to contribute.

I found myself more than once at the library to find out more information on a topic that you mentioned, not because you required it of me, but because you sparked my interest and made me "have" to know. May other professors learn to work as you do!

School of Education administrators have also written very supportive comments:

In my more than thirty-five years of involvement as a professional educator at both the public and university levels, I have not met an individual that I hold in higher regard professionally than I do Mr. Seldin. There is no finer teacher at the School of Education. (Division Chair, May 1991)

I know of no one in the School of Education who cares more about his students or expects more educational growth from his students than Clement Seldin. (Former Academic Dean, 1988)

Honors Relating to Teaching

I am honored to be a recipient of the University of Massachusetts Distinguished Teaching Award (1984–1985). Described as the university's highest faculty honor, just three of approximately 1,400 faculty members are chosen for this award annually.

I am also the recipient of the 1992 Kappa Delta Pi International Honor Society Point of Excellence Award for distinguished contributions to the field of education.

Teaching Improvement Activities

As documented in my Statement of Philosophy, all teachers must seek continuous renewal and growth. I work diligently to improve my knowledge base and instructional methodologies. The following briefly describes my efforts:

+ Researched parent/teacher communication and developed a model for parent/teacher conferences which has been presented for teachers in many communities including: Hadley, Hatfield, Granby, Deerfield, Northfield, Ashfield, Greenfield, and West Stockbridge. This model has also been presented at a research conference and has been published in *Capstone Journal of Education* (see Appendix G).
+ Directed two national studies on off-campus teaching and have presented findings at conferences which have been published in *Educational Research Quarterly and Educational Horizons* (see Appendix H).
+ Request mid-semester student assessments of my courses. These anonymous evaluations help determine course strengths and address student concerns.
+ Presented workshop at the university's Teaching Assistant Orientation titled, "Course Design, the Syllabus, and The First Day of Class," every August since 1989, at the invitation of the university's Center for Teaching.

✦ Search for materials and strategies to enhance my courses. Significant course changes occur every semester. This maintains currency of material presented and interest among students.

Reflective Statement

I often reflect on how fortunate I am to have found a profession that provides a multitude of personal and professional rewards. Pure joy is experienced when I receive letters from former students who express genuine appreciation for my teaching, advising, and general support as they take aim at distant goals (see examples in Appendix I). Great pleasure is derived from the challenge of designing a new component to a course and witnessing the nods and expressions of understanding on the faces of my students.

On the first day of every class I tell my students that "You are my priority." They are. My responsibility as teacher is profound. I strive to improve content and delivery, and to teach at my highest level every day. John F. Kennedy said, "The exemplary teacher instructs in realities and suggests dreams." That is my mission.

Appendices

Appendix A: Course Syllabi
Appendix B: Supplementary Course Materials
Appendix C: Pre-Practicum I Booklet
Appendix D: Student Advising Corps Booklet and Application
Appendix E: Student CIRI Evaluations
Appendix F: Student Evaluation Narratives
Appendix G: Parent/Teacher Conference Model
Appendix H: National Studies
Appendix I: Unsolicited Letters of Support

TEACHING PORTFOLIO
John Zubizarreta
Department of English
Columbia College

Table of Contents
Teaching Responsibilities, Philosophy, Strategies
Collaborative Scholarship with Students
Student Evaluations
Letters from Colleagues
Teaching Awards
Syllabi, Reading Lists, Assignments, Handouts, and Exams
Teaching Improvement
Teaching Related Activities and Committee Work
Letters for Students
Future Teaching Goals
Appendices

Teaching Responsibilities, Philosophy, Strategies

Each semester, I teach four sections of English courses, with three preparations (an average of eighty-three students per semester), and I currently advise nine majors. I have taught specially developed seminars in two May terms, and I have volunteered twice to teach Orientation 190 and Leadership 190. In Spring 1990, I directed a senior honors project and served as second reader of another. In Spring 1991, I again directed a project. In Spring 1992, I supervised an independent study for an outstanding Bulgarian student; at Columbia College, independent studies are considered volunteer work in addition to a full teaching load.

In my relations with students, I have learned that conscientious mentoring is a necessary dimension of careful teaching. Delivering information in the classroom, administering tests, and computing information are superficial acts of teaching which the uninspired but competent teacher can perform. But the outstanding professor knows the value of working patiently with students on personal levels. In the intellectually productive relationship that develops between student and mentor, the teacher advocates the student's whole learning as the student learns not only academic information but social and personal skills that enhance learning. In a sense, the professor teaches more than content; he or she teaches habits of thinking, habits of being. Students discover in the process of engaged learning the rewards of controlled inquiry, the value of reasoned discourse, the delight of intellectual curiosity, and an earned respect for knowledge. Faculty who work vitally with students encourage learning on various levels and contribute to students' lifelong commitment to truth in knowledge.

Excellent teaching must inspire and be inspired. The authentic aim of education is not information—a mean goal—but truth. In order to discover the truth in knowledge, students must insist on the best from teachers. They must demand not only course content and common assessment but the uncommon interactive mentoring that results in genuine learning. The teacher must teach not train. Students must learn, not "perform competencies." Students must know that more should happen in their education than what happens in ordinary classrooms. The outstanding professor extends the teaching moment and inspires students to learn beyond the classroom, beyond facts, beyond "assessment instruments."

I believe that I have lived up to my own standards of teaching. In subsequent categories and appendices, I take care to demonstrate my effectiveness in the classroom and in teaching related activities and my strong commitment to continued development of teaching, to close contact with students, to innovation, to rigorous scholarship, and to the shared act of learning that inspires both teacher and student.

First, I routinely make time for conferences with students to offer them valuable personal attention. Students need such attention in order to learn important skills that carry over to their careers. In composition classes, I meet with students in small groups to teach them word processing or other tactics of writing. For example, I may allow three students to "shadow" me as I underline significant passages in a story, write comments in the margins, make connections among sets of details, and compose a short essay on the computer screen. The small group conference provides an atmosphere of trust and sharing that teaches the students crucial habits. Other times, I meet individually with students to help them revise and edit essays, showing them personally how good writers work.

Second, I use various presentations to engage students in several forms of learning. I particularly encourage discussion, asking students questions, inviting them to participate in vital discourse. I also use portfolios as springboards for dialogue, reading compelling entries aloud so that students become accustomed to analyzing, defending, and challenging ideas. Occasionally, I assign oral reports, use films or slides, and invite guest speakers in order to vary classroom activities. In an honors course in Spring 1991, for instance, I asked a colleague to share with the class a conference paper dealing with a subject we had discussed. She described the process of writing the paper, the many revisions, the discoveries she made in successive drafts, the experience finally of reading the paper at a conference. The students were fascinated with learning that even professors struggle with writing, and they were so delighted and encouraged that they pestered me all term to invite another professor. I believe the students learned something that day that far exceeded the information of the course

Third, my use of student portfolios enhances learning. The descriptions of the portfolio in my syllabi record my methods, and enthusiastic student evaluations testify to the effectiveness of portfolios in encouraging students to develop and test critical thinking and writing skills. One example sufficiently demonstrates the value of portfolios. In my World Literature class of spring 1990, I began to notice in an Iranian student's folder a number of informal entries on an unfamiliar modern Persian poet. I encouraged her to present an oral report to the class, and later she wrote a research paper on Forugh Farrokhzad. In the spring, I collaborated with the student in presenting a workshop at a national conference on teaching methods, highlighting the use of portfolios in teaching intercultural students. Finally, with the help of my student's translations, I have published a paper on Farrokhzad in a prestigious journal. Clearly, portfolios effectively prompt students to practice essential skills without penalties and inhibitions, and the close intellectual relationship that develops between students and teacher is extremely rewarding to both.

Finally, I pride myself on being both teacher and scholar, and I try to teach students respect for scholarship that transfers to other courses and to their professional lives. Professors should be active scholars, and teaching should be informed by research and professional development. My syllabi change regularly to reflect my own continual learning and interests within my discipline. For example, as I developed a scholarly interest in modern Hispanic literature, I incorporated such writers into various courses. When I began teaching at a women's college, I studied more female writers and adjusted my syllabi accordingly. In fact, in summer 1989, I was awarded a fellowship with USC's Institute for Southern Studies, enabling me to study women in Flannery O'Connor's fiction, a topic I now teach in special May terms. I am devoted to the interaction of scholarship and effective teaching, and I try to inspire students with the value of accurate, original research. My beliefs about scholarship and teaching are discussed further in my address at the college's Faculty Convivium; the text is included in Appendix A.

Collaborative Scholarship with Students

A rewarding aspect of teaching has been my involvement with students in producing scholarship that reflects genuine collaborative learning. No student evaluation conveys the extent of learning and influence that results when a professor and student engage in shared research and writing. Both are enriched by the experience.

Appendix A contains a copy of my address at the first Faculty Convivium, a series of talks highlighting faculty research on campus. In order to inaugurate the convivium uniquely, I focused on collaborative ventures between faculty and students, citing three examples of my own involvement with students in presenting workshops, reading papers at conferences, and writing for publication. In February 1991, an Iranian student and I presented "The Written Portfolio: A Collaborative Model for Intercultural Students," a workshop at the Enhancing the Quality of Teaching Conference in Charleston, SC. With the student's translations of Persian, I have published an article on an Iranian poet in the international journal *World Literature Today*. In October 1991, I helped an English major write a paper that was accepted by the Popular Culture Association of the South; I wrote a companion piece, and we read both essays at the conference in Norfolk, VA. In late October 1991, I collaborated with three honors students in presenting "An Honors Approach to Poetry and the Fine Arts" at the National Collegiate Honors Council in Chicago, IL.

In Spring 1991, I had the opportunity to direct a senior honors project, a collection of original short stories. After much close work with the student, I wrote a preface that introduces the talented pieces. I have encouraged this student to send her work to a national contest for eventual publication. I include a copy of my preface in Appendix A.

A more recent example of collaborative scholarship is my association with two Bulgarian students who have read papers at a special session I moderated at the Southern Humanities Council Annual Conference in February 1992. One of the major conference themes was comparative views of the South, and I encouraged both students to write abstracts to accompany my proposal for a session on "The Literature and Sociology of the South from an East European Perspective." Our proposal was accepted, and I helped the students prepare their papers. As moderator, I also wrote a brief response to their unique observations of the South. Appendix A includes a copy of our proposal. Presently, I am helping both Bulgarian students to submit revisions of their essays to an international conference scheduled for Summer 1992, in Italy.

Student Evaluations

Appendix B includes student evaluations from all my classes at Columbia College as well as several from courses I taught at other institutions. My evaluations are consistently high in all categories, and I earn commendations from students about my enthusiasm, knowledge, standards, methods, helpfulness, and fairness. The college's evaluation forms rate faculty on several items, using a scale that defines performance as outstanding, superior, satisfactory, poor, or unsatisfactory. In 1991, I taught multiple sections of four different courses; my ratings are indicated in the following chart:

	Outstanding	Superior	Satisfactory	Poor	Unsatisfactory
Eng. 336	75%	22%	3%		
Eng. 277	86%	12%	2%		
Eng. 150	78%	20%	2%		
Eng. 103	77%	20%	3%		

Such figures are consistent in my evaluation since I began teaching in 1973. Students frequently score me in the upper 97th percentile or better in outstanding teaching.

Students' personal comments on evaluation forms are as generous as their ratings. Students refer to my *enthusiasm*: "Dr. Z makes learning a joy"; "Very energetic and exciting"; "He taught the subject with passion, joy"; "He has an uncanny and exciting way to talk to us"; "He keeps you attentive"; "Dr. Z [has] the capacity to motivate interest and creativity in his students"; "It was obvious that he loves what he does."

But effective teaching is more than showmanship, and students also praise my *high standards* and my emphasis on *scholarship*: "He knew the material extremely well"; "He...looked at the criticism before coming to class to help us understand"; "He could answer all questions accurately and effectively"; "We...were persuaded to do our best and be 'professional'. This caused us to work hard and be proud of our work"; "I know how to do a *tough* research paper now"; "Although he requires a lot of work, I learned a lot...in his class"; "Professor was well-prepared, knowledgeable of subject material, and fair in every aspect"; "Very professional."

Many students focus on my *teaching methods* and my experimentations with the portfolio assignment: "He welcomed and enjoyed our questions"; "Doesn't criticize our thoughts, but encourages us to explore"; "He always listens, offers guidance, gives second chances when needed"; "I have never had a professor take so much time to give students feedback"; "He took time with us in our conferences"; "He is the fairest and best one-to-one professor I have ever had"; "The portfolio method...is the most effective way for me and...others to *learn*"; "He used so many different methods of teaching that one always got through to me."

I expend a great deal of my energy as a teacher on *individual attention*, and students recognize my efforts: "He always made time for me"; "He is dedicated to his students. We all love him"; "He always told us why we got a grade and how we could improve....He always had a personal note to us about our papers"; "Dr. Z was there when I had a question or needed help—that's something great to say about a professor"; "He respects our answers...gives everybody a fair chance"; "He doesn't grade on what skills you should have but on what skills you actually have and [on your] willingness to...do your best"; "He taught...each student...one-on-one. He *cares* about your work and about helping you *learn*"; "I cannot think of any one professor that has left me with a greater thirst for knowledge....I only hope someday I may have as tremendous an impact on a young mind as you have had on mine."

Letters from Colleagues

I enclosed in Appendix C copies of letters from colleagues commenting on my commitment to teaching, my hours with students in conferences, my professional development and scholarship, my devotion to the college, my work with student activities, and my community service. One colleague who has observed me in the classroom and in conferences and who has reviewed my comments on students' papers writes, "He challenges his students to 'be professional'...he exacts high standards from them and refuses to let them get off lightly when they produce second-rate work. Students...sense his genuine respect for and interest in what they have to say." Another colleague who supervises student teachers and who has observed my work says, "John is the consummate professional, the man who gives his all to his career and to his friends....He asks for the best from his students because he always demands it of himself....John is, in a phrase, a 'master teacher.'" A colleague *outside* my department observes, "From day one of his joining our faculty, John has been energetic and enthusiastic as an active participant in student, faculty, and college functions." The *chair* of my department kindly remarks, "John is an exemplary teacher. His successful innovations in...teaching...have spurred forth his students and have inspired his colleagues to emulation. His enthusiasm in the classroom is contagious, so that even his most reticent students gain a new vision of what they may achieve."

Teaching Awards

Appendix D contains evidence of outstanding teaching awards for which I have been nominated or which I have received. While I was a graduate teaching assistant at the University of South Carolina in 1975, I was a finalist for the Amoco Teaching Award, a campus-wide prize for all teaching faculty. And in 1991, I was selected by both faculty and students for the Columbia College Outstanding Faculty Member Award. I also received the 1991 Sears-Roebuck Foundation Teaching Excellence and Campus Leadership Award. Currently, I am the college's nominee for the Governor's Professor of the Year Award, a statewide competition among faculty from all public and private institutions in South Carolina. In addition, I am a nominee for the 1992 Outstanding Teacher Award sponsored by the South Atlantic Association of Departments of English.

Syllabi, Reading Lists, Assignments, Handouts, and Exams

Appendix E includes copies of my syllabi for various courses I have taught over a number of years. I have added some syllabi for classes similar to ones I teach now at Columbia College. These are similar to ones I taught at other institutions to demonstrate my commitment to change and currency not only in my own scholarly development but also in my teaching. The English 201 course I taught between 1979 and 1983 in North Carolina, for example, is identical to the college's English 277. My syllabi reflect continual variety and flexibility in readings, methods, and goals, with increasing evidence of precision in detailing expectations and criteria for evaluation. The syllabi get better overall, though cluttered and lengthy with growing demands of assessment. Yet, the syllabi record progress in my teaching as I try to keep both myself and the courses fresh.

One noteworthy addition to some of my syllabi is the inclusion of a reading list, such as the bibliographies on selected authors for research projects in one class. Such lists reinforce the connection between scholarship and teaching, and provide a useful resource for students. In all classes, I suggest additional readings during discussions, and I plan to add reading lists to all my syllabi.

Appendix F includes copies of representative assignments for freshman classes in which students need extra guidance. I have selected assignments from classes I taught several years ago, and from recent classes, in order to show development in my efforts to be more specific and helpful. For example, the dated sheet labeled "EH 102 Short Fiction Essay" is skimpy in outlining both the topics and the requirements; the "Final Exam Topics," dated and composed several years later, reveals more care and planning, more direction, more instruction; the English 103 and 150 sheets, used in different semesters more recently, also reveal greater detail and more emphasis on using the assignments to teach, not just to test. I have added other assignments that illustrate the value I place on providing models for students. The "Annotated Bibliography" and "Research Paper" sheets offer samples of the style and content of annotated citations and the methods of incorporating research into a critical essay; the assignments also stress the significance of good scholarship, reinforcing a major competency of all my courses. Of course, I provide students with samples of each kind of essay I ask them to write. Finally, the handout "Sample Portfolio Entries" models for students the active learning that comes from maintaining a serious, thoughtful portfolio.

Appendix G contains handouts I use in several classes. Since the portfolio is a major assignment in my classes, I include samples of "Suggested Topics for Out-of-Class Entries," a handout encouraging students to write on a variety of topics. Often embedded in the suggestions are vital issues that enhance students' learning and produce good writing. At the end of a semester, I often reread students' entries on suggested topics and group them according to the issues a student seemed most interested in exploring; then I customize the final exam topics for each student, referring her to selected entries in her portfolio. I add a "Checklist for Oral Reports," which focuses on important features of this particular project, and "Outline of Romantic Tendencies," which helps English 336 students in highlighting key concepts and in seeing a historical overview—skills often lost in rapid survey courses.

In Appendix H, I have placed copies of objective exams I use sporadically, for I prefer essays as a superior means of assessing students' learning. Essays provide students with an opportunity to integrate knowledge; to express their critical thinking about subject matter; to organize, develop, and substantiate ideas. Essays also require students to engage the vital processes of writing, of communication, of invention, and expression of ideas in coherent form. Students must generate knowledge, not just react to it in objective responses. Evaluating essays takes more of the teacher's time than scoring quantitative tests, but I believe essays offer a more valuable index of students' learning.

Teaching Improvement

Just as I stress the importance of ongoing professional activity in my role as scholar, I value the imperatives of experimentation and improvement in teaching. The constant revisions in my syllabi and methods attest to my desire to improve teaching. Also, I have attended workshops and conferences focusing on the enhancement of teaching techniques and goals. In December 1988, I participated in a writing-across-the-curriculum workshop conducted by Dr. Henry Steffens of the University of Vermont. In February 1989, I attended the conference of the Georgia-South Carolina College English Association. In November 1989, I co-presented "Write to Think," a workshop on the use of journals at the meeting of the South Carolina Association of Developmental Educators.

Teaching Related Activities and Committee Work

As part of my service to the community, I frequently extend my teaching to audiences outside of the college. For example, Appendix I contains a copy of a page from my vita which shows that I speak on literary and other topics to several community groups and civic clubs. Also in Appendix I, I include evidence of my membership in the college's speakers bureau and in the South Carolina Humanities Council. In addition, I participate as a teaching scholar in the South Carolina libraries' "Let's Talk About It: Reading and Discussion Program" funded by the National Endowment for the Humanities.

My committee responsibilities at the college involve me in work towards the improvement of teaching, too. I am a member of the Collaborative Learning Steering Committee, which has dutifully sought to enhance teaching by developing ways of incorporating interdisciplinary and collaborative methods into the curriculum. The committee also has taken on the charge of revising the general education program at the college in order to strengthen both teaching and learning. I am also a member of a special committee for reform and improvement of academic advisement.

Letters for Students

A valuable service teachers can provide for students is to write cogent letters of recommendation for scholarships, jobs, or other goals. Appendix J contains letters I have written in recent years at different institutions, demonstrating the continued, serious effort I make to help students.

Future Teaching Goals

1. I feel that because of my academic background, my record of excellent teaching, and my current and vital scholarship, I should teach more upper-level courses in my areas of specialization. I would like to teach modern American literature to majors. Perhaps I will have such a chance this year, for the chair of my department has already begun to press for sharing of courses and has offered his own upper-level courses to serve as a model to the rest of the department.

2. My strengths in comparative literature encourage me to develop more courses in diverse literatures. My department should offer advanced world literature courses for majors. I have published several pieces on works of foreign literatures, and I would like to teach culturally diverse literature in advanced courses. The college's growing emphasis on

curriculum reform may change the English major in the next two years, and I hope to be a leader.

3. I would like to earn a teaching Fulbright in a Latin American country. Such an experience will enrich not only my scholarly background but also my teaching. I already have begun the application process.

4. I hope to find more ways of incorporating word processing technology into all courses. Currently, I build into composition classes days on which I accompany small groups to the Computer Lab in order to teach them basic skills. I would like to discover new ways of devising projects that encourage students to become more proficient with computers. A valued colleague has taught me to use a community computer journal in an honors course (an assignment sheet is attached to the syllabus for that course in Appendix E). I also plan to continue learning from colleagues and conferences.

Appendices
Appendix A: Address at the Faculty Convivium
Appendix B: Student Evaluations
Appendix C: Letters from Colleagues
Appendix D: Outstanding Teaching Awards
Appendix E: Syllabi
Appendix F: Representative Assignments
Appendix G: Sample Assignments
Appendix H: Examinations
Appendix I: Teaching Related Work
Appendix J: Letters for Students

TEACHING PORTFOLIO
Valerie M. Balester
Department of English
Texas A&M University

Table of Contents
Teaching Philosophy
Teaching Responsibilities
Teaching Materials
Teaching Methods
Innovative Teaching Practices and Examples of Student Work
Supervision of GAT's
Assessments of Teaching Effectiveness
Awards
Goals
Appendices

Teaching Philosophy

My grounding in the humanities has made me appreciate the value of traditional Western heritage, yet at the same time has kept me keenly aware of the limitations of traditional knowledge when taught merely as concepts of key words that everyone should know. Just as important is the ability to step outside mainstream traditions. I call this ability to step outside—or see around—a culture's traditional knowledge re-seeing. We literally re-see from more than one perspective something we may otherwise take for granted. Having the ability to re-see is a first step in critical thought, and it is critical thought that I wish to foster. I wish my students to have the ability to analyze a situation and apply various strategies to solving problems or creating something new. In the best humanistic tradition, I wish them to become skeptics—to question where "facts" come from and whose interest they serve—and also activists. I hope they will learn from me to combine action with reflection.

The classes I teach all deal in one way or another with literacy, with reading or writing. One of my primary beliefs about literacy is that it is a humanizing activity, that it should give us the means not only to contemplate but also to transform our world. Reading and writing are worthless unless they provide the means by which we can employ our higher order thinking skills—our ability to analyze, synthesize, and criticize. Likewise, literacy should both prompt us to act and provide us a means by which we can persuade others to act.

Teaching Responsibilities

Although I have taught diverse courses in the Department of English, both graduate and undergraduate, I bring to every class a commitment to active learning and a desire to encourage students to become independent critical thinkers. On the undergraduate level, I have taught Technical Writing (301), Advanced Composition (341), History of the English Language (410), and Survey of World Literature (222). Currently, I teach on a regular basis Approaches to Literacy (201), to which I have added innovations such as computer conferencing, and Minority Women's Literature (394), which I created as a course.

On the graduate level, I created and taught two special topics seminars (689): Research in Rhetoric and Composition, and Computers and Writing. I teach the English Writing Lab seminar (657) every year; I have completely revised it, making it more scholarly and rigorous than it had been. Business Communications (625), which I also teach regularly, is offered exclusively to MBA's and gives me stimulating exposure to graduate students in another discipline.

Teaching Materials

As the sample syllabi in Appendix A illustrate, I always spell out course objectives, methods of evaluation, attendance and participation policies, and a tentative calendar. These details serve to organize my courses and ensure that I have clearly communicated my expectations. For example, since I value active learning highly and see it as essential to improving students performance, I cite participation on my syllabus as a class requirement. By stating how much participation counts toward the final grade (sometimes as much as 30%), I ensure that it will be seen as a concrete measure of performance in the course. Additionally, to clarify and document expectations, I use handouts for major assignments in writing (see sample, Appendix B).

Since some students learn best from visual as opposed to oral cues, and all students seem to enjoy variety, I incorporate visual materials, such as video, charts, diagrams, and photographs, into lectures. In Approaches to Literacy, I show an historical television program titled "Printing Transforms Knowledge" (written by James Burke). Likewise, in The English Writing Lab, I show a training video for tutors produced by former graduate students in the course (Appendix C). I look for materials that demonstrate, clarify, or make memorable my point—scribbles from a three-year-old provide an illustration of preliterate activity (Appendix D), and a chart in handout form summarizes two approaches to literacy instruction (Appendix E).

Teaching Methods

My teaching methods include *lecture, discussion, collaborative learning, writing* and *application*. To introduce new concepts and provide insight and guidance in unfamiliar territory, I turn to lecture. Typically, I: 1) summarize the most important points from class reading, 2) add new or conflicting information to put the topic in context, and 3) problematize the topic.

I use discussion to promote active learning. Discussion forces students to think through the ideas presented in lecture; even better, it forces them to compare their ideas to those of others. Because I want students to do the talking and thus the active learning, I sometimes curb my impulse to lecture by setting aside specific times for discussion.

I turn to collaborative learning in a small group format as a means to stimulate discussion. I find that the more vocal students often act as models for the less vocal, and that most students are willing to disagree with or challenge as well as help peers in a small group setting. Through conflict, groups promote critical stances, and through cooperation, they encourage students to entertain alien ideas.

Writing is not only a way for students to demonstrate their knowledge but also a means by which they can learn. I stress that writing is a process and arrange ample time for prewriting activities, to provide opportunities to invent or develop ideas. I encourage students to revise their writing as well. I especially stress the value of feedback. Through revision, students are pushed into "re-seeing" a subject, into taking a critical stance, and perhaps doing research or conducting some other form of extended inquiry.

Application, like discussion, promotes active learning. Students integrate the theoretical concepts learned through lecture, reading, writing, and discussion with their outside experiences, perhaps to make sense of something, to solve a problem, or to create something. Applying knowledge gives them hands-on experience. There is a different "feel" to concrete experience; it results in a more visceral and, for some, a more fully comprehended and remembered learning.

Innovative Teaching Practices

I commonly use two innovative teaching practices that, I believe, develop critical thinking and promote practical application of theoretical concepts. The first is a semester-long project and the second is computer conferencing.

The semester-long project includes: 1) hands-on experience, either observation or participant/observation; 2) ongoing feedback and reflection, usually in the form of small group discussion, perhaps electronic, or student-teacher conferences; 3) an oral presentation to the class, often with a written or other visual component, such as a video or a handout; and 4) a formal, written report. To accomplish the project, students must "re-see" or problematize an otherwise ordinary event, apply theory to understand it, and express their new understanding (or perhaps solution or creation) to others. The learning is active and experiential, and thus memorable.

Appendices F through J contain examples of student work on semester-long projects done for Approaches to Literacy. In this particular course, students selected a literacy event (i.e., one which involves reading or writing) to observe. For example, one student attended two fourth-grade developmental reading classes and another tutored adolescents at a local high school. To encourage the sharing of views and information, students "discussed" their project on a computer conference with a research group. Membership in groups was based on similarities in literacy events under study, for example, adolescent literacy or adult literacy. (See Appendix F for a sample transcript from one research group.) I encouraged the drawing of connections between class reading and observations. Observations were often discussed in class. Toward the end of the semester, everyone presented an oral progress report and received feedback that would aid in writing the final reports. Students were encouraged to use visual aids, and so we saw books produced by grade school children, videos of preschoolers reading, samples of student writing, posters graphing reading and writing habits, in short, a wide range of material (Appendix G contains some examples of student-produced visual aids). The final assignment was a formal written report presenting students' observations and their subsequent conclusions about literacy (Appendix H contains an A-level report, and Appendix I contains a C-level report). For the final examination, students were encouraged to include examples not only from reading but also from their own and other's projects, and many did so, as the example in Appendix J shows.

Computer conferencing has added an interesting dimension to many of my classes. Appendix K contains a transcript from a synchronous conference held in The English Writing Lab. Appendix L contains some mail messages from a computer bulletin board used in the same course. Computer conferencing of both types allows me to greatly increase my interaction with students. I read all their comments and respond to many. By this means I hope to provide a role model for active discussion, provoke thought, and encourage questioning of authority. I also learn a great deal about what my students think, not only about the subject matter of the course but also about my teaching (Appendix M). Student interaction is certainly increased when computer conferencing is used. In a large class, sociability seems improved. In an end-of-semester survey done in Approaches to Literacy, responses from twenty-six students reveal that students react positively to electronic conferencing. To the question "Overall, I would say that the computer enhanced my learning in this course: 1) not at all, 2) somewhat, or 3) a great deal," sixteen answered "a great deal," nine answered "somewhat," and one answered "not at all."

Supervision of GAT's

Every semester I supervise between one and five GAT's teaching Rhetoric and Composition. I have been consistently invited to fill this role because GAT's have found my constructive criticism helpful. Dr. Joanna Gibson, Coordinator of Freshman English, evaluates my performance as "excellent" (Appendix N).

Assessments of Teaching Effectiveness

Assessments of my teaching effectiveness are available from both students and colleagues. Because both sources of information are invaluable to my growth as a teacher, I solicit such feedback on a regular basis.

Statements from Students

Student comments appear on the back of standard evaluation forms, in unsolicited letters, and in comments made on computer conferences.

From undergraduates in Approaches to Literacy:

+ I like doing the projects and getting firsthand information about how the literacy process works. The articles were informative, but the projects were "real" and more tangible. Also, I enjoyed being able to discuss everyone's project on the [computer]. This added to what I was able to learn.
+ My views changed and I began to think critically.

From graduate students in The English Writing Lab:

+ Dr. Balester aided us in logging onto electronic bulletin boards...one of the most helpful aspects of the class....In that way, we learned from each other's mistakes and had an outlet for our frustrations and enthusiasm.
+ Dr. Balester's course has been one of the most helpful in *applying* what I've learned in class.

Appendix O contains samples of statements from students concerning my teaching effectiveness.

Student Evaluations

During regular semesters, my department requires that I use the standard Instructor and Course Appraisal Form distributed by the TAMU College of Liberal Arts. Below are averages of overall mean scores (on a five-point basis) of standardized student evaluations. Note that statistics are unavailable for two graduate seminars in English (E657, The English Writing Lab, first time taught; and E689, Computers and Writing) and for two undergraduate courses (E410, History of English; and E210, Approaches to Literacy, second time taught). In some cases these figures are pending; in others, standardized evaluations were not done because of a lack of departmental funding.

+ Four sections E625, Business Communications (MBA requirement) 4.02
+ E657, Writing Lab & E689, Research in Rhetoric (seminars)   4.71
+ Three section of E301, Technical Writing (required of non-majors) 4.21
+ One section each of:
    E222, Survey of Western Lit (required of non-majors)   4.08
    E201, Approaches to Literacy (required of non-majors)
    E341, Advanced Composition (required of majors)
    E394, Minority Women's Literature (elective)

See Appendix P for all the summary sheets of courses evaluated by this means to date.

Statements from Peers

Colleagues who have visited my classroom have provided me with written evaluations (Appendix Q). One notes a "nice blend of discussion and instruction" in the Approaches to Literacy class. Another comments approvingly on the "very animated discussion" and my "encouraging students to think for themselves and form their own judgments." All these observers note the high level of student participation in my classes.

Awards

I have received two awards from the Center for Teaching Excellence. With the first, an Incentive Grant of $1,000, I purchased a computer projection panel for my department's Writing Center, which we use for collaborative writing and revising. The second award was appointment as a Center for Teaching Excellence Scholar, which included a $5,000 grant that I have used to research computer conferencing as a teaching method.

Goals

Based on student evaluations, I have set as my goal improvement of how I communicate my expectations to students. I have begun by providing detailed written handouts of assignments and syllabi. I also intend to spend more class time articulating course policy, objectives, organizations, and teaching methods. Articulation of my expectations in writing, and periodic oral review of them in class, reminds me of my part of the contract and gives me a chance to clear up any misunderstandings. Finally, I plan to solicit student feedback throughout the semester. Computer conferencing has proved valuable in this respect, but I will also employ a more formal and anonymous vehicle—an open-ended questionnaire administered in the second, seventh, and eleventh weeks of the semester.

Appendices

Appendix A: Sample Syllabi from Approaches to Literacy and The English Writing Lab

Appendix B: Sample Assignment from Approaches to Literacy

Appendix C: Tutor Training Video from The English Writing Lab

Appendix D: Illustration of Preliterate Activity

Appendix E: Handout Showing Two Approaches to Literacy Instruction

Appendix F: Excerpts from Computer Conference Research Group on Elementary School

Appendix G: Examples of Visual Aids Produced by Students for Oral Presentation of Semester-Long Project

Appendix H: A-Level Formal Report of Semester-Long Project

Appendix I: C-Level Formal Report of Semester-Long Project

Appendix J: Final Examination Citing Observational Research

Appendix K: Transcript From Synchronous Conference in The English Writing Lab

Appendix L: Computer Bulletin Board Messages from The English
             Writing Lab
Appendix M: Summary of Student Evaluations of Computer Conferencing in
             Approaches to Literacy
Appendix N: Comments Concerning Supervision of GAT's
Appendix O: Statements from Students on Teaching Effectiveness
Appendix P: Summaries of Standardized Student Evaluations
Appendix Q: Statements from Peers on Teaching Effectiveness

SECTION TWO

Foreign Language
    Ronald C. Warner
    Ball State University

History
    John R. Barber
    Ball State University

Human Relations
    Elaine K. Ferraro
    Columbia College

Mathematics
    Laurie Hopkins
    Columbia College

    Donald W. Orr
    Miami-Dade Community College

    William L. Perry
    Texas A&M University

TEACHING PORTFOLIO
Ronald C. Warner
Department of Modern Languages and Classics
Ball State University

Table of Contents
Philosophy of Teaching and Statement of Responsibilities
Contribution to University and Department Teaching Mission
Professional Improvement Activities
    Memberships in professional organizations
    Cultural experiences
    Subscriptions to professional publications
    Teaching improvement sessions
Evidence of Good Classroom Instruction
    Unsolicited correspondence from students
    Letters and expressions of gratitude
    Peer evaluations
    Student evaluations
    Special awards and honors
Appendices

Philosophy of Teaching and Statement of Responsibilities

I am a classroom German teacher and for me the teaching of German is a labor of love. I work hard at being the best I can be, and I convey my excitement for my profession and subject matter. I enjoy my classes, and my students do likewise. I am a generalist in my subject area, and my position at Ball State University enables me to teach a wide variety of courses at the beginning through graduate levels. Since a large percentage of many students have traditionally pursued the teaching curriculum, much of my classroom work focuses on providing these future graduate students and teachers with strong backgrounds in the four language skill areas of listening, speaking, reading, and writing. At the same time, I strive to provide my students with a basic knowledge of German behavioral patterns, life, and thought. For these same reasons I sometimes depart from conventional methodology and even approach the subject matter of advanced undergraduate literature classes as an appropriate means of imparting German language and culture skills to my student/future teacher candidates.

My teaching is based on modern research in foreign language teaching methodology and I employ a variety of teaching techniques in the some twenty-five different courses I have taught over the years. I make use of the latest technology, such as the language laboratory, the computer, the BSU Video Interactive System (VIS), the overhead projector, films and video cassettes. At all levels I utilize proficiency-based methodology to encourage the students to speak and write in order to enhance their communicative language skills. At the beginning and intermediate levels, I devote substantial class time to drills based on oral/aural models, and to small group practice for the reinforcement of important linguistic concepts introduced in class. I also require my students to prepare much of their homework with the aid of the computer and the language laboratory so that they benefit additionally from the immediate reinforcement these technologies provide. At the third- and fourth-year levels which are primarily composed of German majors and minors, much of the emphasis shifts to reading, to the refining of grammar skills, and to use of the proper German idiom in written and oral work.

It is a fact that most Ball State University students have grown up in Indiana in single-culture environments, and, for this reason, they are very limited in their understanding of the values of other cultures and the reasons why individuals of different cultures think, believe, and act as they do. One of my most important goals is to acquaint my students as much as possible with German life and thought. My purpose is to open their eyes to the world and to diminish the culture-bound attitudes they typically possess.

In an attempt to relate my students' own experiences to political and social events in Germany, I often bring German news items in to intermediate or advanced classes for brief discussion. On such days, after first preparing a given class with new vocabulary items, I will then divide the class into small groups and encourage the students to utilize their newly acquired vocabulary to describe, discuss, and compare the German events with happenings in their own lives.

My method for motivating students to learn is by displaying genuine interest in them, by being understanding, and by creating a relaxed, non-threatening atmosphere in class. I simply expect different ability levels in my students and I never ridicule or embarrass weaker students when they make mistakes. Instead, I use gentle persuasion to stimulate their thinking and to help them correct their mistakes. In short, I consciously treat all students with equal respect no matter how high or low their aptitudes for language learning might be.

Contribution to University and Department Teaching Mission

Another one of my major goals is to contribute to the university's reputation as a friendly campus and an excellent undergraduate teaching institution. I accomplish this by actively supporting individual students and the activities of student groups. For example, I am currently serving as Faculty Advisor of several student organizations: Lambda Alpha Beta social sorority, the campus chapter of Amnesty International, and Alpha Mu Gamma National Foreign Language Honorary. Also, for twenty-five years, I have served as faculty sponsor or co-sponsor of the Ball State German Club. As Coordinator of German, I am the departmental advisor for all German majors and minors, three of whom recently received Fulbright awards to Germany for study abroad (Appendix A).

Professional Improvement Activities

I remain current in my discipline by actively participating in the activities of several professional organizations:

1. In addition to being a participating member of the Indiana Association of Teachers of German (IATG) and the American Association of Teachers of German (AATG), I am a member of the Indiana Foreign Language Teachers Association (IFLTA). I regularly take part in meetings, conferences and workshops of these organizations, and I am currently serving as Chairman of the Officer Nominating committee for IATG.

2. In order to really understand and to teach German culture, the teacher is almost necessitated to acquire much of his/her knowledge firsthand by spending lengthy periods abroad. Especially a knowledge of everyday or "small c" culture cannot be learned from books. For these reasons, I applied for and received three Fulbright awards over the years. These awards enabled me to totally immerse myself in German society, to teach full time for two years in two different German schools, and to study abroad. In 1974, I also received a Fulbright award to attend a summer seminar in Bonn/Bad Godesberg and, in 1969–70 and in 1986–87, I received Fulbright Exchange Teacher Awards for teaching at Gymnasien in Erding and Erlangen, Germany respectively. On both occasions, I exchanged my position at Ball State and my home in Muncie with teacher counterparts from Germany. The linguistic and cultural knowledge I acquired from the Fulbright experiences have proved invaluable to my German teaching career.

3. In addition to the three Fulbright awards, I also received an award in the summer of 1989 from the Berlin City Parliament to participate in a conference for American teachers at the Europaeische Akademie in Berlin.

4. I also subscribe to *Die Unterrichtspraxis* (The Teaching Profession), the national pedagogical journal for my field, to the *German Quarterly*, one of the preeminent journals for German literary studies worldwide, and to *The Teaching Professor*.

5. To further develop my teaching effectiveness, I regularly attend teaching improvement workshops sponsored by the Center for Teaching and Learning on the BSU campus.

Evidence of Good Classroom Instruction

Letters, greetings and other correspondence from students here and abroad.

1. Certainly one measure of success as a teacher is how well you are remembered through the years by students after they leave your class. Each year I receive letters and cards from former students who are now graduates and are engaged in their own professional careers. An example is a letter I received in 1990 from Diane Pflaum Neumann, a student I had in several classes during 1970–71: "Dr. Warner, you may not

remember me, but I remember you....I always enjoyed my German classes and having you as a teacher....Just want you to know that you weren't forgotten—you made an impression." (Additional items related to my teaching are found in Appendix A.)

Congratulatory letters and expressions of gratitude from government officials, colleagues, and administrative personnel.
1. Congratulatory letter from US Senator Richard Lugar
2. Letter from the German Ministry of Education. (In addition to these items, Appendix B contains an array of items related to my Fulbright teaching assignments and other teaching activities.)

Peer Evaluations.
1. Translation of German letter from Headmaster Schneider and Asst. Headmaster Kiesling concerning my teaching at Ohm-Gymnasium, Erlangen, Germany, 1986-87: "Of the numerous exchange teachers...at Ohm-Gymnasium during the past years, Mr. Warner is certainly one of the most notable....The pupils...treasured Dr. Warner's unpressured, yet goal-oriented classroom manner....He motivated his pupils, and made them enthusiastic for learning English....His friendliness...and receptivity to his German partners opened many doors for him...This exchange year was a success for all." (Complete letters and additional items found in Appendix C.)

Student Evaluations.
1. In accordance with departmental guidelines, I have my courses evaluated each semester using the standard university faculty/course evaluation instrument which includes fifteen additional items required specifically by my department from the departmental core. For all items, my median scores rank among the highest in the College of Sciences and Humanities. The response frequency categories range from the value 5, indicating the number of students who strongly agree (SA) with the item, to the value 1, indicating the number who strongly disagree (SD). Median values exceeding 3.0 represent a positive evaluation. Median values of less than 3.0 are associated with items for which the evaluations are negative. The following summary provides median scores for what is generally recognized as the two most important core items from several classes at the beginning, intermediate, and advanced undergraduate levels over several years:
Core Item: "OVERALL THIS INSTRUCTOR IS AMONG THE BEST TEACHERS I HAVE KNOWN."
1990–91 (Autumn)
GER 101 – 4.8   GER 202 – 4.7   GER 338 – 4.5   GER 363 – 4.8
(Spring)
GER 101 – 4.8   GER 101 – 4.8   GER 201 – 4.5   GER 403 – 4.3

1989–90 (Autumn)
GER 101 – 4.6   GER 338 – 4.6   GER 401 – 4.6
(Spring)
GER 101 – 4.6   GER 335 – 4.8   GER 402 – 4.8
1988–89 (Autumn)
GER 202 – 4.6   GER 334 – 4.4   GER 317 – 4.8
(Spring)
GER 101 – 4.6   GER 201 – 4.3   GER 362 – 4.8
1987–88 (Autumn)
GER 101 – 4.8   GER 201 – 4.4   GER 317 – 4.8
(Spring)
GER 103 – 4.7   GER 204 – 4.5   GER 330 – 4.7

Core Item: "OVERALL THIS COURSE IS AMONG THE BEST I HAVE EVER TAKEN."

1990–91 (Autumn)
GER 101 – 4.3   GER 202 – 4.2   GER 338 – 4.2   GER 363 – 4.5
(Spring)
GER 101 – 4.5   GER 101 – 4.6   GER 201 – 4.1   GER 403 – 4.3
1989–90 (Autumn)
GER 101 – 4.7   GER 338 – 4.3   GER 401 – 4.7
(Spring)
GER 102 – 4.6   GER 335 – 4.7   GER 402 – 4.6
1988–89 (Autumn)
GER 202 – 4.5   GER 334 – 4.7   GER 361 – 4.6
(Spring)
GER 101 – 4.8   GER 201 – 4.8   GER 362 – 4.5
1987–88 (Autumn)
GER 101 – 4.7   GER 201 – 4.6   GER 317 – 4.6
(Spring)
GER 103 – 4.8   GER 202 – 4.2   GER 319 – 4.8

2. Sampling of written student comments from the evaluation form, all levels, 1989–1991:

"Dr. Warner is probably the best professor I've had at BSU....If there's a problem, he covers it until it's clear with everyone. He made German a very enjoyable class."; " The professor is sometimes absent-minded but he never gives up! He's very interested in German and teaching, and you can see this in class."; "Herr Warner is definitely an asset to this university...he is by far one of the best teachers I have had...he is very concerned about his students. He is just a great guy!"; "Mr. Warner is definitely one of the best teachers I have ever had. He motivates his students and seems to care about each one...what I really like is that no question is a dumb one to him. He takes time out to help someone understand."; "This is my fifth year at BSU, and I found Dr. Warner to be one of the best teachers I have had."; "Herr Warner is one of the best profs here when it comes to caring about his students and their work...he's a great man." (Appendix D includes samples of student evaluations as well as copies of the above and many more written opinions provided by students on their evaluation forms.)

Special Awards and Honors (Appendix E).
1. Recognized as "Outstanding Ball State Faculty Member" by the Clavia Chapter of Mortar Board in November, 1990.
2. Chosen as an "Esteemed Member of Ball State University Faculty" by Sigma Kappa Sorority, November, 1990.
3. Designated "University-Level German Teacher of the Year" for 1991–92 by the Indiana Association of Teachers of German (IATG).

Appendices
Appendix A: Correspondence from Students and Former Students
Appendix B: Congratulatory Letters and Expressions of Gratitude from Government Officials, Colleagues, and School Administrative Personnel
Appendix C: Peer Evaluations
Appendix D: Student Evaluations
Appendix E: Special Awards and Honors

TEACHING PORTFOLIO
John R. Barber
Department of History
Ball State University

Table of Contents
Portfolio Plan
Teaching Responsibilities
A Description of the Western Civilization Course
Course Development
Course Evaluation
Future Course Development Plans
Appendices

Portfolio Plan

This portfolio concentrates on a single class (HIST 150: Western Civilization) and is intended mainly for use in course enhancement—a guide to improvement and support for development grant applications.

Teaching Responsibilities

Each term I usually teach one freshman Western Civilization class, offer an upper division course (Soviet History or Europe Since 1945), and devote one-fourth of my time to research or work as an instructional development consultant. My HIST 150 is always a large class (over 500 autumn, over 200 spring) and counts as two sections. The total load is equal to twelve semester hours. My agreement with the department for the Western Civilization class includes the understanding that I will carry-on a personally designed program of curricular experimentation and will involve my HIST 150 sections in institutional teaching innovations such as writing-across-the-curriculum.

A Description of the Western Civilization Course

The purpose of the course is to encourage students to gain a new knowledge and deeper awareness of the main features of European history since ancient times but especially since the late 1700s. A particular concern is to help students use this knowledge to better understand themselves and their times. The curriculum is also designed to achieve these other student learning goals: advance in critical thinking, improvement in communication skills, and the cultivation of problem-solving and values-clarification techniques. (For a detailed description of all aspects of the course summarized in this section of the portfolio, see the syllabus, Appendix A.)

The course work planned to help students attain these learning goals includes the following: daily reading assignments in the text and collateral sources; twelve short essays (five to ten minutes in class) related to assigned reading; ten pop quizzes and three one-hour multiple-choice tests; three map tests; and optional special topic reports. (For sample quizzes and tests, see Appendix B. Examples of student essays and special reports comprise Appendix C. Appendix D charts test scores and course grade patterns.)

Class sessions are important in conveying course content and implementing learning goals. Students in this class encounter quite varied methods. In every session they experience a sequence of visual presentations, lecturettes, demonstrations, and expression activities designed to gain maximum attention and involvement. The variety achieved in this way is further enhanced by changes in the length of presentations and alterations in the pace of activities. Handouts and commentary in class indicate the relationship between the presentations and the reading and other assignments.

Course Development

Since the latter 1960s, I have experimented with visuals, drama, simulations, expression actions, and demonstrations that I could use along with lectures and discussion to produce a more effective class session. When HIST 150 became one of my assignments five years ago, I continued my established practice of regularly assessing and adjusting all techniques. From that point on, however, I devoted special attention to visual methods and made videotapes rather than slide programs the primary AV instrument. This alteration enabled me to restructure session plans and gain much more variety in content and pace within each period and over the course of the semester. Thus far, I have indexed several hundred videotapes, produced twenty new slide programs, and prepared over forty demonstrations and simulations for this class.

Specific development steps during the past year included the following: 1) Used fewer short videos and more often played long segments; 2) Presented the videotapes in a pattern designed to achieve much greater variety in the length of presentations; 3) Linked the videos much more directly to lecturettes and structured discussions, often accomplished by the distribution of "unfinished notes;" 4) Redesigned short essay and other student activities in class to ensure achievement of specific purposes: emphasize points, convey information, develop critical thinking, etc.; 5) Thoroughly revised all study guides and other supplementary material; 6) Restructured map assignments and multiple-choice tests; and 7) Began trials of new instruments for student evaluation in the course.

Course Evaluation

In order to assess the effectiveness of these methods developed during the past twenty years, I have used personal observation, an analysis of student data from my classes, and a survey of pedagogical literature. After teaching HIST 150 for several semesters, I composed a detailed description of the techniques and summarized my assessment of them in a fifteen-page paper that I presented in a national conference (see Appendix E). I also have prepared a videotape that depicts class session methods. (The format of the video allows a review of one or more brief class presentations or a complete session. It is available in the history department office, if it does not accompany this portfolio.)

Every term I have arranged student evaluations of this course using a departmental instrument that includes twelve objective items (each ranges from high of 1 to low of 5). It also contains a section that calls for comments on strengths and weaknesses of the instructor and course. The overall rating five years ago was 1.6 and now is 1.2. I also have quantitative data on student perceptions of the effectiveness of the various methods used to teach content and unsolicited student letters commenting on this course. (For a summary of student evaluations during the past three years and other quantitative data, see Appendix F. Photocopies of all letters pertaining to this course are available on request.)

Twice during the past two years, I have used an instrument provided by the National Center for Research to Improve Post Secondary Teaching and Learning (NCRIPTAL, University of Michigan), to compare student perceptions of my course goals and student personal goals in taking the course. NCRIPTAL research indicates that when teacher and student course goals are mutually understood and are adequately compatible, learning is enhanced. Information from this study has influenced many of the changes in course content and methods in recent semesters. (See Appendix G for survey data and an outline of related curriculum alterations.)

Six faculty colleagues have observed my teaching in HIST 150. Two of these professors attended all sessions of the course and subsequently wrote evaluations. Within the past three years, four departments and six other faculty groups have invited me to conduct seminars on techniques used in the Western Civilization class, thus allowing about 250 other professors to consider descriptions of the methods developed for this course. Participants in these sessions composed brief reactions to the seminar presentations. (For peer observations, see Appendix H.)

Future Course Development Plans

The improvement steps that I plan to carry out, beginning with the most important, are these: 1) Improve the evaluation program by selecting instruments to provide the specific information needed for course development; 2) Develop a more complete program of activities to encourage improvement in critical thinking skills; 3) Complete the organization of the video database—review recently acquired tapes and develop a single topical index; 4) Reassess study aids, revise further if needed, and incorporate into a unified course guide; and 5) Conduct a trial run of a library instruction project similar to the one I used in more advanced courses in previous terms—Appendix I.

Appendices
Appendix A: Course Syllabus
Appendix B: Samples of Quizzes and Tests

Appendix C: Examples of Student Writing: Essays and Reports
Appendix D: Chart of Test Scores and Course Grades
Appendix E: "The Montage Class": A Report on Course Methods
Appendix F: Summary of Student Course Evaluations
Appendix G: NCRIPTAL Survey Report
Appendix H: Peer Observations
Appendix I: Library Instruction Project Assignment Model

TEACHING PORTFOLIO
Elaine K. Ferraro
Department of Human Relations
Columbia College

Table of Contents
Teaching Responsibilities, Strategies & Objectives
Representative Course Syllabi & Materials
Record of Student Evaluations of Teaching
Record of Student Performances
Peer Evaluations of Teaching from Outside the College
Statement from Department Chairperson
Statement of Student Readiness for Graduate School
Description of Efforts to Improve My Teaching
Goals for the Next Five Years
Appendices

Statement of Teaching Responsibilities, Strategies & Objectives
Teaching Responsibilities
The Department of Human Relations offers majors in three related disciplines: psychology, social work, and sociology. My primary teaching responsibilities are the courses required for the social work major. Because the disciplines are related the department cross-lists several courses, i.e., social work/psychology, social work/sociology. Thus, several of my courses are cross-listed. Additionally, I teach the senior honors seminar on women's studies, administer the Social Work Program and advise twenty-five to thirty social work majors. My teaching load is four different courses each semester:

HUMAN BEHAVIOR
SW/SOC 268   Ethnic and Minority Groups
PSY/SW 301   Human Development and the Social Environment I
SOC 325   Gender Roles
SOCIAL PROBLEMS, POLICY, AND SERVICES
SOC 163   Social Problems
SW/SOC 255   Introduction to Social Welfare
SW 380   Social Welfare Policy and Services
RESEARCH METHODS
SW/SOC 385   Social Research I
SW/SOC 472   Social Research II
SW/SOC 473   Senior Research Project

Strategies and Objectives
Rather than discussing the strategies and objectives for the nine different courses that I teach over an academic year, I am going to write a brief statement

about my teaching philosophy which undergirds the methods that I use in all my courses. I will then describe the strategies and objectives for these courses, one from each curriculum area. The courses I have selected include an introductory-level course that may be taken for general education credit and upper-level courses required for a social work or sociology major. This will provide an overview of my teaching strategies and objectives for the courses in each curriculum area. (See Appendix A for a description of the other courses.)

My professional training is in social work. In addition to my academic preparation, I have clinical practice experience. Both arenas have influenced my teaching style. Social workers must engage clients in problem solving in the context of relationships that empower clients to accept responsibility for their own solutions. I believe the same process applies to student learning. Consequently, I use a variety of teaching methods designed to move students from being passive "receivers" to active "doers" both in and out of the classroom. I do this through assignments that require students to use the knowledge from the classroom in applied situations. For example, in my social welfare course students assess a social service program. To complete the assignment students must spend some time in a social service agency. Assignments also require students to make evaluative judgments based on what they have learned.

Social workers are licensed in South Carolina. While I do not believe that multiple-choice tests are always the most effective measure of student learning, the state uses such tests for licensure. Therefore, in my courses I include evaluative methods that require recall and application of information in a multiple-choice test format.

The courses described in the following paragraphs represent the ideas and methods that guide my teaching in each of the curriculum areas:

HUMAN DEVELOPMENT AND THE SOCIAL ENVIRONMENT I (PSY/SW 301) is the first course in a two-semester lifespan sequence. It is required for social work majors and an elective for psychology majors. The enrollment is generally twenty to twenty-five students, and I teach the course each fall semester.

The primary goal of the course is to help students acquire and apply knowledge of individuals as they develop from birth through adolescence. I use the Behavior Assessment Model to teach the course. This model requires acquisition of substantial knowledge in four areas: normal developmental milestones, common life events, effects of diversity, and resulting coping behavior. I use a variety of teaching methods (such as videotapes, contemporary literature, professional journals) and assignments to help students identify developmental issues, possible causes and appropriate responses. The culminating assignment is a case analysis using a contemporary novel. Students are required to analyze the various factors that shaped the main character's individual development and behavior. Most recently students read *I Know Why the Caged Bird Sings* by Maya Angelou.

INTRODUCTION TO SOCIAL WELFARE (SW/SOC 255) is a required course for social work majors and an elective for sociology majors. It is also elected by a number of students to fulfill a general education social science requirement. The normal student enrollment is twenty to twenty-five.

The principal purpose of the course is to introduce students to the social welfare institution and the social service delivery system as responses to human need. One goal for the course is for students to understand that we are all consumers of social welfare services and that we all play a role in determining what and how resources are distributed to respond to human need. To help students develop some sense of personal responsibility for the social welfare institution they are not allowed in their discussions to blame problems on "society," "those people," or the ever popular "they." My aim is to explore social problems so that students see the individual and the multiple factors that influence service provision. A variety of assignments are required, including a self-statement as a social welfare consumer.

SOCIAL RESEARCH II (SW/SOC 472) is the second course in a three-course research sequence required for the social work or sociology major (enrollment twelve to fifteen). The focus of Research II is on research methodology and the application to social problems and human behavior. This is probably the most difficult course I teach because students approach it with anxiety and mental blocks which impede learning.

One of my first tasks is to reduce the anxiety so that students are open to learning. I begin with a class demonstration involving water, alcohol, and ice cubes. Students write descriptions of what they think will happen when ice cubes are placed in unknown liquids. They describe what they observed, develop hypotheses, and research questions based on the demonstration.

Each class follows a similar format: lecture and discussion of a research concept followed by an opportunity to practice the concept. This provides students the opportunity to apply the theoretical framework of research to a concrete, familiar situation.

Representative Course Syllabi & Materials

Appendix A contains current course syllabi for each course that I teach and a brief description of my teaching strategies for each course. Also included in Appendix A are samples of instructional materials, assignments, guided class discussions, and a sample lecture.

I recently completed a doctoral course, Principles of College Teaching. One requirement was a syllabus of a course that I was currently teaching. I submitted the syllabus for Human Development and the Social Environment I. The instructor had the following comments: "You've thought of everything! Your objectives have been consistently carried out through your instructional strategies and your tests...." See Appendix A for the complete evaluation.

Record of Student Evaluations of Teaching

Appendix B contains summaries of student evaluations of my teaching over the past five years as reflected by the use of the Columbia College course evaluation form. In the Fall of 1991, seventeen of seventeen students on a scale of "very good to poor" gave me the highest rating and fifteen of the seventeen students indicated the course had "greatly" increased their knowledge in the subject area. Similarly in the Spring of 1992, twenty-two of twenty-five students "strongly agree/agree" with the statement that the "instructor taught this course effectively." Sample comments include: " I liked the class because it made me think....I thoroughly enjoyed the professor...."

Also included are letters and short notes from current students and alumni. These are unsolicited and are only a sample that I have received over the years. Comments include: "Thanks for being such a great teacher...you really made an impact on my life....An extra thanks for inspiring me and giving me some self-confidence....As an instructor, you're the 'best'....I really appreciate your sharing of knowledge and wisdom with me....I am also grateful for the encouragement and 'warm fuzzies' that I received from you....I could never be the person I am today without your support and guidance...."

Record of Student Performance

In Appendix C are representative samples of written student assignments; an example of a good paper and a poor paper are included. The criteria for grading student written work are also included. I have also included sample objective exams with a summary of student performance. I want to work on helping students acquire test-taking skills.

Evaluations of Teaching from Outside the College

I recently (May of 1991) completed my doctoral degree in social work. The program I completed had as one of its major goals preparation of social work educators. As part of the program students were required to teach selected portions of courses. I have included in Appendix D four statements evaluating my teaching in three different courses.

Statement from Department Chairperson

Appendix E contains statements from my department chairperson regarding my role in and contribution to the department over the past five years. On my most recent evaluation (calendar year 1991), he wrote: "As much a complete faculty member as one could want. Go down through the categories in this self-report and notice the activities of substance in each one...I appreciate and admire her deep integrity."

Statement of Student Readiness for Graduate School and Performance in the Profession

Approximately two-thirds of our graduates attend graduate school. Appendix F contains a statement from the Associate Dean at the University of South Carolina's College of Social Work regarding Columbia College graduates' preparation to pursue a master of social work degree. Also included in the Appendix is a list of graduates' professional employment.

Description of Efforts to Improve Teaching

I am continuously trying to improve my teaching. I do this through attendance at workshops, seminars, and lectures. I also read educational texts and journals pertaining to education in my field and higher education in general. I carefully read the student evaluations of my courses and try to incorporate suggestions as appropriate. In fact, my policy regarding late papers came as a student recommendation. I also try to submit one abstract annually for a presentation at an educational conference in my field.

Appendix G contains a list of the workshops and seminars I have attended in the past two years, journals to which I subscribe, abstracts submitted for presentation, and programs of conferences where I have presented.

Goals for the Next Five Years and Reflective Comments

My most immediate goal relates to my administrative responsibilities as Director of the Social Work Program. The social work major is accredited by the Council on Social Work Education. As the director, I am responsible for the self study process leading to reaccreditation. The Columbia College Social Work Program is scheduled for review in June 1993. My goal is successful reaffirmation of accreditation for the maximum eight-year period.

I have also set more long-term goals. These relate to my own professional development. Once the reaccreditation process is complete, I would like to focus on the following:

1. I want to use different assessment procedures to measure student learning. I would like to begin to evaluate not only mastery of content but cognitive growth and development. Sometimes I think we spend too much time concerned with what students know rather than how they think and perceive knowledge. Beginning in the Fall of 1993, I plan to begin some research in ways to do more meaningful assessment of what students learn in class. My initial plan is to begin with two courses: Ethnic and Minority Groups, or Gender Roles and Introduction to Social Welfare.
2. I want to submit one article for publication in a refereed journal within the next two years.
3. Beginning in the Fall of 1994, I plan to evaluate one course each academic year in terms of curricular validity. I also want to make sure that I address the issues of multiculturalism and gender. I will do this with either a colleague at the college or an educator outside the college.

Appendices

Appendix A: Sample Syllabi, Instructional Materials and Assignments
Appendix B: Student Evaluations of Teaching
Appendix C: Evidence of Student Performance
Appendix D: Evaluation of Teaching from Outside the College
Appendix E: Statement from Department Chairperson
Appendix F: Student Readiness for Graduate School
Appendix G: Efforts to Improve Teaching

TEACHING PORTFOLIO
Laurie Hopkins
Department of Mathematics
Columbia College

Table of Contents
Teaching Responsibilities
Personal Philosophy and Strategies for Teaching
Future Goals
Course Descriptions
Teaching Improvement Activities
Student Products
Teaching Recognition
Appendices

Teaching Responsibilities

My primary area of teaching responsibility is the upper-level computer courses; I teach all of the courses that are offered beyond the introductory programming course. I also teach one of the calculus courses, some upper-level math courses, general education courses, the math course for business majors, and one of the developmental math courses. I have designed or revamped several courses for the department and I designed and coordinate the minor our department offers in microcomputer studies. I advise most of the math majors who do not plan to certify to teach and have served as advisor to several contractual studies students with an emphasis in computer science. I also supervise honors projects regularly, direct the senior project for the contractual studies advisees and have offered numerous classes on an independent study basis to facilitate scheduling for students in their major or minor courses.

Since the number of math majors and the number of math or computer minors is fairly small, we offer only one section of upper-level courses in both areas either annually or biannually. Consequently, I typically have taught four different courses each semester. In the past three semesters, I have taught eight different courses.

Personal Philosophy and Strategies for Teaching

I want my students to see themselves as problem-solvers, with mathematics or computer science as a tool for them to use. For this reason, most of my classes involve projects in which my role is that of resource/support to enable the students to solve complicated realistic problems. Much of my teaching involves presenting problems and their solutions for the same reason.

In a world in which technological changes abound, students of mathematics and computer science must be able to continue to learn and develop their understanding of this technology beyond their college careers. Therefore, the ability to read and understand narratives of this nature is an essential skill. To encourage students to acquire the ability to decipher writings about math and computer science, I choose the most readable texts possible. I assign specific readings and daily in-class writings to reflect on what they have read. A sample of such writing, with my comments, is in Appendix Gi.

I often prepare a set of incomplete notes which I distribute to the students to correspond to the overhead transparencies that I use in class. This method allows me to cover lecture material efficiently without needless copying and encourages maximum student involvement in the lectures. An example of incomplete notes is included in Appendix Gii.

To encourage students to receive the practice and understanding they need from the homework, I collect and grade all assignments. I spend class time answering questions about assignments and am available to students outside of class, either in person or by phone. I return all student work promptly, usually the next class period. I prepare an assignment sheet listing all homework assignments, the dates on which they are due, and all test dates. Each student receives this sheet on the first day of class. Although flexibility requires that some adjustments be made to these assignments on occasion, the basic framework for each class remains unchanged.

Student writing encourages student learning. Utilizing writing in many different ways has been an exciting challenge for me as a math teacher. Daily in-class writing assignments require students to put concepts and processes into their own words, to explain the rationale behind techniques, to explore their attitudes toward mathematics and to examine their study habits. Longer take-home assignments provide an opportunity for students to relate the material in the test to their own experience. I frequently use summarizing discussion questions on tests and exams, often telling students in advance exactly the kinds of questions they will need to answer on the tests. In some classes, students design these discussion sections of the tests themselves, in consultation with me, as part of a class meeting. Sample questions include "Describe the numerical techniques for integration," for a numerical analysis course and "Compare and contrast the use of linked and sequential lists for storing ordered data," for a data structures course. Additional student writing is contained in Appendices Gi and Giii. Comments from students indicated that writing helps them to organize their thoughts and to locate concepts with which they need more help.

In general education courses and in developmental courses, math anxiety and poor self-image play a major role in the performance of many students. I try to combat these problems with reassurance, availability outside of the classroom, and many opportunities for success. In all freshman and sophomore classes, I develop a practice test to help students prepare for the testing experience and allow students who want to improve their grade to take a retest with no penalty. Although constructing multiple tests is quite time-consuming, the benefits in decreasing anxiety about the tests have been well worth the effort.

Future Goals

My primary goal for future teaching is to develop a connection with the Harvard Calculus Consortium, a group of university and college professors who are interested in changing the way that calculus is taught. To that end I have submitted an abstract to the planners of the conference that will be held this summer by the HCC. I will attend and present a paper.

My second goal is to begin to develop my own texts for use with the computer course and the numerical analysis course. I would like to have a preliminary version of the computer text to use by Spring of 1993 and a version of the numerical analysis text to try the following Spring.

I would also like to develop a set of incomplete notes to be used in each class I teach in which lectures comprise fifty percent or more of classroom time. Finally, I would like to implement library use into more upper-level math and computer courses.

Course Description, Materials and Syllabi

The appendices contain syllabi, prepared course materials and some student products for four courses chosen to be representative of the classes I have taught over the past three semesters.

I teach Math 261, Calculus II each Fall. It is the second of a three-course sequence required of all math and chemistry majors. The course sequence is fairly standard at colleges and universities and the material covered in each semester is prescribed by this tradition. To help students master the large amount of content, I structured the course to allow time for many examples in class and much practice on the homework. Daily writings focused on giving the students the chance to express the concepts and techniques in their own words. Giving a test after each chapter kept the students from feeling overwhelmed by the magnitude of the material. I designed a practice test for the students to use as they studied for each of the tests and offered a retest for any interested student. The tight schedule precluded class time spent on group projects, so I have a difficult practical application of the material in each chapter as a bonus assignment. Students were encouraged to cooperate on the solution of these extra credit problems which were turned in one week after the test on the chapter. The appendix contains the syllabus, assignment sheet, practice test, test retest and extra credit for one chapter, and one student's writings.

One of my favorite courses to teach is Math/Comp 450, Applications of Abstract Algebra. The material in this course focuses on the use of abstract structures to design machines. The actual machines are predominantly theoretical, although the logical circuits can actually be constructed. The major hands-on experience of the course was the creation of such a circuit which could add small binary numbers. It was quite exciting for the students to hook up the myriad wires and gates in the prescribed complex fashion and then actually see that the resulting machine worked. I developed an incomplete notes set for this class so that there would be ample time in class for working examples. The appendix contains the syllabus, assignment sheet, a set of the incomplete notes, and one student's final exam.

An Introduction to Artificial Intelligence, Comp 440, was offered for the first time in the Fall of 1990. In designing this course, I tried to integrate the history and philosophical development of this topic with the current practices in the field. I could find no single text which covered both aspects. Therefore, I used two different books. The first was an extremely well written and thought provoking analysis of man's attempts to create a thinking machine. Students were required to read one chapter per week and to write a two-page response to the material. One class period per week was devoted to sharing these responses, first in small groups and then with the whole class. The second text was an introduction to the language of Turbo Prolog and its use in the creation of expert systems, the predominate application of artificial intelligence. Students worked independently with my supervision to master the language and to construct an expert system. The final requirement of the course was a presentation on the newest developments in the field. Each student researched current practices and chose a topic to study and present to the class. The appendix contains a syllabus, daily class outline and one student's weekly writing assignments. In addition, I have included a program written in conjunction with the course by two contractual studies students for their senior project.

The final course under consideration is Math 017, Preparatory Mathematics for Education Majors. I designed this course, with the help of two other members of the math faculty, to prepare students to pass our state's Educational Entrance Exam (EEE). This test is given to all prospective teachers in the state before they are allowed to enroll in a teacher education program. A student may take the test at most three times. Math 017 reflects the objectives of this exam together with math proficiency as defined by the department. No text could be found to adequately address these goals. Therefore, we developed many handouts and activities to provide the necessary learning experiences. Homework assignments were extensive and were graded promptly. Writing assignments allowed students to explore attitudes and study habits as well as concepts. Tests were given in the areas of arithmetic, measurement, geometry, algebra and problem-solving. As discussed previously, practice tests and retests were also available. These tests were made to mimic the types of questions which students could expect to see on the EEE. The final exam was designed to serve the student as a pretest for the EEE. I have included the syllabus and assignment sheet in the appendix as well as the handouts I developed for the measurement section and all tests related to that section.

Teaching Improvement Activities

In March of 1988, I attended a Chautauqua course led by Dr. Charles Wales on "Teaching Decision-Making in the Math and Sciences." More than any other single experience, this course has had a profound effect on my teaching.

As a result, I led an effort to completely revise the general education math courses around the theme of problem-solving and to incorporate problem-solving into all math courses. As a follow-up experience, I attended the annual conference of the International Society for Effective Teaching Alternatives (ISETA) in the Fall of 1988. Presenters from all disciplines were there to share ideas about non-traditional methods of teaching. This conference reinforced my desire to incorporate projects and student-centered activities into the learning experiences in my classrooms.

My teaching has also benefited from my involvement with the campus-wide effort to incorporate "Writing Across the Curriculum." In December of 1987, Dr. Henry Stefan presented a workshop for several members of our faculty on using writing in all disciplines. Since that time, I have used many writing techniques in most of my classes. Specifically, I use informal in-class writings on a daily basis in most classes to encourage students to reflect on the mathematical content we are considering. I also use discussion questions and longer writings as evaluative tools.

In the Summer of 1989, I attended a week-long institute on using computers in the mathematics classroom sponsored by the National Science Foundation, led by Dr. David Kraines and held at Meredith College. My desire to incorporate technology into the learning experiences of my students led me to attend this institute. Specific software, appropriate for particular courses, was available for experimental use. As a result of this course, we acquired some of the software, and I have been using it in my classes with regularity.

In March of 1990, most of the math department attended a one-day workshop presented by Dr. D. R. LaTorre of Clemson at UNC-Charlotte on the use of the hand-held graphics calculator in the classroom. This was followed by an intensive week of work during the summer by all the math faculty to incorporate this important new tool in math majors classes beginning in the Fall of 1990. Students have commented that this use of technology in the classroom is very effective.

In January of 1990, I attended a seminar presented by faculty from Lesley College on the assessment of collaborative learning. This experience was helpful to me in implementing the problem-solving component into more classes. It also reinforced the importance of collaborative activities in structuring learning experiences for women.

In February of 1991, I went to a meeting on "Enhancing the Quality of Teaching." Both collaborative learning and technology in the classroom were topics of interest at this meeting.

Finally, the preparation of this document has been an effort to enhance my teaching. I have met with colleagues from my own campus and from other locations to discuss the content of the portfolio and ways that it might be improved. The conversations with others and the time I have spent alone thinking about my teaching have had a direct and positive impact on what I do in the classroom.

Student Products

I have not given pretests in my classes because the nature of the subject matter precludes students understanding of the material before a section is covered. I do believe that student performance on my tests is an indication of what they have learned in my classes. A copy of my calculus exam is in Appendix Gi. The grades on that exam were 71, 81, 82, 83, 84, 91, 93, and 95. No student failed the exam or the course.

The results of the EEE can demonstrate the effectiveness of my teaching of Math 017. Twenty-four (24) out of twenty-six (26) students passed the course. This is a very good record for students requiring remediation of this type. Of the students who passed the course, fifteen (15) took the EEE in February. Fourteen of the fifteen (or 93%) passed.

The source code for a program written in Comp 440 for a contractual studies project is included in Appendix Giii. The students who wrote this program were not the brightest or best in the class, but actually were the students whose performance was most average.

The exam for Math 450 is included in Appendix Giv. The lowest grade on this exam was 88.

Teaching Recognition

I have been invited to talk at the annual South Carolina Council of Teachers of Mathematics (SCCTM) meeting for each of the past three years. In 1989, I gave a presentation on writing in the mathematics classroom. I was invited to repeat that talk the following year, but I requested the opportunity to present a talk on collaborative learning instead. That talk was very well received and I was asked to present it again in the Fall of 1991. Unfortunately, personal responsibilities prevented my attendance at the fall meeting. I have been invited to present a workshop at the meeting for Fall of 1992.

I received the 1989 Outstanding Faculty Award at Columbia College. This award is predominantly based on good teaching and is given annually to a faculty member elected by students and faculty. As the 1989 recipient, I was also the college nominee for the CASE Professor of the Year Award and for the Governor's Distinguished Professor Award. I was also asked to be speaker for the summer commencement as a result of this award. The certificates for these honors are contained in the Appendix as are copies of letters from several people in support of the nominations solicited by the dean. Dr. David Sumner taught me and supervised my graduate teaching at USC. Dr. Strickland is chairman of another department in my building. Dr. Day has advised several students who were math minors. Roni Samaras is currently working for a bank in Roanoke, Virginia.

I have asked Lucy Snead and Memi Kinard to write letters evaluating my teaching. Both of these fellow faculty members have taken classes that I have taught. I have also asked three former students to write letters about my teaching. Trudy Hartzog is currently in her last year of law school. Nella Huntley is pursuing a master's degree in computer science from Georgia Tech. Linda Ramsey will graduate in the spring, but she has only her student teaching left to complete this semester. I would encourage the interested reader to examine these letters carefully. Comments include, " ...she distributed 'incomplete notes'. This was the first time I had ever been given this teaching aid. I found it to be extremely helpful, not only in helping us make effective use of class time, but also in guiding me to read the textbook with understanding," and, "My background in mathematics and analytical reasoning has been very beneficial to [my work at law school]. Dr. Hopkins gave me this strong mathematical foundation to build upon. More importantly, she instilled in me the desire to want to learn..." and, "She indeed possesses an outstanding knowledge of content. In my personal experience, she has always known the answer to my questions."

I have also included my student course evaluations for the past four semesters in an appendix. On the question about the effectiveness of tests, examinations and required papers, 94% of the respondents rated me 4 or 5 (Outstanding or Superior), with the average score being 4.6. When asked how effectively the instructor communicated subject matter, 88% responded either 4 or 5 with an average answer of 4.5. Similarly, when asked for an overall evaluation of the instructor, 88% responded "very good" from the choices very good, fair and poor. There were many very positive comments in the evaluations. My favorite comment is, "Dr. Hopkins loves to teach and I love to learn from her."

Over the years, I have received several unsolicited notes from students thanking me for the help that I have given them. A sample of these are included in Appendix E. One student wrote, "You have helped me understand math for the first time in my life." Another said, "You gave me the help and encouragement I needed to continue in math."

Appendices
Appendix A: Documentation of Awards
Appendix B: Letters from Administrators
Appendix C: Letters from Fellow Teachers
Appendix D: Letters from Former Students
Appendix E: Unsolicited Notes from Current Students
Appendix F: Student Evaluations
Appendix G: Course Materials
        i. Math 261
            syllabus
            assignment sheet
            practice test, test and retest for one chapter
            student writings
            final exam

ii. Math/Comp 450
    syllabus
    assignment sheet
    incomplete notes
    one student's final exam
iii. Comp 440
    syllabus
    daily class outline
    one student's weekly writing
    source code for a program written by two students
iv. Math 017
    syllabus
    assignment sheet
    measurement handout
    practice test, test and retest

TEACHING PORTFOLIO
Donald W. Orr
Department of Mathematics & Physics
Miami-Dade Community College

Table of Contents
Teaching-Learning Philosophy
Classroom Techniques
Self-Assessment
Statement of Performance Goals
Appendices

Teaching-Learning Philosophy

The fundamental premise of my teaching/learning philosophy is that none of us can be forced to learn. Learning is a process through which we adapt to the world around us: it is something we do; it's not something done to us. Learning requires effort, and like all human efforts it is a matter of choice. So the crucial first step in learning is choosing to make the effort.

It follows that in our role as teachers, the first thing we must do is to persuade our students to accept responsibility for their own choices. All students want to succeed academically, and I have yet to meet a student whom I considered incapable of learning. But many do not realize the extent to which their own choices govern their performance—especially the seemingly insignificant daily choices about whether and when to study. We as teachers must constantly remind our students of the power they exercise over their own progress. My personal preference is to avoid framing this message to the students as a moral prescription. It is not my style to tell my students that they ought to invest any particular amount of time or energy into their studies, nor do I feel inclined to scold them like children if they do not live up to their academic potential. I would rather present the idea to them as a simple observation regarding cause and effect: if they want to excel, then they must practice self-discipline and make the appropriate effort; contrapositively, if they don't do the required work, their performance will suffer. Most of our students are in the process of learning to function as adults. The best way for us to help them is to give them room to make choices, and then to point out the connections between those choices and their consequences, both desirable and undesirable.

If learning is the students' job, then the teacher's job is to make the students' job easier. Although we can't make our students learn, we can make it possible for them to learn. As teachers, we do so much more than merely present material to our classes. We can either ignite or extinguish our students' curiosity, depending on how we choose to respond to their questions. We can either fertilize or sterilize their imagination and creativity, depending on the attitudes we project. And perhaps one of the most essential things we do is to impose expectations upon our students. I have found that students generally live up (or down, as the case may be) to our expectations of them. So we should try always to expect more of our students than they would have the ambition to demand of themselves. And we should be prepared not only to lavish them with praise when they succeed, but also to lend them our support and encouragement when they fall short of those expectations, our patient assistance when they become disoriented, and our confidence when they lose faith in their own abilities.

For myself, this is by far the most challenging aspect of the teaching profession: to cultivate that delicate and peculiar relationship with the student in which one functions simultaneously as admirer and critic, advocate and judge. Teaching is a stimulating occupation to which I feel singularly well-suited, and I hope to be afforded the opportunity to practice it for many years to come.

Classroom Techniques

In all of the classes I teach, the time is spent partly in lecture and partly in responses to students' questions. A typical class period begins with questions from individual students over material covered and problems assigned during the previous meeting. The amount of time devoted to questions varies with the level of the course. Generally speaking, in the lower-level algebra courses I may choose to allow as much as half of the period to be utilized in this way, while in the calculus and differential equations courses I am often constrained to limit the question-and-answer sessions to as little as twenty minutes, in order to reserve sufficient time for lecture over more intricate and more complex material (see Appendix A for list of courses taught). The results of recent Student Feedback Surveys indicate that 97% of my students either agreed or strongly agreed with the item "The instructor encourages questions in class," with a mean response of 1.28.

It is often necessary to prepare supplementary materials for the higher-level students in the form of solutions to difficult exercises and detailed treatments of subtleties for which the allotted class time is insufficient. I have found that the more advanced students are generally very aggressive about seeking assistance outside of class. This is fortunate, because the sheer volume of material that must be covered in our higher-level math courses precludes the possibility of satisfying all of the students' instructional needs during the formal class meetings.

Mathematics is by its nature extremely precise and well-defined. The ability to present ideas clearly is therefore critical for a good math teacher. I believe I possess that ability; in fact, I consider it to be one of my greatest strengths. This has been confirmed by the Student Feedback Surveys, where 85% of the students surveyed strongly agreed with the item "The instructor presents course material clearly." The main response was 1.17. A student in Business Calculus remarked:

> "I am very confused about math and especially calculus, and if it weren't for the teacher, I wouldn't know what to do. He is the best teacher (by far) out of any teacher I have had in my entire educational experience so far. *He explains things very well and is very exact about everything.* He is also extremely fair about the tests. I enjoyed the class because of him."

At the beginning of each term, I distribute to all of my classes a course outline that spells out on a week-by-week basis which topics will be covered, what the assignments will be, when the exams will be administered, and what the grading policy will be (see Appendix B). Any time a student is absent from a class meeting, they know from the course outline exactly which sections of the textbook were covered that day and what work should be done to avoid falling behind. I have prepared literally hundreds of pages of detailed lecture notes (see Appendix C) so that I always know, when I enter the classroom, precisely which topics I need to address, how they are to be presented, and which examples I will use to illustrate them.

Student feedback indicates that 98% of my students strongly agreed with the item " The instructor is prepared for class." (The other 2% agreed, but not strongly.) The mean response for this item was 1.02 (see Appendices D and E). A student in Calculus III testified as follows:

> "Professor Orr is by far one of the most competent professors on campus. Orr's teaching methods are quite excellent. Mr. Orr shows great mastery of the material; he is a professional. *Mr. Orr always comes prepared with the day's lesson.* In grading tests he is quite fair. The material isn't easy, but Professor Orr *explains it very clearly.* Professor Orr is definitely one of the finest math professors I have ever had!"

The nature of the subject I teach makes it necessary to *set challenging performance goals* for my students. By simply following the guidelines established by the Math Department, I set goals that many students are unable to achieve on their first attempt. Despite my constant efforts to help them in every way possible, the result is that a significant percentage of my students withdraw each semester to avoid the risk of a low grade. I don't have access to the statistics, but I would assume that the withdrawal rate for my classes is about average for the Math and Physics Department, particularly among those faculty who teach the higher-level courses. However, one need only glance briefly at the results of the Student Feedback Surveys to see that those students of mine who do withdraw most emphatically do not perceive themselves to be fleeing from the shadow of incompetent instruction. Particularly in a discipline where the courses are arranged in sequential order, with the earlier courses establishing prerequisite skills for the later courses, we owe it to our students to ensure that they are not simply ushered along without having demonstrated a fairly sound understanding at each level.

Both of the students quoted above made reference to my fairness in evaluating them. The following student feedback results document this quality.

Question	Mean Response	Scale
The objectives agree with what is taught.	1.25	1 = Strongly agree
The assignments help me learn the course material.	1.22	2 = Agree
The exams are related to course material.	1.22	3 = Disagree
The exams are graded fairly.	1.20	4 = Strongly disagree
The instructor discussed the grading system.	1.18	
The instructor makes the grading system clear.	1.22	

In addition to the mean responses listed, it is worth noting that on each of the above items, at least 96% of the students surveyed either agreed or strongly agreed, with at least 78% expressing strong agreement.

One of the factors that cause my students to feel they are treated fairly is that I spend enormous amounts of time correcting their exams (see Appendix F for example), as they can tell by reading the lengthy corrections and comments I write on their papers. A student in first-semester calculus offered the following observation:

> "The instructor is very well qualified to teach this class. Not only is he very patient and understanding with first-time calculus students, but he is also very enthusiastic about his and our work. *His testing is fairly hard, but fair.* The instructor is very dependable. He is always on time and in class. He has an awesome grading system in which he *spends time on individuals' papers to tell what's incorrect.* I will in the future try to take the follow-up courses with this instructor."

Another practice of mine that the students like very much is to show them the distribution of scores earned by the class on each exam and the cumulative averages for all students in the class (anonymously, of course—that is, they get to see this list of numbers for the entire class, but only the individual student knows which number is his or hers). My students gave a mean response of 1.26 on the item "The instructor informs me about my progress," with 98% either agreeing or strongly agreeing. A trigonometry student commented:

> "It is my personal opinion that Prof. Orr is an excellent math teacher, probably the best I've had. He teaches with patience, which makes the student feel comfortable. Also he encourages questions and *listens attentively.* One of the best things he does is *constantly inform the student of his/her progress in class,* so that the student always knows their average. Great job, Prof. Orr."

Self Assessment
1. *Performance in the classroom.*
A. *Strengths*
   ✦ *Clarity.* I believe my greatest strength as an instructor of mathematics lies in a capacity for clear explanation of the topics I present to my students. Although this is but one of many talents that a good

instructor must strive to cultivate, it is, at least in the area of mathematics instruction, the one that is most indispensable.

+ *Preparation.* I spend many hours preparing my lectures and exams. I never enter a classroom without knowing exactly which topics I plan to present and which examples I plan to use to elucidate those topics.

+ *Concern for students.* I try to impress upon my students that my sole professional concern is to help them to learn. I consistently encourage them to seek out my assistance during office hours, and I do everything in my power to reinforce that encouragement by being kind, courteous, patient and genuinely helpful to those who come to me. It seems to me that there is little point in inviting students to take advantage of office hours unless one is willing to be hospitable toward those who respond to the invitation.

+ *Enthusiasm.* I enjoy teaching mathematics, and I think most of my students pick up on this. I try not to be 'pushy' by insisting that they share my enthusiasm; indeed, I am sometimes guilty of allowing my students' lack of enthusiasm to color my own presentations (a point which is further discussed below under the heading of weaknesses). But on the whole, I like to persuade myself that none of my students left feeling any less excited about mathematics than he/she was before having encountered me.

+ *Fairness.* I am almost fanatical in my effort to evaluate all students in each course by precisely the same standards. Since this means, in part, that none is to be permitted any unfair advantage over any others (such as, for instance, the extra study-time that would be gained by any students if he/she were permitted to take a make-up exam), my policies are occasionally misinterpreted by some students as being quite 'unfair'.

+ *Breadth of knowledge.* Since my arrival at M-DCC I have taught courses ranging from Introductory Algebra to third-semester Calculus and Differential Equations. I consider myself qualified to teach every course that we offer.

+ *Use of personal computer.* I make extensive use of a personal computer (acquired at my own expense) in the daily performance of my teaching duties. All of my exams, and most of the numerous handouts, problems solutions and study aids that I make available to my students, are prepared at home, on my own time, with the aid of a scientific word-processor.

B. Weaknesses

+ *Shyness.* I am not a 'people-person' by nature. I do not take naturally to anything resembling public speaking. I suppose the dark side of my tendency toward extensive and meticulous preparation is that I dread the thought of having to extemporize. I find it difficult to infuse wit and personality into my lectures, falling back instead on a matter-of-fact and business-like approach. In short, I am not an entertainer.

◆ *Passivity*. I am not possessed of a dynamic personality. As a result, I tend to be greatly influenced by the energy level of each group of students I encounter. If I am fortunate enough to be presented with a class in which at least a few of the students are intensely interested in learning and sufficiently gregarious to let it show, I am capable of responding in kind, with the result that a very high level of energy is generated and a very positive learning environment is created. On the other hand, if I am presented with a class in which most of the students are distinctly not interested in learning, and/or in which those few alert and ambitious students are not inclined to step forward and confess their interest through active participation in the teaching/learning process, then I tend to permit the classroom environment to become rather dull and the energy level to remain low. I am either unable or unwilling to attempt to manipulate the attitudes of my students. In short, I am not a salesman.

◆ *Elitism*. In reading over the written comments submitted by my students from the past semester, I was pleased to note that a majority could think of nothing "bad" to say. A the same time I was a little disappointed at the concomitant lack of constructive criticism. There was, however, one remark that struck me as being particularly eloquent in its simplicity: "...sometimes he teaches for those who know—not for those who need to learn..." I have reflected at length on this comment, trying to determine exactly what it is about my approach to teaching that would prompt the student to offer it. That same student gave me a rating of "10" on a scale from zero to ten; so the comment was clearly intended as a gentle suggestion rather than as part of an all-out assault on my character. I suspect that I do carry, albeit nowhere near the surface, a conviction that one ultimately should teach to the very best students in any class, leaving the rest to follow along as best they can. Although I make a concerted effort never to act on that conviction, it may be that sometimes I fail in that effort. If so, then this is certainly a point on which I need to improve.

2. *Performance in other departmental responsibilities*

   A. *Advisement*. I have spent a great deal of time advising students during the past semester. I have learned much about the sequence of coursework in mathematics at M-DCC, and in particular about the math requirement imposed on students by the various other departments. I have found that the secret to gaining an opportunity to advise a lot of students is simply to be present in one's office with the door open and to appear interested in any student who appears to have a question.

B. *Committees*. I have contributed to the work done by the course-outline committee during the past semester. I personally composed the newest course outline for MAC 2311, and I have also volunteered suggestions concerning the outlines for MAC 1140, MAC 2312 and MAC 2313. I worked in conjunction with Professor Sanders in designing the departmental final exams for MAT 1033.

C. *Textbook selection*. I have routinely examined all new textbooks that have been brought to my attention, passing along opinions and recommendations to other interested faculty members.

Statement of Professional Goals

In the broadest sense, my only professional goal is to evolve as an educator, which means to do a better job of helping students learn. I believe that 'learning' is an activity in which the teacher does not and cannot directly participate. The teacher is merely a catalyst in the learning process. My goal as an educator is to illuminate the path I wish my students to follow—to remove obstacles from that path, to find ways to lure my students in the proper direction, to cheer them on, to encourage them to right themselves when they stumble, and orient themselves when they stray from the path—but always to resist the temptation to walk the path for them.

On a more concrete level, my primary professional goal is to do everything in my power to combat the perception that math students at Miami-Dade are 'weak'. It is true that a disproportionate number of our entering students are 'underprepared' in mathematics. So it is up to us to place them at an appropriate level and to lead them forward from there. But we must acknowledge that from that point onward those students will have been prepared by us, with the result that if they continue to be 'underprepared', we have let them down. It behooves us to ensure that, however 'weak' our students may be when they come to us, those who leave our institution with an associates degree are thoroughly prepared for their subsequent endeavors and will be perceived as 'strong' students thereafter.

I hope to promote this philosophy first and foremost in my own classes, and secondarily in my efforts to influence the attitudes of my colleagues and the development of our mathematics curriculum in the years to come. I aspire to continue my involvement in 'non-required' campus and college activities, but with the stipulation that those activities must never be allowed to interfere with the daily execution of my primary professional responsibilities.

Appendices

Appendix A: List of Courses Taught
Appendix B: Syllabus and Course Outline
Appendix C: Lecture Notes
Appendix D: Student Feedback: Numerical Data
Appendix E: Student Feedback: Written Comments
Appendix F: Sample Exams

TEACHING PORTFOLIO
William L. Perry
Department of Mathematics
Texas A&M University

Table of Contents
On the Portfolio
Statement of Teaching Responsibilities and Methods
Syllabus
Summaries of Course-Instructor Evaluations by Students
Teaching Improvement Activities
Closing Statement
Appendices

On the Portfolio

This portfolio focuses on improvement of my teaching in a single course, Mathematics 131: Mathematical Concepts - Calculus. As Associate Provost and Dean of Faculties, I have retained my tenured professorship in the Department of Mathematics and teach a small (35-45 students) section of the course every semester. I do this because of my love of teaching and belief in the centrality of undergraduate education to the mission of the university. With time constraints as they are, I must be efficient in my efforts to improve teaching. By concentrating my portfolio on improvement of this course I have gained renewed enthusiasm and purpose. In essence, the portfolio now serves as a dynamic planning document—channeling my efforts and forming the foundation for improving instruction.

Responsibilities, Strategies and Objectives

My current responsibilities include teaching one section of calculus per semester and serving on two Ph.D. committees as a member. My methods of teaching are geared to foster interaction with the students. Because my classes are small (35-45), interaction is possible. I try to have student response and input average one or more per minute. To facilitate this I set aside an "interaction area" in the classroom (for example, the front row) through which the students rotate. For instance in Spring 1992, my classroom was equipped with three rows of tables with twelve chairs each; the students in the front row were the students I interacted with. Thus once every three class sessions the students in the front row received very personal instruction with at least five questions to answer or responses to give. The students called this the "rolling row" method and received it favorably.

My lectures are based on examples and attempts to draw general conclusions from the students. In the development of the examples, I obtain from the students not only answers to "bite size" leading questions, but also let the students choose specific examples within broad contexts. I teach using these methods because they make teaching more enjoyable than any other way I have tried. Presentation of applications related to the students' majors is an important part of my teaching. Typically the majority of my students are from biomedical sciences. I present applications from population dynamics, drug infusion, and radiotherapy to maintain interest and enthusiasm. When discussing rates of change, functions, and velocity and acceleration, I construct my examples using tax tables, newspaper articles, hang-time for punts, and so on. Praise for good performance in the classroom and on exams is an important motivational technique that I use. Also by showing the students applications that relate to their major, motivation is further enhanced. I bring in examples from the current press and media to illustrate how mathematical knowledge allows one to respond more effectively as a citizen. My primary objective is for the students to learn problem-solving techniques and in particular the importance of re-casting difficult problems in terms of smaller more easily solved problems that approximate the original.

Syllabus

The syllabus for the course is contained in Appendix A. It has changed little over the three semesters I have taught the course. The syllabus states objectives, prerequisites, information regarding grading and examinations, and daily section coverage. I try to present my openness to the students by giving my home telephone number and stating that the students are welcome to use it. I believe the syllabus sets the tone for the course; in a very real way, it forms much of the students' first impression of the instructor. As will be remarked later, I will be making additions to the syllabus to further improve that first impression.

Summary of Course-Instructor Evaluations by Students

Appendix B contains a sample Course-Instructor Survey Instrument and numerical data for the last two semesters. I consider these evaluations to provide baseline data to measure future improvement. I consider the students' opinions to be the most important data for me in determining activities to improve the course. The university exists to educate students — they are our primary constituents and we must be assiduous in bringing the highest quality instruction to them.

The evaluations indicate that in the areas I consider to be of most importance I am performing well, but there exists room for improvement. I consider the written comments of the students to be of primary importance and use them to modify my teaching from semester to semester, whenever a significant number address the same issue. For example, one semester enough students remarked that I was digressing too often from the topics at hand ("getting off on tangents," in their words). I have made sure since then to keep digressions related to the subject matter, to illustrate important points.

Selected evaluation questions and mean responses are listed below.

Question	Fall 1991 Mean	Spring 1992 Mean
*5 Compared with all the instructors I have had in college this instructor was:	4.44	4.56
**7 Given your natural ability, background preparation and the amount of time that you spent on the course, you are being given a fair grade.	4.18	3.97
**9 The instructor seemed well-prepared for lecture or discussion.	4.56	4.66
**12 The instructor was in control of the direction of the class.	4.47	4.72
**13 The instructor lectured well.	4.29	4.53
**14 The instructor genuinely tried to help the students learn the material and showed concern for their progress.	4.62	4.56
**16 If I were required to take a final exam in this subject made out by another instructor, I would feel that this teacher had prepared me well.	4.03	4.19

* Responses are:
  5-One of the best 4-Above average 3-Average 2-Below average
  1-One of the worst
**Responses are:
  5-definitely agree 4-agree 3-neutral 2-disagree 1-definitely disagree

Teaching Improvement Activities
I will be engaging in eight specific activities to improve my teaching.

1. *Videotaping of classroom teaching.* Every semester, I will use the services of the Center for Teaching Excellence to videotape and analyze my classroom teaching, following up with consultation with the staff. I will use this process at intervals recommended by the CTE and measure progress in the areas addressed by the staff in their evaluation.
2. *Peer visitation of class and evaluation of syllabi, exams and assignments.* I will ask colleagues to visit my class and also evaluate course materials each semester.
3. *Pre- and post-tests.* I will investigate for suitability of use in Spring 1993, the ETS BASIS examinations to measure student knowledge gained each semester.
4. *Syllabus development.* In Spring 1993, I will add a section in which I explain some of my methods and point out how former students have received them. This should give confidence to the students and alert them to my methods so they can prepare accordingly.

5. In 1992–93, I will conduct a random poll of former students to obtain their evaluations of my course from their perspectives as either upper-classmen or alumni.
6. I will continue development of the "rolling row" method of individual-izing instruction.
7. I will continue to add articles to the "find the calculus" file (see Appendix C). Whether in the long run the collection will be of use to colleagues remains to be seen. However, once a substantial number (annotated, of course) are pulled together, I will share them and obtain evaluations as to usefulness to other teachers of calculus.
8. I will, in Spring 1993, develop new questions for the course-instructor survey. In particular I will develop questions focusing on the syllabus, "rolling row" and "find the calculus."

Closing Statement

I am driven to do the best possible job for the students of the university. Consequently I strive to be the best I can be in my teaching, research, and service. In teaching, improvement can only be made by means of honest assessment (self, student and peer) of performance and planned efforts at strengthening teaching methods, techniques and abilities. The portfolio offers a concrete assessment and planning document for that purpose—I simply wish I had adopted this approach about twenty years ago—my students would have benefited.

Appendices

Appendix A: Course Outline
                    Syllabus for Mathematics 131:
                            Mathematical Concepts – Calculus
Appendix B: Course-Instructor Survey and Responses
Appendix C: "Find the Calculus" Examples

SECTION THREE

Medical Ethics
    Donnie J. Self
    Texas A&M University

Physical Education
    Richard C. Krejci
    Columbia College

Religion
    Vivia L. Fowler
    Columbia College

Veterinary Surgery
    Theresa W. Fossum
    Texas A&M University

Voice
    Charlotte Suzanne Nelson
    Shenandoah University

TEACHING PORTFOLIO
Donnie J. Self
Department of Humanities in Medicine
Texas A&M University Health Science Center

Table of Contents
Statement of Teaching Responsibilities and Objectives
Syllabi, Exams and Handouts from Courses Taught
Description of Efforts to Improve My Teaching
Peer Evaluation of Both My Teaching and Teaching Skills
Student Evaluation Data from Previous Courses Taught
Measures of Student Achievement
Other Evidence of Good Teaching
Future Teaching Goals
Appendices

Statement of Teaching Responsibilities and Objectives

I teach both undergraduate and graduate students in the College of Liberal Arts and professional students in the College of Medicine. In both places my teaching is primarily in medical ethics although I teach various other elective courses in moral development, social issues in medicine, human sexuality, and so forth. The undergraduate course is taught through the Department of Philosophy each Spring semester and typically has thirty-five to forty students. Each year several graduate and undergraduate students take individual directed tutorials with me. The forty-eight first-year medical students each year take a required medical ethics course that I coordinate for the first two quarters of their first year.

I incorporate personal growth and development in my teaching because I believe that every teacher has a responsibility to foster the student's personal development regardless of the subject matter content. Therefore, I frequently use quotes and other materials which are intended to reduce prejudice and promote tolerance of differing values as well as promote peace and reduce violence in the world. While this may be easier with my subject matter content which focuses on values, I believe that it can and should be done with any subject matter content. We should serve as mentors for our students, not just information processors. Specific objectives for my courses include the following:

1. *Critical thinking.* You should be able to identify and apply the major ethical principles to biomedical cases using reflective inquiry to support or refute the various positions on a given ethical issue.
2. *Knowledge about ethical and social issues in medicine.* You should be able to display a basic working knowledge of the social and ethical issues in medicine including an understanding of the terminology and distinctions that arise within them.

3. *Effective oral communication.* You should be able to orally communicate information clearly and precisely about a social or ethical issue, including a precise statement of the issue and your reasons for the position you advocate.
4. *Effective writing skills.* You should be able to express clearly and effectively ethical issues and reasoning in your writing. This skill is essential in documenting treatment decisions and in entering progress notes into the medical record that have ethical and legal implications.
5. *Self-knowledge.* You should enhance your self-knowledge through opportunities to clarify your attitudes, values and beliefs with respect to ethical issues in medicine.
6. *Tolerance.* You should become more tolerant of alternative perspectives involved in the complexities of health care.

In my teaching I use a lot of case study discussion to make the material in the course practical and relevant. This requires the students to take a stand on important issues and develop a rationale to support and defend their positions. It promotes introspection and reflection which help accomplish the goal of personal growth. I use a lot of audiovisual materials in my teaching because I believe that the younger generation has been so brought up on television that they are primarily visual learners and expect to be entertained. Furthermore, they relate more to audiovisual learning since almost anything is better than the lecture method.

I incorporate case studies in each class in order to help the students better understand the social issues in medicine so that they can be more aware of these things when they are patients or when their relatives or friends are patients. Several examples of case studies are included in Appendix B. Students report this to be a very desirable teaching strategy. Since most of the undergraduate students are premedical students, some of them are paramedics or, frequently, hospital volunteers. Case studies often relate to their experience outside of class. The medical students are all interested in how the case studies better prepare them for their clinical duties.

I begin each undergraduate class with a brief personal growth and development segment which includes the use of motivational quotes, audiotapes or videotapes. Students report this to be a very helpful and positive experience. Several examples are included in Appendix B. Frequently I have the students participate in breathing exercises, guided fantasy or meditations. The medical students are exposed to numerous motivational quotes in my teaching and are given a journal to keep which has motivational quotes on each page. I often talk to my students about stress management and the mind-body relationship. This past year just prior to an exam I had the students participate in a seven-minute meditation with quiet music. At the conclusion I told them that I *believed* they would do well on the exam—not that I *expected* them to do well which would have just increased their stress. I frequently do things to help program students into high performance.

Syllabi, Exams and Handouts from Courses Taught

Appendix A includes copies of my syllabi for the various courses that I teach. Each syllabus clearly states the course content and objectives as well as the work requirements or assignments, the grading system, texts, supplementary readings, and class format. Copies of earlier syllabi are included for comparison to demonstrate changes and improvements that I have made in the courses over the years. These changes include moving from a lecture format only to the use of small group discussions as well as clarifying more explicitly the course objectives and updating the textbooks and supplemental readings. In addition, new assignments such as writing letters to the editor have been devised to help ensure that the course objectives regarding communications skills are met. I use extensive course handouts in all of my teaching. Sample copies of exams and other course materials are included in Appendix B.

Description of Efforts to Improve My Teaching

I have attended many Philosophy of Education Society annual meetings which addressed issues in teaching. Perhaps more importantly I have attended many Society for Health and Human Values annual meetings and other professional meetings in which ideas are exchanged through networking. I regularly attend the annual meeting of the Association of American Medical Colleges and participate in sessions on medical education. Several years ago I participated in a week-long workshop on cooperative education led by the Johnson brothers at the University of Minnesota. Similarly I have recently participated in a teaching portfolio workshop led by Peter Seldin. I have attended many personal growth and development workshops and listened to many audiocassette programs on personal growth and development from which I have incorporated teaching techniques. Certificates and documentation of some of these activities are included in Appendix C.

I have conducted a series of projects examining the teaching of medical ethics. Several of these have resulted in publications and are included in Appendix C along with a list of other publications related to teaching. One project looked simply at the influence of medical education on moral development where students were tested at entry and exit. Another project looked at the influence of teaching a course in medical ethics with pre- and post-testing to demonstrate the improvement of moral reasoning skills. Another project assessed methods of teaching medical ethics comparing lecture and small group case study discussions. Another project assessed the use of films in teaching medical humanities. A project on cooperative education is still under analysis.

On several occasions I have given presentations on the educational philosophies behind the various approaches to teaching medical ethics and the applications of cognitive moral development theory to medical education. Some of these presentations have subsequently appeared as publications and are listed in Appendix C.

I keep up to date in my discipline by extensive attendance at professional association annual meetings at which I frequently present my work and learn what others are doing. In addition I scan the current literature and serve on the editorial boards of three journals in my field. The journals are *Theoretical Medicine, Cambridge Quarterly of Health Care Ethics,* and *Adult Development Journal.* Also important is the fact that I have regular and frequent exposure and interaction with practitioners in clinical medicine which gives me firsthand knowledge and experiences with the issues in medical ethics.

Peer Evaluation of Both My Teaching and Teaching Skills

For several years I have invited colleagues both from within my department and from other departments to visit and/or participate in my courses. They have been an important source of encouragement and support. I have learned from their suggestions and/or participation in class. I have received written evaluations on my teaching from some of them. Examples of these written peer evaluations are included in Appendix D. These evaluations indicate that I have been innovative, organized, creative, and good at developing rapport with the students. They cite my effective use of audiovisual materials in teaching. They state that I am a good role model for other faculty in improving teaching. For example, one says, "Don relates extremely well to students of all backgrounds. He has the ability to make students think and to allow them to explore their values in a non-threatening way. He makes himself available to all students not only for help with his course, but with life." Another evaluator states as my strength "his ability to adapt teaching to the individuality of a class as well as to the differences of each individual student." Another one states "students receive a very effective combination of audiovisual and substantive teaching—a combination most effective for learning. Too, he works well with both large and small groups." Lastly, one peer evaluator says, "His ability to deal with all values, morals and beliefs without 'preaching' is unbelievable. He needs to be teaching teachers to teach."

Student Evaluation Data from Previous Courses Taught

My undergraduate course in medical ethics is evaluated by the university teaching evaluation process. It consists of having students fill out a questionnaire at the conclusion of each course. It is comprehensive in the aspects of teaching that it evaluates, including teacher preparations, promptness, fairness, availability outside class, and so forth. I am consistently scoring very high in all aspects of my teaching. This is demonstrated in the following table based on a scale from 1 to 5 with 5 being the best score possible.

	Phil. 480H Medical Ethics Means by year			
Sample Questions	1991	1990-A	1990-B	1989
1. The instructor seemed well prepared.	4.97	4.74	4.86	4.87
2. The instructor seemed to care about students learning.	4.97	4.78	4.95	4.61
3. The instructor seemed enthusiastic about teaching.	5.00	4.74	4.76	not asked
4. The instructor was an effective teacher	4.93	4.70	4.90	4.94
5. I would take another course from this instructor	4.90	4.74	4.86	not asked

Other written evidence from these student evaluations is included in Appendix E. In addition to the university evaluation there is also department and/or instructor initiated evaluations. Results of these evaluations are also included in Appendix E. The medical student course in medical ethics and other electives are evaluated only by the department. Examples of these evaluations are included in Appendix E.

Measures of Student Achievement

In addition to the usual evaluation of students through exams, outside written assignments, and so forth, I get an objective measure of moral reasoning skills of my students each year by having them fill out a pre- and post-test in moral reasoning (The Defining Issues Test) based on cognitive moral development theory. Possible scores range from 0 to 95. Consistently the students show a statistically significant increase in their moral reasoning after having been exposed to my course. Pre-test means are 47.3 and post-test means are 54.9. A comparable control group that has not taken my course shows no change in their moral reasoning skills. Data to support this change have been published on several occasions, and examples are included in Appendix C.

Other Evidence of Good Teaching

In addition to measures of student achievement, other evidence of good teaching includes the fact that my elective undergraduate courses are always over subscribed and fill up the first day of registration. I frequently get students in my courses upon the recommendation of former students. In addition I frequently get cards, letters and telephone calls from past students who just want to stay in touch and let me know what they are doing now. For example they say that they learned a lot about medical ethics and a lot about themselves and are recommending the course to others. They frequently mention their appreciation for the caring support they received. Examples of these materials are in Appendix F.

I have been chosen to receive several grants to develop new courses or explore alternate teaching methodologies. A recent grant from the Texas

Veterinary Medical Foundation was for the development of curriculum materials for a new course in veterinary medical ethics through the use of case studies and homework problem sets relating to case studies. I have been asked to present my work on teaching research at several national conferences over the years. I frequently have other faculty colleagues sit in on my classes and have received many compliments from them on my teaching ability. Last, but by no means least, I was chosen as a Teaching Scholar by the Center for Teaching Excellence. Documentation of the grants and presentations are included in Appendix G.

Future Teaching Goals

One goal that I plan for the future is to devise ways to do more small group instruction and more cooperative education activities. The undergraduate course will probably focus more on case study discussions in small groups within the class. The medical student course will probably be subdivided into small groups with the recruitment of some of my colleagues to lead the discussions in separate rooms. I plan to conduct some workshops to teach the small group leaders the principles of small group interaction since most of them have no previous training in small group work. The estimated completion date for this will be June, 1993. The undergraduate course will likely involve cooperative education assignments which will automatically lend themselves to small group work. I plan to do further reading in the area of cooperative education and begin collecting appropriate materials for cooperative projects.

In addition, as a second goal I plan to develop an annotated bibliography of appropriate audiovisual materials for my teaching. I will build a videotape and audiotape library which will support and enhance my ability to incorporate personal growth and development into all my teaching. I plan to have the annotated bibliography completed by December, 1992, although it will be a continually growing and expanding project.

Appendices

Appendix A: Course Syllabi
                Medical Humanities 911
                Medical Humanities 989
                Philosophy 480H Medical Ethics

Appendix B: Representative Exams and Course Materials
                Exams
                Class objectives
                Case studies
                Motivational quotes

Appendix C: Documentation of Efforts to Improve Teaching and Publications
                Related to Teaching

Appendix D: Peer Evaluation Materials

Appendix E: Student Evaluation Materials
Philosophy 480H Medical Ethics
Medical Humanities 911
Medical Humanities 989
Appendix F: Former Student Correspondence
Appendix G: Documentation of Grants and Presentations on Teaching

TEACHING PORTFOLIO
Richard C. Krejci
Department of Physical Education and Health Promotion
Columbia College

Table of Contents
Statement of Teaching and Departmental Responsibilities
Description of Teaching Methodologies
Representative Course Syllabi, Laboratory Activities, Exams and
    Workbooks for Courses Taught
Summaries of Course Evaluations by Students
Letters from Alumni
Description of Efforts to Improve My Teaching
Statements from the Department Chairperson
Goals for Next Five Years
Appendices

Statement of Teaching and Departmental Responsibilities

As a member of the faculty in the Department of Physical Education and Health Promotion I have had a variety of teaching responsibilities in both the professional program and in general education service courses. My primary teaching responsibility is in the biological sciences including Anatomy for Physical Education Majors (PE 349), Kinesiology (PE 350), and Physiology of Exercise (PE 460). These courses service both the Physical Education Department and the Department of Dance. Every other year I teach Test and Measurements (PE 372) and Health Education courses including Personal and Community Health (PE 265), Human Sexuality (PE 262), Personal Health and Wellness (PE 266), and Drug Education (PE 261). Each semester I teach three to four general education activity courses including Concepts of Fitness (PEA 100), Beginning Golf (PEA 104), Weight Training (PEA 105), Beginning Tennis (PEA 107), Intermediate Tennis (PEA 108), Archery (PEA 116), and Aerobics and Weight Control (PEA 123). I have also taught the freshman orientation course (ORI 190) on four occasions and I taught the freshman leadership course (Lead 190) in the Fall of 1991.

In addition to teaching these courses, I have served as the interim department chairman during the spring semesters of 1987 and 1992. I will assume permanent department chairman responsibilities in the Fall of 1992. As department chairman, I have the responsibility of scheduling courses as well as evaluating teacher performance in this department.

I also coordinate the Faculty and Staff Wellness Program. Responsibilities in the Wellness Program include conducting and supervising exercise stress testing, coordinating adult fitness classes and special guest speakers, and directly supervising the laboratory fitness program. I also have the responsibility in the department of coordinating the requisition of library books, computer software, and A-V materials.

Description of Teaching Methodologies

In the classroom I utilize a variety of instructional methodologies including demonstrations, lectures with A-V support, collaborative (both large and small group) classroom assignments, group discussion, individual research projects, and laboratory reports. I incorporate the methodologies according to the course content, goals, objectives, and preparedness (background) of the students. For example, in teaching Anatomy or Kinesiology, I tend to use more demonstrations with the use of anatomic models, charts or slides to better clarify difficult concepts. I use lectures more frequently when it is imperative to clarify many concepts in a relatively brief period of time. In the exercise physiology course, students may work in a collaborative fashion on the preparation of laboratory reports while most classroom time is devoted to lectures, demonstrations, and small group discussion.

In contrast, while teaching health education courses in which the underlying goals are to clarify values and to develop decision making and communication skills, I have the tendency to use small group discussion, role playing strategies, and collaborative projects. In teaching skill or activity courses, I use lectures, demonstrations, and small group activities while allowing maximum time for motor skill practice and development.

Representative Course Syllabi, Laboratory Activities, Exams and Student Workbooks for Courses Taught

Appendix A contains syllabi for the Anatomy, Kinesiology, and Physiology of Exercise courses. Included in each syllabus are course and instructor goals, course objectives and competencies, a detailed list for course content, required reading, methods of evaluation, and general course policies. There are also detailed indications of the weighing of individual assignments in the determination of final grades.

The laboratory guide for Physiology of Exercise along with examples of student work with my comments can be seen in Appendix B. Representative course examinations are in Appendix C. A student workbook which I wrote for Weight Training (PEA 105) is contained in Appendix D. Finally, a student workbook that I also wrote for Aerobics and Weight Control (PEA 123) is in Appendix E. Other members of the department have evaluated these workbooks and one member is also using the aerobics and weight control workbook.

Summaries of Course Evaluations by Students

Summaries of my academic-year course evaluations by students are kept in the department chairperson's office. The student evaluations of my teaching are reflected by use of the standard faculty evaluation form used by Columbia College. I have included the results of a physiology course (Fall 1990), an anatomy course (Fall 1991), and two activity class evaluations (Fall 1990 and Fall 1991) in Appendix F.

The following chart reflects my average ratings on a 5-point modified Likert Scale (5 being outstanding and 1 being unsatisfactory) for the three courses:

	Anatomy	*Physiology*	*Golf*	*Tennis*
Knowledge of subject matter	3.2	3.9	4.5	4.7
Class preparation	4.0	3.2	4.4	4.6
Effective communication	3.3	3.0	4.4	4.4
Stimulate student interest	3.9	3.7	4.4	3.8
Fairness	4.6	3.9	4.4	4.4

I have used these evaluations to modify learning strategies in many of my courses. For example, in the Kinesiology course students cited a need for more use of anatomical models and laboratory experiences. I now incorporate six laboratory experiences using new models and charts in this course. Examples of these laboratory experiences can be seen in Appendix G. In the Fall of 1992, I constructed a special instrument to evaluate my Anatomy and Physiology course. The students rated the overall effectiveness of all of the instructional methodologies used in the course on a 6-point Likert Scale. The average rank for my lectures was 4.1 out of 6.0. This instrument has been an important tool in helping to plan for future health science courses. In order to improve teaching effectiveness, I now incorporate demonstrations, small group tasks, independent tasks and open discussions with my lectures. Results from this instrument can be seen in Appendix F.

Letters from Alumni

In Appendix H, I have included letters from Alumni who have evaluated my teaching ability. One letter stated, "Dr. Krejci's courses were some of the most challenging faced at Columbia College. It was not only that the content was more challenging, but the manner in which Dr. Krejci presented information required me to use higher cognitive skills in order to gain a working knowledge and understanding of the material." Another alumnus wrote, "His instruction in such classes as Anatomy, Kinesiology, and Exercise Physiology have given me a solid base of knowledge and skills to perform my job as a professional at the YMCA."

Description of Efforts to Improve My Teaching

I have great enthusiasm and pride in my teaching and I take every opportunity possible to improve my classroom performance. I attended a two-day workshop on writing across the curriculum at Columbia College in 1989, and I learned how to utilize creative writing to enhance student learning. I also attended a two-day workshop on Health Education for the 1990s in Norfolk, Virginia, in March of 1990. At this workshop I was able to recognize the important factors contributing to the way that I conceptualize things most efficiently.

At the same time I was able to see that students learn best in a variety of environments, many of which differed from those in which I learn best. I felt as though this workshop helped my understanding of how people learn in various ways. Documentation for this workshop is contained in Appendix I.

I frequently attend teaching performance sessions at the State Health and Physical Education Convention in Myrtle Beach, South Carolina, and I had the opportunity to attend several sessions at the national convention in New Orleans in April, 1989. In New Orleans I gained invaluable experience on new computer technologies being utilized in health education. In May of 1992, I attended an all-day conference on professional preparation of school health educators at the national convention in Indianapolis, Indiana. At this conference I learned about new and innovative instructional resources in health education as well as ways of preparing future teachers in the profession. The specific sessions attended during these workshops can be seen in Appendix I.

I read professional journals in *School Health, Research Quarterly for Exercise and Sport,* and the *International Journal of Sport Nutrition.* I frequently share information from the most recent research studies with my students and in professional courses I have students read and critique articles for classroom discussion. I encourage my students to attend at least one professional conference each year and I always allow for time to discuss information relevant to the health and physical education profession. I also incorporate an incentive grading system for those who attend conferences and report what they learned to the class. In addition, I subscribe to *Health Line* and *The Connection,* two state publications from the Office of School Health Education at the University of South Carolina. These publications provide the most up-to-date information on teaching resources in health education.

Statements from Department Chairperson

I have compiled a list of statements from my overall annual evaluations from the department chairperson. These statements are included in Appendix J. Particular note should be taken of comments concerning not only classroom teaching but also in the areas of curriculum revision, participation in student activities, departmental and committee responsibilities, and professional development. Dr. Kemp states, "Richard is an enthusiastic and conscientious teacher. The physical education majors indicate that his courses are excellent and under his guidance they learn the content as well as the skill of making practical application of the content."

Goals for Next Five Years

1. My immediate goal is to develop further specialization in two primary areas of health and physical education, exercise physiology and nutrition. I plan to continue to conduct and publish research articles in the area of eating disorders and to attend workshops, seminars, and on occasion take additional graduate courses in these two areas.

2. During the 1992–93 academic year, I will further develop my expertise in computer software in the areas of health and physical education. By the end of 1993, I would like to develop a small computer center within our department and to have students utilize these computers in all of my academic classes.
3. By the end of 1994, and with the help of my department colleagues, I would like to have developed and implemented a revised and much improved undergraduate curriculum in Health Promotion and Wellness. This curriculum will include new course offerings such as Health Psychology, Worksite Wellness Program Planning, and Pedagogical Issues in Health Education.
4. By the end of 1995, I would like to develop an activity curriculum which better addresses the issue of motor impairment in young adults. I believe that we, as a service department, still have a long way to go to better meet the needs of these individuals.

Appendices

Appendix A: Course Syllabi for PE 349, PE 350, and PE 460
Appendix B: Lab Manual for PE 460 and Example of Student Lab Work
Appendix C: Representative Exams for PE 349, PE 350, and PE 460
Appendix D: Student Workbook for Aerobics and Weight Control
Appendix E: Student Workbook for Weight Training
Appendix F: Examples of Student Course Evaluations
Appendix G: Examples of Laboratory Exercises in Kinesiology
Appendix H: Letters from Alumni
Appendix I: Documentation on Workshops Attended
Appendix J: Statement from Department Chairperson
Appendix K: Products of Good Teaching

TEACHING PORTFOLIO
Vivia L. Fowler
Department of Religion
Columbia College

Table of Contents
Statement of Pedagogical Philosophy
Statement of Teaching Responsibilities and Objectives
Representative Course Syllabi
Evaluation of Instruction
Invitations to Teach from Outside the Department
Efforts to Improve Instruction
Future Teaching Goals
Appendices

Statement of Pedagogical Philosophy

I consider it a real privilege to engage in the teaching/learning process with students. It is exciting to be a continuing learner myself and it is exciting to expose students to new ideas and information. As a teacher of religion, I find that students are frequently faced with real cognitive and emotional dissonance; they often begin to examine their own faith or that of their family or peers or tradition as a result of the learning experience. This, in fact, is an important young adult developmental task. I consider it my responsibility to encourage students to think critically and analytically about religious issues in order to both own their faith (in other words, identify and articulate it) and to value the faith of others—to be able to disagree with me and with each other without building barriers between us. I believe that classroom environment is an important factor in creating a climate in which such development might best occur; therefore, activities are included during the first few sessions to allow me to get acquainted with my students and them to become acquainted with each other.

I consider it critical to student learning that students feel that they can ask questions and make comments in a supportive environment. In the initial sessions students share information with a small group (from totally non-threatening topics to more personal statements of understanding of religious issues); as the semester continues, many students seem to feel increasingly comfortable articulating their ideas at least to "their" small group. I provide many handouts, outlines, review notes, etc., especially in courses with heavy freshman enrollment, in order to aid students in their processing of information and free them from unnecessary note-taking.

I approach most courses using a whole-part-whole approach. I offer an overview of the course (using student-generated themes, time lines, etc.) then break the course into themes or topics, relating the "part" to the "whole" all along. While I find that a certain amount of knowledge and understanding of information is required, particularly in survey courses, I have tried to encourage students to focus on application of information and analysis of concepts. In other words, I want students to *think*: to generate new ideas, draw conclusions, and make connections between religion and literature, history, human relations, and (the list goes on and on). That is what I hope for as a teacher!

Statement of Teaching Responsibilities and Objectives

My primary responsibility is teaching biblical and non-biblical courses in religion which students may take to earn General Education credit, with secondary responsibility for courses for Christian Education majors. I teach the following on a rotational basis:

RELIGION 127 (An Inquiry into the Nature of Religious Experiences). This course considers the origin, development, and expression of religious experiences with primary emphasis on Judaism, Christianity, Islam, Hinduism, Buddhism, Confucianism, and Taoism. I try to convey a sense of human and historical connectedness through an understanding of the relationship between present and past religious rituals and traditions as well as the relationship of one religious tradition to another. Current events with religious implications (wars, legal issues, etc.) are highlighted in an attempt to raise students' awareness of the influence of religious experiences on world events. One of the most popular segments of the course involves slide presentations from my 1988 trip to India; students seem surprised to find that many practices that they imagined to be obsolete around the world are, indeed, both current and prevalent.

RELIGION 128 (Biblical Religion). This course presents an overview of the Old and New Testaments and the Apocrypha. The course covers a broad range of information (details, dates, events, people, etc.), but the terminal objective of the course is not to simply know those details (however important they may be); rather it is to develop an understanding of the bible as a reflection of the faith of people (their understanding of and relation to God). This course helps students understand the impact of culture, history, and personal experience on a person or a group's faith.

RELIGION 350 (Women and Religion). From primitive times through the 20th Century, from Mother Goddess to ordination, religious attitudes of and toward women are examined. Students relate current practices (laws, social customs, ritual, stereotypes, advertising, etc.) to themes of womanhood that have developed within the religious traditions. While our primary emphasis is on the Judeo-Christian tradition, we also touch on the role of women in Islam, Hinduism, and Chinese religions. Other aspects of the course include weekly journal entries, book reviews, student-directed attitude surveys, and many collaborative experiences. Student assessment is based on two restricted essay exams, a book review, and a journal.

RELIGION 360 (Women in the Bible). This course provides an overview of the Bible with primary emphasis on the stories, experiences, and faith of the women, both named and unnamed, in the Bible. Each student researches (and provides written and oral character sketches of) at least two biblical women. Character sketches and weekly written study guides as well as formative tests are used for assessing student performance.

RELIGION 310 (The Sexual Experience in Religious Perspective). Team-taught with Harris Parker and still in the early evolutionary stages, this course has been a real challenge and learning experience for the co-instructors as well as the students; at times the learning has occurred through personal and group confrontation with very controversial and personal issues. We have made an effort to be truly collaborative in this venture; we refer in the syllabus to each of us (Harris, Vivia, and student) as instructor/learner. The course is based primarily on reading, reflection, discussion, and research, focusing on themes of sexuality from a religious perspective. I developed a simulation experience based on ethical dilemmas in reproductive technology. Students contract for a grade which is based on completion of a journal and a chosen number of research papers (from 0 to 4) as well as class participation.

RELIGION 376 (Christian Education in the Local Church). In this course I attempt to acquaint students with the practical application of Educational Ministry as well as leadership skills and resources which will assist them in an introductory-level position in a local church. This course is designed to help the student develop skills needed to become a "leader of leaders" in the local church. Through discussion and role play, we explore styles of leadership, communication, planning and coordination skills, recruitment of volunteers, etc. Each student must develop a detailed training program for a particular group of church leaders.

RELIGION 379 (Age Level Ministries in the Local Church). In this course students observe age level activities, conduct interviews with persons at each age level, and develop a proposal for a short-term local church program which offers learning experiences for each age level (either separate or intergenerational). Ten years of experience working in local churches provides relevant insight and resources.

For the past three summers, I have taught courses in the Evening College. I have been very impressed with these classes; they are a good bit more vocal than our"typical" daytime classes and the wide range of experiences of the students provides a helpful background for our study of religion. These experiences have required me to shape courses with a distinct population in mind.

In addition to these teaching responsibilities, I normally supervise Christian Education majors in their required practicum experiences. I have developed guidelines for practicum experiences which include evaluative instruments for the student, the on-site supervisor, and the supervising instructor (Appendix A).

Appendix B contains course syllabi for four representative courses: Religion 128, a survey course; Religion 350, a course which includes many nontraditional forms of instruction; Religion 310, a team-taught, collaborative course; and Religion 379, a course for Christian Education majors. Each syllabus includes instructor's goals, course goals and objectives, learning activities, and information about attendance and grading. In addition, syllabi normally include a schedule of reading assignments and class topics, as well as session/unit outlines. A bibliography may also be included. Appendix C includes representational course materials such as handouts, tests, and guidelines for special assignments.

Evaluation of Instruction

Appendix D contains a statement from the chairperson of my department and co-teacher for Religion 310, commenting on my contributions to the department as well as my teaching ability. This colleague has had the opportunity to observe my teaching for a full semester during each of the last three years. Appendix E reflects results of student evaluations during my six years of teaching at Columbia College using the college's Student Evaluation Form. Since joining the faculty in 1986, an average of 89% of all students who evaluated my courses gave the highest response of "Very Good" to the question, "What is your overall evaluation of this instructor?" Evaluations since 1989 (when I became full-time) have averaged 92% responding "Very Good" to the same question. Included in Appendix F are mid-semester anonymous comments solicited from students in an effort to improve the instruction/assessment process, as well as written comments from final course evaluations. Among the latter was the following example: " ...This course made me think, and it also helped me to answer questions I had. Mrs. Fowler challenged my mind while letting me know that I was learning. This class interacted well together, and we had really good class discussion." Appendix G contains copies of letters from former students. Appendix H includes examples of graded student work.

Invitations to Teach from Outside the Department

Each year I receive at least a dozen invitations to teach within South Carolina, from local churches to district and conference training events to community organizations. In 1991, I provided a workshop on the role of women in the ancient Hebrew culture for the Speech and Drama Department as it planned for the performance of "Michal, Wife of David."

Efforts to Improve Instruction

During the past five years at Columbia College I have been continuously trying to improve as a teacher. The first two years (when I was employed part-time) were spent frantically developing six of the seven courses I teach. Subsequent years have been spent improving and adapting courses, evaluating textbooks, and experimenting with new courses (see Appendix I for an example of the evolution of a course). I always look for news of relevant current topics and events to bring to my students' attention, and I am trying to add to both library and media center holdings to complement our courses.

The most beneficial experiences I have had as a teacher have come by way of (of all things!) my doctoral studies. I anticipate completing a Ph.D. in Foundations of Education in 1993—a program which has pushed me to pay special attention to how I teach and how students learn. For one major project I developed a simulation experience for Religion 310 (Appendix J). For another major project I revised and analyzed tests for Religion 128 (Appendix J), attempting to better relate this course's assessment with my curriculum goals and instruction. I plan to share my knowledge of item analysis with members of my department this semester.

In 1988, I spent six weeks in India under the auspices of the Fulbright Faculty Development program. This experience continues to bring relevance to my teaching (see slide presentation script in Appendix J). In 1990, I attended a seminar on collaborative learning and completed "Writing To Learn" training; I am continuing to integrate those techniques in my courses (see Appendix J for instruction for students' journals). I attended the 1991 "Enhancing the Quality of Teaching in Colleges and Universities" and I serve on (and have learned a great deal from) the Collaborative Learning Steering Committee. In addition, I have served for three years on the Instruction Committee and have recently assisted with the creation of a new student evaluation process.

Future Teaching Goals (Five Years)

Anticipating the imminent end of coursework for my doctoral program (and, I hope, an increase in available time!), I have established a few personal and professional goals.

1. Each year I intend to select a topic for research and spend the majority of the summer completing my studies.
2. I intend to submit at least one article for publication each year in areas of expertise, focusing on teaching in those areas.
3. Finally, I will select one course each semester to scrutinize using a Curriculum-Instruction-Assessment model of analysis

1992–1993: Harris Parker and I intend to collaborate on a book which will be used as a resource for our course titled The Sexual Experience in Religious Perspective. We will begin this year and continue next year.
1993–1994: Complete Dissertation.
1994–1995: Increase knowledge of Liberation Theology and develop course.
1995–1996: Investigate the role of the Sunday School in the education of blacks in the South.

Appendices
Appendix A: Practicum Requirements and Evaluative Instruments
Appendix B: Representative Course Syllabi

Appendix C: Representative Course Materials
Appendix D: Statement from Chairperson of Department
Appendix E: Student Evaluation Summaries
Appendix F: Student Comments
Appendix G: Letters from Former Students
Appendix H: Graded Student Work
Appendix I: Example of Course Evolution
Appendix J: Examples of Creative Work
           Simulation
           Item analysis project
           "India" script
           Journal instructions

TEACHING PORTFOLIO
Theresa W. Fossum
Department of Small Animal Medicine and Surgery
Texas A&M University

Table of Contents

Statement of Teaching Responsibilities and Objectives
Representative Course Syllabi, Reading Lists, Exams and Handouts from Courses Taught
Description of Efforts to Improve My Teaching
Statement of Department Chairperson and Peer Evaluation of Classroom Teaching
Student Evaluation of Clinical and Laboratory Teaching
Record of Supervision of Students in Graduate Programs
Unsolicited and Solicited Letters from Clients, Referring Veterinarians, Surgery Residents/Graduate Students, Interns and Professional Students
Teaching Awards and Funded Research Grants in Education
Future Goals
Appendices

Statement of Teaching Responsibilities and Objectives
Professional Curriculum

As a veterinarian whose primary teaching responsibility is to students in the professional veterinary curriculum, my teaching obligations comprise three somewhat different roles. The majority of my teaching time is spent in the clinical setting with the fourth-year students. Clinical teaching is different from didactic teaching in a number of ways. Student teacher contact time is generally 8–10 hours per day. I usually have three to four students on my clinical service for two weeks. During this time, I am responsible for teaching the students surgical techniques, diagnostic and technical skills, problem-solving skills, and patient management. Our patients are the clients and cases that are referred to our veterinary teaching hospital.

In the clinics my primary goal is to teach the students to become independent problem-solvers. Therefore, I spend a great deal of time allowing the students to work cases up as a group or alone. I then go through their work-up and try to help them develop a rational plan for arriving at diagnosis. I also spend time with the students making sure that they are comfortable with history taking and physical examination procedures. In the surgery suite, the amount of hands-on experience that the students get is limited because of the complicated nature of most of the cases that are referred to me. Therefore, I try to ask the students questions that will at least challenge their minds, as I explain the procedures being performed to them. I also try to always act as a good role model for these students by being honest, considerate, compassionate and ethical in dealing with my clients.

Additionally, I co-teach several courses and laboratories for the first-, second- and third-year veterinary students. Didactic lectures included among these are: 1) VMID 930 Integumentary Course for third-year students where I give 5–6 hours on surgical management of skin disorders in small animals; 2) VMID 935 which is the third-year surgery course where I provide orientation and instruction for students performing surgical procedures for the first time; 3) VMID 937 Cardiovascular, Respiratory and Hemolymphatic Systems Course for third-year students which is designed to instruct the students in specific small animal respiratory diseases and surgery of the respiratory system; and 4) VMID 923 Introduction to Surgery for second-year students where I provide four hours of didactic lecture on general surgery surgical principles such as antibiotic use and patient preparation.

It is somewhat difficult to be innovative with didactic courses in which there are 128 students and you teach only a small segment of the course. However, because I believe that pure lecturing is not the best method by which to impart knowledge, I have tried to depart from this practice whenever possible. In some of my lecture courses, I have given the students reading assignments and questions ahead of the scheduled lecture period; the lecture itself then consists of a discussion period in which the questions are deliberated. In other lectures I sometimes bring in case examples that exemplify the principles that I want the students to learn from the assigned reading material (see Appendix A for examples of case materials used).

Laboratory courses that I instruct include: 1) VMID 935 Operative Techniques in Small Animal Surgery, (Junior Surgery Laboratory Course) where I teach 40–60 hours per year, and 2) VMID 923 Introduction to Surgery for second-year students where I provide 24 hours per year of laboratory instruction.

In the third-year operative laboratory course I have attempted something new in the past few years. In these laboratories the students work in groups of three. One student is assigned as the surgeon, one as the assistant surgeon, and one as the anesthetist. The laboratory is generally preceded by an orientation that consists of a videotape demonstration or oral discussion of the procedure to be performed. I have tried to encourage cooperative learning in this laboratory by performing a live demonstration for the surgeon of the group immediately prior to the laboratory and asking that student to return to their group and teach the procedure to the other members of their group. This gives the surgeon an opportunity to increase their confidence regarding the procedure, and also allows them to act as instructor and mentor, something they seem to enjoy (see videotape and written description of laboratory exercise in Appendix A).

Graduate Student Teaching

In addition to the aforementioned responsibilities, I also am responsible for the training of graduate students and residents in the surgical program. Additionally, I teach six hours in a newly devised course on education in veterinary medicine for graduate students (VTAN 685 – Education in the Veterinary Medical Environment). This course has been devised to help improve the quality of education in the veterinary curriculum by providing lectures on pedagogical methodology to graduate students wishing to pursue a career in academics. I have also taught a surgical anatomy course for residents which provided approximately 20 hours of laboratory time. My goals in teaching clinical residents are to provide one-on-one surgical training, to be a good role model, and to help them develop research and critical thinking skills that they will need to continue their careers in academia.

Representative Course Syllabi, Reading Lists, Exams and Handouts from Courses Taught

Appendix A includes the course syllabi, reading lists, exams and handouts from a representative course that I have co-taught in the College of Veterinary Medicine's professional curriculum. It also contains the syllabi and handouts from a graduate course that I co-taught in Veterinary Education.

Description of Efforts to Improve My Teaching

In the past three years, I have attended nine workshops and seminars devoted to improving teaching skills. The first workshop that I attended was a Clinical Educator's Course at the University of Illinois. After attending this course, I began a collaborative research project with the College of Education at Texas A&M devoted to improving clinical teaching and evaluation. These collaborative efforts are ongoing and have resulted in several publications and continuing research. I have also attended several workshops on problem-based learning. I believe that as instructors of professional students we need to improve students' critical thinking skills so that they can solve clinical problems that are presented to them following graduation. These workshops have enabled me to encourage problem-solving in my students in both the classroom and in the clinics by improving my small group discussion skills. I have also attended two teaching improvement seminars (TIPS) workshops which were valuable in teaching me how to write course objectives, improving my lecture skills, and showing me ways to better organize my classroom teaching. Appendix B contains a detailed list of the teaching workshops and seminars that I have attended. In addition, I have included documentation of my attendance, such as Certificates of Attendance, at these workshops.

Because I feel strongly that in order to improve and reward teaching, it must first be evaluated, I have been instrumental in developing a method for evaluating clinical teaching (see below under funded research projects). I have found the comments from students to be extremely helpful because they enforce my ideas of what I do well in my clinical teaching, while at the same time pointing out the things that I need to improve.

Statement of Department Chairperson and Peer Evaluation of Classroom Teaching

I have solicited a statement from the departmental chairperson regarding my contributions to the department as a faculty member. This statement appears in Appendix C. Particular note should be paid to the comments not only on my teaching, but also on my contributions to the instructional programs of the college. He notes that "as a part of her interests in investigating new methods of instruction in the clinical setting, Dr. Fossum has had a very positive and pervasive effect on faculty attitudes in general toward this subject." He also notes that I have organized a number of successful workshops for clinical faculty who wish to enhance their teaching skills.

During the past three years I have had one colleague from the College of Veterinary Medicine and the head of my department attend my classroom lectures in two of the didactic courses that I teach. Although detailed written evaluations of my teaching were not given, my department head noted that he found my lectures to be very well organized and well prepared. He also stated that I made every effort to keep the students involved in an active way during lectures. His evaluation appears in Appendix C.

I have also been invited to participate as a lecturer in a course that was designed to improve the quality of education in the veterinary medical environment (see syllabus in Appendix A). I give approximately six hours of lecture in this course.

Student Evaluation of Clinical and Laboratory Teaching

Prior to March of 1992, the clinical departments at Texas A&M University did not evaluate clinical teaching. I have been instrumental in developing student evaluation for clinical teaching. It was my perception that there were very few instruments for evaluating clinical teaching available in the literature that applied to our teaching situation. Therefore, we have developed a student evaluation form which we are in the process of testing. I have tabulated the student assessment of my clinical teaching for Spring semester, 1992. The table below gives my score and the mean score for all clinical instructors in the Department of Small Animal Medicine and Surgery and the Department of Large Animal Medicine and Surgery for representative questions concerning my teaching effectiveness (4-point scale, 4 being the best). Appendix D contains a complete summary of the student evaluations.

My clinical instructor on this rotation:	My median score	Overall median score of all clinical faculty
Created an environment in which I could apply my pre-clinical education.	3.75	3.39
Gave me an opportunity to develop my ability to solve clinical problems.	3.38	3.26
Appeared to be knowledgeable.	4.00	3.70
Encouraged student input into the clinical decision making processes.	3.50	3.26
Overall, I learned a lot from this instructor during this rotation.	3.75	3.39
On the whole, this is a good instructor.	3.88	3.52

Student comments of clinical teaching:

> *Dr. Fossum is very enjoyable to work with. She is very evidently knowledgeable both in education and clinical experience.*
> *All in all, this has been one of the most enjoyable and educational rotations I have had in the small animal clinics.*

As noted previously, I have incorporated some techniques of cooperative learning into my laboratory teaching of surgery. Some representative comments from the students regarding this experience include the following:

> *This laboratory was great—especially since Dr. Fossum took the time to care—showing the surgery to the surgeons beforehand—the lab went very smoothly and quickly.*
> *The demonstration before the surgery was extremely helpful. It made the surgery more time efficient and a more effective learning experience. It gave me more confidence when I did the procedure.*
> *Excellent. How could a student ask for more? It was the most enjoyable lab we've had this semester..*

Appendix E contains further evaluations on this laboratory experience.

Record of Supervision of Students in Graduate Programs

Appendix F contains a record of my participation in the graduate training program at Texas A&M University. During this time I served as graduate chairperson for two residents in the Master's Degree Program and for one in a Ph.D. program. I have also served as a diplomat advisor to nine surgical residents and numerous interns.

Thus far, only one resident for which I have been the major advisor has presented his research at a national meeting. Dr. Carlos C. Hodges presented the results of his study entitled "Lymphoscintigraphic evaluation of the canine thoracic duct" at the American College of Veterinary Surgeons meeting on

February 21, 1990. His presentation was judged to be the best research abstract presented by a resident at the meeting (of twenty-six presenters selected based on the quality of their written abstracts). Documentation of his award is given in Appendix F.

Unsolicited and Solicited Letters from Clients, Referring Veterinarians, Surgery Residents/Graduate Students, Interns and Professional Students.

Appendix G contains unsolicited letters from clients and professional students in the veterinary curriculum regarding my teaching effectiveness. One client stated:

"We recently lost our 14-year-old to kidney failure, and wanted to let you know what a great job Dr. Paul Brandt (a former student of mine) did with her prior to our decision to put her down. You definitely gave him good lessons in caring and compassion and it's nice to see the younger vets handle the animals showing that care and compassion. You are doing a wonderful job, from what we've seen with your students."

A referring veterinarian said:

"I just received the packet of chylothorax information, and I simply wish to thank you for your prompt reply and your above and beyond attitude toward practitioner consultation. If not for you and people like you, the field veterinarian would not be able to afford clientele the quality care which we hope to promote and maintain."

Included in Appendix G are solicited letters from residents and interns that I have taught at the College of Veterinary Medicine. One of the residents notes that I have been one of the most effective educators that she has been associated with in six years of professional and post-professional training. An intern notes that I have a tremendous ability to motivate students, residents and interns to want to learn.

Teaching Awards and Funded Research Grants in Education

I have received several teaching awards in the past few years. In May of 1991, I received the MSD AGVET Creativity in Teaching Award. This award is given annually to one faculty member at each Veterinary Teaching School in the United States who has contributed to innovation and excellence in teaching veterinary medicine. Last year, I was named as the Center for Teaching Excellence Scholar from the College of Veterinary Medicine. Through this award I have had the opportunity to work with other scholars from different colleges in the university to enhance my teaching skills. I also received a $5,000 grant to pursue my interest in cooperative learning. In May of 1992, I received the Richard H. Davis Teaching Award. This award is presented annually to an early-career faculty member who has shown outstanding ability, interest and promise as a teacher. Appendix H contains documentation of my receipt of these awards.

Appendix I contains a list of funded research projects in the field of education where I have been either principal or co-principal investigator. In the last three years, I have had five funded research grants in education totalling

$76,983. These projects have been aimed at improving clinical education through faculty development and improving methods of evaluating clinical faculty. Not only has this research benefited me, but it has also been devised to benefit the entire clinical faculty. Our efforts in evaluating clinical teaching have allowed me to obtain input on my clinical teaching effectiveness and improve my teaching based on the student comments. We are also implementing a peer evaluation process for clinical teaching which will provide both external and internal peer evaluation through assessment of videotapes that document our clinical teaching in different settings. Working with educators and fellow clinicians on these projects has made me more aware of my own clinical teaching style and has given me the impetus to improve my teaching.

Appendix J contains several publications that I have authored or co-authored on the results of our research in clinical education. One of these publications was published in the *Journal of Veterinary Medicine Education* in 1991. The other has been accepted for publication in the same journal. In addition, we have three other manuscripts in press discussing the results of our research efforts.

Future Goals
1. Formal peer evaluation of my classroom teaching is something that I would like to expand in the future. I plan to ask two of my colleagues to critique my teaching this upcoming year. I would also like to have a representative of the Center for Teaching Excellence attend my lectures and formally evaluate them.
2. In order to better evaluate my clinical teaching effectiveness, I plan to implement pre- and post-testing of my students in September, 1992. On the first day of each rotation, the students will be given an examination over selected material that they should know in soft tissue surgery. The last day of the rotation they will be given another examination over similar material and their performance compared between tests. The pre-test will also be used to help individualize my instruction during the rotation to apparent weaknesses in their education.
3. I plan to complete testing and modification of the student evaluation forms for clinical teaching by September, 1992. As a part of this process, we will develop norms for clinical teaching effectiveness at Texas A&M University.
4. We have devised a peer evaluation manual for faculty to use to critique their clinical performance (Appendix K). I plan to finalize procedure for videotaping clinical faculty for evaluation and faculty development purposes using this guide. By Fall 1992, we plan to complete a pilot of this procedure and should be ready to analyze whether it appears to be an effective and worthwhile method of assessing clinical teaching.
5. I plan to organize a workshop for clinical faculty on "Faculty evaluation of student performance in the clinical setting" for October, 1992.

While working with students in developing the student evaluation form for clinical faculty evaluation, one comment that I heard repeatedly was that as faculty we presently do a poor job of evaluating student performance. "Therefore, why should students evaluate faculty?" Hopefully, this workshop will enable us to improve our evaluation of student performance.

6. I plan to attend the Johnson and Johnson Cooperative Learning Workshop sponsored by the University of Minnesota this year and bring information back to my college regarding how we can use cooperative learning to enhance student learning in the clinical setting.

7. Over the next several years I would like to present our research in clinical education and evaluation at a national meeting. We also hope to publish these results in a peer-reviewed journal.

Appendices

Appendix A: Course Syllabi, Reading Lists, Exams and Handouts

Appendix B: List and Documentation of Attendance at Workshops and Seminars on Educational Methodology

Appendix C: Statement from Department Chairperson

Appendix D: Student Evaluations of My Clinical Teaching

Appendix E: Student Evaluations of Cooperative Learning Laboratory Experience

Appendix F: Record of my Participation in the Graduate Training Program at Texas A&M University

Appendix G: Unsolicited and Solicited Letters from Clients, Referring Veterinarians, Surgery Residents/Graduate Students, Interns and Professional Students

Appendix H: Documentation of Receipt of Teaching Awards

Appendix I: List of Funded Research Projects in the Field of Education

Appendix J: Publications in Veterinary Medical Education

Appendix K: Peer Evaluation Manual for Clinical Teaching

TEACHING PORTFOLIO
Charlotte Suzanne Nelson
Voice Division
Shenandoah Conservatory of Shenandoah University

Table of Contents
Statement of Teaching Responsibilities
Philosophy and Teaching Methods
Methods to Motivate Students
Description of Efforts to Improve My Teaching
Evaluations
Closing Comments
Appendices

Statement of Teaching Responsibilities
My teaching responsibility is to give vocal instruction to graduate and undergraduate voice majors and minors who are pursuing a variety of degrees in the field of music. Since 1979, I have taught private voice and related subjects such as French and Italian diction. Due to the needs of the voice division, my teaching load has included only private voice instruction since Spring 1991.

Philosophy and Teaching Methods
Teaching private voice means that one's teaching is often molded to suit each individual student. My teaching load is usually eighteen one-hour students per week. In general, my method is to treat each student in a friendly and warm manner. My goal is to let the students know that I am completely committed to their vocal development, but that ultimately they are each responsible for their own progress. This progress will be positively affected if they follow my instructions regarding the amount of practice required per week and if they practice the technical exercises I teach them in their lessons. My expectations are outlined in the course description which I distribute at the beginning of each semester (Appendix A), and the conservatory requirements for their particular course of study are also outlined in the voice student handbook which they are given in their fist semester of voice study.

Each one hour voice lesson begins with twenty to thirty minutes of vocal exercises and is followed by thirty minutes of work on their vocal repertoire. The vocal exercises are designed to teach students healthy and accurate coordination of the vocal mechanism so that they will be able to perform to the best of their ability. It is imperative that the student practice these exercises during the week between lessons so that the muscle coordination will become second nature. The exercises are a combination of exercises which I have learned from my voice teachers during my training, and some are of my own creation. The "creations" are usually in response to a particular student with a specific vocal problem and are adaptations that apply to particular situations. Teaching private voice is similar to performing in that it is not all planned and executed one step at a time. A good voice teacher is constantly responding to the moment just like a good performer. What a student does in a lesson at any given time determines what one does as a teacher to guide the singer in the right direction; this cannot possibly be planned. However, there is always the ever guiding ear of the teacher and the clear picture of exactly where the teacher intends to lead the student in vocal use and artistic achievement.

After vocalizing the student, I teach the student to apply technical concepts learned in the exercises to the repertoire that they are preparing for the semester. For instance, if I am teaching a student how to release his or her tongue while ascending in pitch, it is then necessary to apply this concept to a melody in a specific song. It is also usually necessary for a student to learn to breathe and support the sound correctly. This particular coordination must then be applied and mastered during the singing of a song or aria.

I select the large part of the student's repertoire to suit the needs of the student. It is important for a singer/musician to understand the performance practices for all periods of music, and I emphasize that a breadth of musical periods should be explored. However, I do believe it is a primary responsibility to guide the student to the point where he or she is able to choose their own repertoire. Therefore, from the very beginning of a student's study, I encourage them to explore songs that they enjoy and/or find challenging.

Voice students are required each semester to learn and then perform for their final exam a certain amount of song/opera/oratorio repertoire. The literature chosen is often material that they will perform as soloists in campus performances of recitals, musicals, operas or oratorios. There are also other performance opportunities such as voice division recitals and voice studio classes, as well as some outside employment in the surrounding communities. It is important that all of the students' performing experiences be integrated with the techniques being learned in the voice lesson.

Methods to Motivate Students

Through discussion and work in voice lessons, I help each student see their own strengths and weaknesses as a singer. No one can change anything until one becomes aware of what should be changed. They must clearly understand the direction I see for them and how it meshes with the direction they see for themselves. Specific exercises are assigned that will help improve their singing; if they do the exercises, their singing will improve. In time students come to realize the need to practice and are motivated to work in order to achieve better performance.

Good singing requires a great deal of self-confidence. This is strengthened through positive performance experiences. These experiences can be found in studio classes held monthly by me for my students, in voice division recital required of all voice majors, or in a recital, musical or operatic production on the campus. It is also possible for the performance experience simply to be in the lesson. If the voice lesson is a positive and joyful experience for the student, the level of self-esteem rises, and then the level of singing improves. Once the student experiences the vocal improvement that can be achieved in one lesson he or she is usually motivated to continue on that track. To summarize, I would say that motivation for improved performance is created when I teach the student how to improve their singing, and that can be accomplished in our work together.

Description of Efforts to Improve My Teaching

It is my firm belief that a singer's ability is either improving or deteriorating. I have made it part of my work to continue to grow and improve as a singer myself. In so doing, I continue to improve as a teacher. Continuing my private study greatly enhances my teaching because I am always in the process of learning; consequently, my ideas are kept fresh and alive. Continued study keeps me from getting set in my ways as a teacher because I am always being pushed to expand and deepen my own artistic ability. I share these realizations with my students by discussion and by teaching them either my newly learned concepts or the refreshed steadfast ones. Appendix B contains a complete list of all workshops and classes I have attended. The most recent of these were made possible with faculty development grants from Shenandoah University and include:

1. 1988–1989: Private coaching sessions with Dr. Robert McCoy from the University of Maryland. These sessions enabled me to study specific 20th Century American vocal repertoire.
2. 1990–1991: Study with Ms. Edith Bers from the Julliard School of New York. My work focused on vocal technique.
3. 1991–1992: Study with Mr. John Fiorito, a member of the Metropolitan Opera Company of New York. This work has been a positive influence on my teaching because I am able to incorporate the new techniques I now use in my own singing into my teaching through improved vocal exercises and applications into the repertoire.

Future efforts to improve my teaching include continued study with Mr. Fiorito as well as continued performance of vocal repertoire. In an effort to keep communication with my students, I intend to schedule voice studio classes where my students have an opportunity to perform each semester. In these classes, I will have open discussion sessions centering around vocal technique and performance practice issues.

Evaluations

Student evaluations are conducted annually in each course. Shenandoah Conservatory faculty who teach applied study use a form that can be tailored to suit the specific needs of the faculty member. All of the available data from my student responses are in Appendix C. The table below shows the median scores for several key questions. The responses range from 1.17 to 1.35 on a 5-point scale, with 1 representing the best response (strongly agree).

Items	Median Score
#2) Course objectives are clear.	1.17
#9) Connection between technique and performance is clear.	1.35
#17) Verbal communication of concepts is effective.	1.17
#18) There is continuity from lesson to lesson.	1.23
#20) Lesson time is used efficiently.	1.29
#29) I have earned the student's respect as a musician and teacher.	1.35

As a teacher I find the written comments on the course evaluation forms very informative. Selected typical comments include:

1. "My teacher is supportive, friendly, encouraging, and fair."
2. "I can tell my voice is changing because of what I am doing in my lessons."
3. "The atmosphere in my lesson is mutually respectful, relaxed, new and fresh."
4. "She knows my potential and chooses music accordingly. She realizes my needs."

It is my goal to continue to assess my teaching by observation and by anonymous questionnaires so that I may continue to deepen my understanding of how best to communicate to young singers.

Peer evaluation is not usually conducted at Shenandoah University. However, I personally feel that input from colleagues who are familiar with my work can serve to document the effectiveness of my teaching. Therefore I have requested comments from peers on the Shenandoah faculty and from colleagues outside the university. All of these musicians have had ample opportunity to either observe my students in performance during their study with me or they have actually worked with my students after they have graduated. The complete letters can be found in Appendix D. Representative comments from the letters include: "She is a very organized and responsible teacher whose students always seem to be well prepared for their juries and performances....", "Her students would rank in the top ten percent of those students who place in competitions I judge", "I have never ceased to be amazed by the growth in vocal ability of her students", and "Dr. Nelson is a thoughtful and very effective teacher of the art of singing."

Closing Comments

My career as a teacher over the past thirteen years has been tremendously fulfilling. Teaching has provided the opportunity for me to use my musical talent to help aspiring singers improve their skills. Every lesson is a new experience where two people are working for a common goal. The goal is to bring music to life through the development of the individual student's talent.

My own growth as a teacher is constantly enriched by my students. One way in which I am rewarded is when I receive unsolicited notes of appreciation. I have included copies of some of the notes I have received over the past years in Appendix E. Perhaps these are the best reward I can have because it so clearly demonstrates that what I am doing can touch the very souls of those I aspire to teach.

Appendices
Appendix A: Course Description
Appendix B: Workshops and Classes Attended
Appendix C: Student Assessment
Appendix D: Peer Assessment
Appendix E: Unsolicited Student Feedback

INDEX

Administrators   11, 16, 17, 28, 30,
  31, 66, 67, 71, 87, 89, 91, 95, 97, 98
Agricultural Education
  Department   103
Alexander, P.A.   117
Annis, L.F.   9, 19
Appendices   90
Arreola, R.   52
Attitudes, faculty   96
Balester, V.M.   136
Ball State University   144, 150
Barber, J.R.   150
Biology Department   110
Bird, T.   4, 14
Bok, D.   4, 42
Boyer, E.   4, 14
Canadian Association of
  University Teachers (CAUT)   63
Caris, N.   110
Cartwright, J.   76
Cheney, L.   4, 14
Choosing items   6
Clark, H.C.   37
Columbia College   4, 28, 127, 154,
  159, 186, 191
Committees   90
Dalhousie University   33, 75
Definition   2

Edgerton, R.   3, 5, 9, 11, 14, 61
Educational Psychology
  Department   117
Elementary Teacher
  Education Program   122
English Department   66, 74, 127, 136
Evaluate, forms to   77
Evaluating, models for   74
Evaluation, pitfalls   74
Faculty endorsement   29
Faculty report   87
Ferraro, E.K.   154
Forms, evaluation   77
Fossum, T.W.   197
Fowler, V.L.   191
Fund for the Improvement of
  Post Secondary Education
  (FIPSE)   63, 67
Gaining acceptance   10
Getting started   75
Gordon College   39
Harvard University   42
History Department   150
Hopkins, L.   159
Human Relations Department   154
Humanities in Medicine
  Department   179
Hutchings, P.   3, 5, 9, 11, 14, 61

Improve teaching   9, 91
Institutional climate   11
Institutional introduction   92
Items for evaluating   73
Items, mandated   72
Jenrette, M.   48
Kennedy, D.   4
Knapper, C.K.   37
Krejci, R.C.   186
Lemm, R.   3, 14
Marquette University   8
Mathematics Department   17, 159,
    167, 174
Mentor   16, 19, 22, 23, 89
Miami-Dade Community
    College   4, 48, 75, 164
Millis, B.   14, 62
Modern Languages &
    Classics Department   144
Mooney, C.   14
Murray State University   4, 8, 52, 74
Narveson, R.D.   66
Nelson, C.S.   205
New Community College   4
O'Neil, C.   5, 10, 11, 14, 33, 37, 38
Orr, D.W.   167
Other purposes   10
Ownership   88
Pace University   8
Perry, W.L.   15, 174
Personnel decisions   8, 71
Physical Education Department   186
Posey, M.   52
Questions, common   87
Quinlan, K.   3, 5, 9, 11, 14, 61
Raymond, J.S.   39
Religion Department   191
Roundtable discussion   95
Savory, J.J.   28
Seldin, C.A.   122
Seldin, P.   1, 3, 5, 8, 9, 11,
    13, 14, 19, 21, 25, 30, 53, 58, 61, 63,
    71, 76, 87

Self, D.J.   179
Self-evaluation   15
Shackelford, R.   22, 25, 95
Shenandoah University   205
Shore, M.B.   5, 14
Similarities   88
Small Animal Medicine &
    Surgery Department   197
St. Norbert College   4, 56
Stanford Teacher
    Assessment Project   63
Steps to create   5
Student learning   89
Teaching dossier   34
Texas A&M University   4, 103, 110,
    117, 136, 174, 179, 197
Thoughts   12
Three-meetings process   21
Time to prepare   88
Townsend, C.D.   103
University of Colorado   8
University of Maryland   4, 62
University of Massachusetts   122
University of Nebraska   4, 66, 74
Voice Division   205
Warner, R.C.   144
Wilkinson, J.   42
Wright, A.   5, 10, 11, 14, 33, 37, 38
Zahorski, K.J.   56
Zubizarreta, J.   127